For Marion

State Trials

By the same author

A Long Time Burning: The history of literary censorship in England

Points of Contact: A collection of poems 1958–1961

Volume 2

State Trials

The Public Conscience

Edited by

Donald Thomas

Routledge & Kegan Paul

London and Boston

*First published 1972
by Routledge & Kegan Paul Ltd
Broadway House, 68–74 Carter Lane,
London EC4V 5EL and
9 Park Street, Boston, Mass. 02108, U.S.A.
Printed in Great Britain by
Butler & Tanner Ltd, Frome and London
© Donald Thomas 1972*

*No part of this book may be reproduced in
any form without permission from the
publisher, except for the quotation of brief
passages in criticism*

Library of Congress Catalog Card Number: 72–81447
ISBN 0 7100 7326 7

Contents

	Introduction	1
	The Public Conscience	
One	A Trial of Witches at Bury St Edmunds (1665) with an account of the Salem Witch Trials (1692)	4
Two	The Trial of John Huggins, Warden of the Fleet Prison, for the murder of Edward Arne (1729)	74
Three	The Trial of Thomas Picton, sometime Governor of Trinidad, for causing the torture to be inflicted upon Luisa Calderon (1806)	158
	Notes	245

Illustrations

facing page

1. Witches apprehended, examined and executed (1613)
   (Courtesy of the Curators of the Bodleian Library)   102
2. The Representations (1729)
   (Courtesy of the Trustees of the British Museum)   103
3. Luisa Calderon being tortured by order of General Picton (Courtesy of the Trustees of the British Museum) 118
4. The Court of King's Bench
   (Courtesy of the Trustees of the British Museum)   119

Introduction

The demands of the public conscience, as illustrated by *State Trials*, were not always as straightforwardly admirable as one could wish. Certainly in the eighteenth and nineteenth centuries there were increasingly strong currents of opinion which insisted that civil or criminal prisoners were entitled to humane treatment and sanitary conditions; that the trade in Negro slaves was an abomination in a Christian society; that officers of state were not entitled to plunder the public revenue, and that inhabitants of territories conquered by British arms were no less entitled to justice and mercy for having had the misfortune to be on the losing side. All these matters of public debate are reflected in the collections of *State Trials*.

No less clearly reflected are those occasions when the public conscience demanded that suspected witches should be interrogated, pressed to death by weights if they refused to plead, or summarily tried and hanged. The hunting and killing of witches was as clearly a social duty to men in one age as the freeing of slaves or the rebuilding of prisons might be in another. It is not surprising that the language of witch-hunting bears a close resemblance in some respects to the terminology of those who later fought social injustice. Here, for example, is Henry Boguet in *An Examen of Witches* (1590).[1]

> I say nothing, too, of the fact that the only delight of witches is to do ill, and that they gloat over the sickness and death of persons and cattle. This is but another reason why we should naturally be incited to punish them, provided that there is any humanity in us and if, to speak more strongly, we are at all worthy of the name of man. For even the most irrational beasts do not suffer amongst

Introduction

them those which league and conspire together against the rest, as we know from experience. Nature, or to speak more correctly, the Author of nature, naturally impresses this common duty on our minds; for otherwise the world could not continue. For these reasons, therefore, it is necessary that everybody should bear a hand in so good a work.

However inconvenient it may be to certain historical theories, the hunting of witches cannot be explained as the consequence of evil bigots scheming to seek out and kill innocent men and women for dark purposes of their own. All too often the tragedies at Salem or Bury St Edmunds involved good intentions on the part of scientifically enlightened or humane men, anxious to do what was correct according to the rule of law and beneficial to the communities in which they lived. Sir Matthew Hale had the reputation of a humane judge; Cotton Mather was a Fellow of the Royal Society; Sir Thomas Browne, apart from his literary genius, had studied medicine at the universities of Padua, Montpellier, and Leyden. It is dangerously easy to look back and feel, with some indignation, that men who were the contemporaries of Dryden, Boyle, and Wren should have known better than to lend their authority to such proceedings. In other respects, their conduct illustrates that instinctive arrogance which every age feels collectively in respect of its own intellectual achievements and moral innovations.

Equally inconvenient is the conduct of Lord Chief Justice Mansfield, who, so far as the press is concerned, might be so easily dismissed as the judicial implement of repression in the service of an unenlightened oligarchy. Yet Mansfield's conduct in the case of James Somersett, a Negro slave, in 1771–2 was all that any abolitionist could ask.

James Somersett's master, Charles Steuart, had brought him to England from Jamaica. On the eve of their return, Somersett managed to escape but was later taken again and put on board the ship in irons. Before the ship could sail, Somersett's sympathizers took legal action on his behalf and Mansfield allowed a writ of *habeas corpus* so that Somersett could be brought before him. There was a lengthy hearing, which concluded with Mansfield remarking that the system of slavery was 'so odious, that nothing can be suffered to support it, but

Introduction

positive law'.[2] In the absence of 'positive law' he set an important precedent by giving Somersett his freedom.

State Trials is rich in such cases as Somersett's, which illustrate the political and social issues of public life in the seventeenth and eighteenth centuries. A few of these, which established the most important principles, are unfortunately little more than a succession of legal arguments or sets of accounts, which would hardly make stimulating reading in any form. This applies to Somersett's case, as it does to those of fraud or embezzlement on a grand scale, as when the Lord Chancellor, the Earl of Macclesfield, was fined £30,000 for corrupt practices after charges were brought against him in 1725. Yet such proceedings as those against General Picton, Governor of Trinidad; John Huggins, Warden of the Fleet Prison, and the witchcraft trials at Salem and Bury St Edmunds illustrate most vividly the public life of Stuart and Hanoverian England.

As the trials of Huggins and of Picton show, the improvement of society in the eighteenth and early nineteenth centuries was as often to be brought about by the prosecution, if not conviction, of a defendant as by any acquittal of the innocent. Indeed, the Fleet Prison scandal of the 1720s and the trials of General Picton eighty years later, when imperial policy and humanitarian concern came into public conflict, mark the chronological limits for cases of this kind in *State Trials*. Certainly the Cobbett and Howell edition shows, by its contents, as clearly as Salmon's first edition of 1719 that 'the best and bravest of mankind are far from being exempted from Criminal Prosecutions'. Yet it adds the second public theme, the theme of 'The Public Conscience', which was to be sounded even more loudly by the Victorians with their concern for the condition of society. Without ceasing to deplore the tyrannical use of law to manipulate charges of treason or intimidate the press, the reformers of the eighteenth and nineteenth centuries were well aware that in certain areas of social concern, whether these involved the slave trade, the prisons, or the colonies, the law might be the support of justice rather than its bane. Often the reformers were to be disappointed in the verdict but the facts of the case had been heard by a far greater audience than the few who attended the Court of King's Bench at Westminster, or the Sessions House in the Old Bailey.

Chapter One

A Trial of Witches: Bury St Edmunds and Salem (1665 and 1692)

The witch mania of the Tudors and Stuarts was in part the operation of a new orthodoxy after the English Reformation. In 1541 witchcraft became punishable as a statutory rather than an ecclesiastical offence, and though this law was repealed in the reign of Edward VI, another was imposed with the accession of Elizabeth. There were at least five trials for witchcraft in 1560–97, and when James I succeeded Elizabeth the law was strengthened by another Act, which remained in force until witch trials were finally made illegal in 1736. One witch was executed in Scotland as late as 1722, and one in Bermuda in 1730. The last conviction in England was in 1712 but the defendant was pardoned.

At first sight, the condemnation of the two accused women at Bury St Edmunds in 1665 seems remarkable, even though there had been a witch hunt in East Anglia twenty years earlier which would have done credit to some of the proceedings at Salem in 1692. The courts of Stuart England were not always as credulous as they have since been thought to be and at a Lancashire trial in 1634 the seventeen defendants were saved by the trial judge who discovered the perjury which had been committed against them.

Two of the most eminent Englishmen of the seventeenth century were involved in the Bury St Edmunds trial. 'Dr Browne' is Sir Thomas Browne, the author of *Religio Medici* and *Hydrotaphia: or, Urn Burial*, who was celebrated among his contemporaries for *Vulgar Errors* (1646), in which he described many misapprehensions over natural phenomena and attributed some of these to Satan's attempts to mislead the human race. *Vulgar Errors* was to be referred to in the discussion of scientific evidence when Spencer Cowper and his co-defendants were tried for the murder of Sarah Stout in 1699. In the Bury St Edmunds trial, Browne attributed the symptoms shown by the 'afflicted' to witchcraft, though as a doctor he saw this as witchcraft which produced the symptoms of a known illness.

The underlying thesis of *Vulgar Errors* may have made Browne more susceptible to belief in the guilt of the accused women but the case of the trial judge, Sir Matthew Hale, is harder to explain. Hale was generally regarded as the model of an English judge. In difficult times, he had scrupulously avoided becoming the creature of any political faction. Though a Puritan by upbringing, he had defended Archbishop Laud and during the Commonwealth he appeared for the defence of men prosecuted by the state. In 1654 he became a Justice of Common Pleas, yet in the following year he refused to preside over the trial of Colonel Penruddock for treason. In 1660 he became Chief Baron and was generally admired for the equitable and expeditious way in which he settled claims after the fire of London. He was the friend of latitudinarian churchmen like Isaac Barrow and John Tillotson as well as of such Nonconformists as Richard Baxter and John Bunyan, whose imprisonment he regarded as a miscarriage of justice and whom he did his utmost to assist.

That Hale should have condemned to death the two defendants in the present case was, understandably, horrifying to a nineteenth-century biographer and jurist like Lord Campbell. Yet it is less an indication of some moral deformity on Hale's part than an illustration of the degree to which men are prisoners too frequently of a fashionable human system, whether intellectual or cultural. This explains Hale's conduct but does not necessarily excuse it.

Central figures in such witch trials as those at Bury St Edmunds or Salem, men like Sir Matthew Hale or Cotton Mather, have become the easy focus of anger or guilt which might more properly be applied to a whole society. Mather, who was a Fellow of the Royal Society as well as a Puritan clergyman, attempted to restrain the enthusiasm of some of the witch hunters at Salem in 1692, even though he offered a partial defence of the proceedings in his *Wonders of the Invisible World* in 1693. Yet even by the standards of witch mania, the events at Salem are remarkable as an example of collective hysteria rather than as the application of contemporary theories of law, science, or theology.

Thomas Hutchinson's presentation of the documents of the Salem witch hunt, which he published in his *History of the Province of Massachusetts Bay* in 1750, forms a preface to the Bury St Edmunds case in *State Trials* and is reprinted in the present edition. Hutchinson does not include all the documents of 1692 but a selection of those which seem to be most significant. By the end of that year, one prisoner had died in gaol and another, Giles Corey (who gave his name to Longfellow's play *Giles Corey of the Salem Farms*), had been pressed to death for refusing to plead. Nineteen others had been hanged.

At the beginning of 1692, Elizabeth Parris, the nine-year-old daughter of the Rev. Samuel Parris, and his eleven-year-old niece, Abigail Williams, were 'afflicted' with fits or convulsions, which might now be diagnosed as hysterical illness. All the evidence suggests that the fits were genuine rather than feigned. Dr William Griggs diagnosed witchcraft and in due course the children accused a cantankerous old woman, Sarah Good, as well as Sarah Osborn and Tituba, a Carib Indian slave belonging to Parris. Other girls then claimed to be afflicted, including twelve-year-old Ann Putman Jun., and four more whose ages ranged from sixteen to twenty: Mary Walcot, Elizabeth Hubbard, Mercy Lewis, and Mary Warren.

The afflicted girls and the alleged witches were examined before John Hawthorne, or Hathorne, the great-great-grandfather of the novelist Nathaniel Hawthorne, and before other magistrates. At the sight of their supposed tormentors, the children again fell into fits. As the panic spread, defendants began to accuse one another and members of families gave evidence against each other. A few inhabitants of Salem retained their commonsense. John Proctor, who employed Mary Warren, promised to thrash her if the fits recurred, and her 'affliction' then disappeared with miraculous rapidity. Yet the result was that both Proctor and his wife Elizabeth were accused of witchcraft. He was one of those hanged on 19 July 1692, condemned as a wizard. Elizabeth was pregnant and therefore respited until after the child should be born. Fortunately, by the time that happened it was the witch hunt itself which was being investigated.

A Trial of Witches

At the time of the trials, Massachusetts was awaiting its new charter, following the Glorious Revolution of 1689 in England. On 14 May 1692 the Governor, Sir William Phips, and Increase Mather, father of Cotton Mather, landed in Boston with the charter. A special court, a Commission of Oyer and Terminer, had been set up to deal with the witches at Salem. From June until September 1692 there were four batches of executions, condemnations coming more easily once John Hawthorne had ruled that if a person were seen by a witness in spirit form, it was conclusive proof that that person had a pact with the devil and required no further evidence. The witch hunt began to spread from Salem to other areas of New England until a rather unspiritual citizen of Boston, when accused, promptly issued a writ for £1,000 damages for defamation against those who alleged that he 'afflicted' them. The spread of accusations ceased almost at once.

Some of those executed maintained their innocence, a few hoped for vengeance on their accusers. At the gallows, Sarah Good said to the Rev. Nicholas Noyes, who urged her to confess, 'You are a liar. I am no more a witch than you are a wizard, and if you take away my life, God will give you blood to drink.' Twenty-five years later, Noyes choked to death on blood pouring from his mouth. Yet the real drama of Salem took place in court, as Hutchinson shows. The witchcraft often occurred there as part of the proceedings, as did accusations and the confessions of those who believed that incriminating others was the only way to save themselves.

In what has become an American tradition, miscarriage of justice was followed by public remorse and well-advertised investigations or remedies. The Commission of Oyer and Terminer, the evidence of guilt, the credibility of witnesses, were all discredited. In England, Robert Calef attacked the Mathers in *More Wonders of the Invisible World* (1700). In 1697 one of the magistrates, Samuel Sewall, and twelve jurors confessed themselves guilty of shedding innocent blood in the trials. In 1706 Ann Putman confessed that she had been misled by Satan. A day of fasting throughout Massachusetts had been appointed in 1697 and in 1710 a committee was set up to award compensation to those survivors who had suffered in 1692. For two centuries, accounts of the Salem trials, like

Hutchinson's, tolerated no exoneration of those responsible for the prosecutions. Only in the twentieth century, after the investigation of hysterical illness, is it possible to contemplate the most horrifying of all hypotheses: that the events at Salem were not determined by malice or falsehood but remained, ultimately, as uncontrollable as an earthquake or a hurricane.

A Trial of WITCHES at the Assizes held at Bury St Edmunds for the County of Suffolk: 17 CHARLES II. A.D. 1665 before Sir Matthew Hale, Knight, then Lord Chief Baron of His Majesty's Court of Exchequer. Taken by a Person then attending the Court.

[*As a further illustration of witchcraft in the seventeenth century, the* State Trials *account of the Bury St Edmunds case is prefaced by contemporary descriptions of the Salem witch trials, as presented by Thomas Hutchinson in his* History of Massachusetts Bay *(1750).*]

New England seems to have had its share of witchcraft in the 17th century. The following account is extracted from Hutchinson's *History*.

'The confusion the country was in from the supposed witchcrafts seems to have occasioned an adjournment of the general court on the 2nd of July, to the second Wednesday in October, 1692; very little public business having been done during the session.

'The great noise which the New England witchcrafts made throughout the English dominions, proceeded more from the general panic with which all sorts of persons were seized, and an expectation that the contagion would spread to all parts of the country, than from the number of persons who were executed, more having been put to death in a single county in England, in a short space of time, than have suffered in all New England from the first settlement until the present time. Fifteen years had passed, before we find any mention of witchcraft among the English colonists. The Indians were supposed to be worshippers of the Devil, and their powows [*medicine men*] to be wizards. The first suspicion of witchcraft among the English, was about the year 1645; at Springfield upon Connecticut river, several persons were supposed to be under an evil hand, and among the rest two of the minister's children. Great pains were taken to prove the fact upon several persons charged with the crime, but either the nature of the evidence was not satisfactory, or the fraud was suspected, and so no person was convicted until the year 1650, when a poor wretch, Mary Oliver, probably weary of her life from the general reputation of being a witch, after long examination was brought to confession of her guilt; but I do not find that she was executed. Whilst this inquiry was making, Margaret Jones was executed at Charlestown; and Mr. Hale mentions a woman at Dorchester, and another at Cambridge about the same time, who all at their death asserted their innocence. Soon after, Hugh Parsons was tried at Springfield and escaped death. In 1655 Mrs. Hibbins, the assistant's widow, was hanged at Boston. In 1662, at Hartford in Connecticut, about thirty miles from Springfield upon the same river, one Anne Cole, a young woman who lived next door to a Dutch family, and no doubt had learned something of the language, was supposed to be possessed with demons, who sometimes spake Dutch and sometimes English, and sometimes a language which nobody understood, and who held a conference with one another. Several ministers who were present, took down the conference in writing, and the names of several persons, mentioned in the course of the conference as actors or bearing parts in it; particularly a woman then in prison upon suspicion of witchcraft, one Greensmith, who upon examination confessed and appeared to be surprised at the discovery. She owned that she and the others named had been familiar with a demon, who had carnal knowledge of her, and although she had not made a formal covenant, yet she had promised to be ready at his call, and was to have had a high frolic at Christmas, when the agreement was to have been signed.

> ['The Egyptians suppose a divine spirit may possibly approach a woman and produce in her the principles of generation; but on the other side, that it is impossible for a man to have any such intercourse with a goddess. It is however altogether irrational to believe that any god or demon is capable of a sensual love for human bodily form or beauty. Plutarch's life of Numa.' Hutchinson.

A Trial of Witches

The scheme of Grecian mythology, replete as it is with intrigues between gods and women, goddesses and men, seems scarcely to admit the possibility of such congress being effected by those deities, in their proper persons. Homer tells us, that when Mars was knocked down by Minerva, 'επτὰ ἐπέσχε πέλεθρα πεσών [*Fallen he covered a couple of acres*]', *Iliad*, book 21, l. 407.]

'Upon this confession she was executed, and two more of the company were condemned at the same time.

['20 January 1662, three witches were condemned at Hartford. 24 February after one of the witches was hanged, the maid was well. Goffe[1] the regicide's Diary.' Hutchinson.]

'In 1669, Susanna Martin of Salisbury, was bound over to the court upon suspicion of witchcraft, but escaped at that time. She suffered death in 1692.

'In 1671, Elizabeth Knap, another *ventriloqua*, alarmed the people of Groton in much the same manner as Anne Cole had done those of Hartford; but her demon was not so cunning, for instead of confining himself to old women, he railed at the good minister of the town and other persons of good character, and the people could not then be prevailed on to believe him, but believed the girl, when she confessed she had been deluded, and that the devil had tormented her in the shape of good persons; and so she escaped the punishment due to her fraud and imposture.

'In 1673, Eunice Cole of Hampton was tried, and the jury found her not (legally) guilty, but that there were strong grounds to suspect her of familiarity with the devil.

'In 1679, William Morse's house at Newbury, was troubled with the throwing of bricks, stones, &c. and a boy of the family was supposed to be bewitched, who accused one of the neighbours; and in 1682, the house of George Walton, a Quaker at Portsmouth, and another house at Salmon Falls, both in New Hampshire, were attacked after the same manner.

'In 1683, the demons removed to Connecticut river again, where one Desborough's house was molested by an invisible hand, and a fire kindled nobody knew how, which burnt up great part of his estate; and in 1684, Philip Smith, a judge of the court, a military

A Trial of Witches

officer and a representative of the town of Hadley, upon the same river, an hypochondriac person, fancied himself under an evil hand, and suspected a woman, one of his neighbours, and languished and pined away, and was generally supposed to be bewitched to death. While he lay ill, a number of brisk lads tried an experiment upon the old woman. Having dragged her out of her house, they hung her up until she was near dead, let her down, rolled her some time in the snow, and at last buried her in it, and there left her, but it happened that she survived, and the melancholy man died.

'Notwithstanding these frequent instances of supposed witchcrafts, none had suffered for near thirty years, in the Massachusetts colony. The execution of the assistant or counsellor's widow in 1655, was disapproved of by many principal persons, and it is not unlikely that her death saved the lives of many other inferior persons. But in 1685, a very circumstantial account of all or most of the cases I have mentioned, was published, and many arguments were brought to convince the country that they were no delusions nor impostures, but the effects of a familiarity between the devil and such as he found fit for his instruments; and in 1687 or 1688, began a more alarming instance than any which had preceded it. Four of the children of John Goodwin, a grave man and a good liver at the north part of Boston, were generally believed to be bewitched. I have often heard persons, who were of the neighbourhood, speak of the great consternation it occasioned. The children were all remarkable for ingenuity of temper, had been religiously educated and were thought to be without guile. The eldest was a girl of thirteen or fourteen years. She had charged a laundress with taking away some of the family linen. The mother of the laundress was one of the wild Irish, of bad character, and gave the girl harsh language; soon after which she fell into fits, which were said to have something diabolical in them. One of her sisters and two brothers followed her example, and it is said, were tormented in the same part of their bodies at the same time, although kept in separate apartments, and ignorant of one another's complaints. One or two things were said to be very remarkable; all their complaints were in the day-time, and they slept comfortably all night; they were struck dead at the sight of the Assembly's Catechism, Cotton's *Milk for Babes*, and some other good books, but could read in Oxford Jests, Popish and Quaker books, and the Common Prayer, without any difficulty.[2] Is it possible the mind of man should be capable of such strong

A Trial of Witches

prejudices as that a suspicion of fraud should not immediately arise? But attachments to modes and forms in religion had such force that some of these circumstances seem rather to have confirmed the credit of the children. Sometimes they would be deaf, then dumb, then blind; and sometimes all these disorders together would come upon them. Their tongues would be drawn down their throats, then pulled out upon their chins. Their jaws, necks, shoulders, elbows and all their joints would appear to be dislocated, and they would make most piteous outcries of burnings, of being cut with knives, beat &c. and the marks of wounds were afterwards to be seen. The ministers of Boston and Charlestown kept a day of fasting and prayer at the troubled house; after which the youngest child made no more complaints. The others persevered, and the magistrates then interposed and the old woman was apprehended, but upon examination would neither confess nor deny, and appeared to be disordered in her senses. Upon the report of physicians that she was *compos mentis*, she was executed, declaring at her death the children should not be relieved. The eldest after this was taken into a minister's family, where at first she behaved orderly, but after some time, suddenly fell into her fits. The account of her affliction is in print; some things are mentioned as extraordinary, which tumblers are every day taught to perform; others seem more than natural, but it was a time of great credulity. The children returned to their ordinary behaviour, lived to adult age, made profession of religion, and the affliction they had been under they publicly declared to be one motive to it. One of them I knew many years after. She had the character of a very sober virtuous woman, and never made any acknowledgment of fraud in this transaction. The printed account was published with a preface by Mr. Baxter, who says, "The evidence is so convincing, that he must be a very obdurate Sadducee who will not believe."[3]

['In the year 1720, at Littleton in the County of Middlesex [*Massachusetts*], a family was supposed to be bewitched. One J[*oseph*] B[*lanchard*] had three daughters, of eleven, nine, and five years of age. The eldest was a forward girl, and having read and heard many strange stories, would surprise the company where she happened to be, with her manner of relating them. Pleased with the applause, she went from stories she had heard, to some of her own framing, and so

A Trial of Witches

on to dreams and visions, and attained the art of swooning and of being to all appearance for some time breathless. Upon her revival, she would tell of strange things she had met with in this and other worlds. When she met with the words, "God", "Christ", "the Holy Ghost", in the Bible, she would drop down with scarce any signs of life in her. Strange noises were often heard in and upon the house; stones came down the chimney and did great mischief. She complained of the spectre of Mrs. D—y [*Dudley*], a woman living in the town; and once the mother of the girl struck at the place where the said D—y was, and the girl said, "You have struck her on the belly," and upon inquiry it was found, that D—y complained of a hurt in her belly about that time. Another time the mother struck at a place, where the girl said there was a yellow bird, and she told her mother she had hit the side of its head; and it again appeared that D—y's head was hurt about the same time. It was common to find her in ponds of water, crying out she should be drowned; sometimes upon the top of the house, and sometimes upon the tops of trees, where she pretended she had flown; and some fancied they had seen her in the air. There were often the marks of blows and pinches upon her, which were supposed to come from an invisible hand.

'The second daughter, after her sister had succeeded so well, imitated her, in complaints of D—y; and outdid her in feats of running upon the barn, climbing trees, &c. and, what was most surprising, the youngest attempted the same feats, and in some instances went beyond her sisters. The neighbours agreed they were under an evil hand, and it was pronounced a piece of witchcraft, as certain as that there ever had been any at Salem; and no great pains were taken to detect the imposture. Physicians had been at first employed, but to no purpose; and afterwards ministers were called to pray over them, but without success. At length D—y, not long after the supposed blows, took to her bed, and after some time died, and the two eldest girls ceased complaining; the youngest held out longer, but all persisted in it, that there had been no fraud. The eldest, not having been baptized, and being come to adult age, desired and obtained baptism, and the minister then examined her upon her conduct in the affair, and she persisted in her declarations of innocency. In 1728, having removed to Medford, she offered to join the church there, and gave a satisfactory account of herself to the minister of the town; but he knew nothing of the share she had in this transaction. The Lord's day before she was to be admitted, he happened to preach from this text, "He that speaketh lies shall not escape." The woman supposed the sermon to be intended for her, and went to the minister, who told her nobody had made any objection against her; but being determined to confess her guilt she disclosed the fraud of herself and her sisters, and desired to make a public acknowledgment, in the face of the church; and accordingly did so. The two sisters, seeing her pitied, had become actors also with her, without being moved to it by her, but when she saw them follow her, they all joined in the secret and acted in concert. They had no particular spite against D—y; but it was necessary to accuse somebody, and the eldest having pitched upon her, the rest followed. The woman's complaints, about the same time the girl pretended she was struck, proceeded from other causes, which were not then properly inquired into. Once, at least, they were in great danger of being detected in their tricks; but the grounds of suspicion were overlooked, through the indulgence and credulity of their parents. MS. of the Rev. Mr. Turell minister of Medford.' Hutchinson.]

'It obtained credit sufficient, together with other preparatives, to dispose the whole country to be easily imposed upon by the more extensive and more tragical scene, which was presently after acted at Salem and other parts of the County of Essex [*Massachusetts*]. Not many years before, Glanvill published his Witch stories in England; Perkins and other nonconformists were earlier;[4] but the great authority was that of Sir Matthew Hale, revered in New England, not only for his knowledge in the law, but for his gravity and piety. The trial of the witches in Suffolk was published in 1684. All these books were in New England, and the conformity between the behaviour of Goodwin's children and most of the supposed bewitched at Salem, and the behaviour of those in

England, is so exact, as to leave no room to doubt the stories had been read by the New England persons themselves, or had been told to them by others who had read them. Indeed, this conformity, instead of giving suspicion, was urged in confirmation of the truth of both; the Old England demons and the New being so much alike. The Court justified themselves from books of law, and the authorities of Keble, Dalton and other lawyers, then of the first character, who lay down rules of conviction, as absurd and dangerous as any which were practised in New England. The trial of Richard Hathaway the impostor, before Lord Chief Justice Holt, was ten or twelve years after.[5] This was a great discouragement to prosecutions in England for witchcraft, but an effectual stop was not put to them, until the Act of Parliament in the reign of his late Majesty.

['I remember to have heard a gentleman, who in other respects was very sensible, express his surprise upon the first news of this Act. The Parliament, he said, had in effect declared that there were no evil spirits, he was afraid they would declare by another Act that there are no good ones.

'From 1694 to 1701, there were eleven persons tried for witches before Lord Chief Justice Holt, all of whom were acquitted. In Scotland seven were executed for witches in 1697, upon the testimony of one girl about eleven years old.' Hutchinson.]

'Even this has not wholly cured the common people, and we hear of old women ducked and cruelly murdered within these last twenty years. Reproach then, for hanging witches, although it has been often cast upon the people of New England by those of Old, yet it must have been done with an ill grace. The people of New England were of a grave cast, and had long been disposed to give a serious solemn construction even to common events in providence; but in Old England, the reign of Charles II was as remarkable for gaiety as any whatsoever, and for scepticism and infidelity, as any which preceded it.

'Sir William Phips, the Governor, upon his arrival, fell in with the opinion prevailing. Mr. Stoughton, the Lieutenant-Governor, upon whose judgment great stress was laid, had taken up this notion, that although the devil might appear in the shape of a guilty person, yet he would never be permitted to assume the shape of an innocent person.

A Trial of Witches

[' "A gentleman of more than ordinary understanding, learning and experience, desired me to write to New England about your trials and convictions of witches, not being satisfied with the evidence upon which some who have been executed were found guilty; he told me that in the time of the great reformation Parliament, a certain person or persons had a commission to discover and prosecute witches. Upon these prosecutions many were executed, in at least one county in England, until, at length, a gentleman of estate and of great character for piety was accused, which put an end to the commission, and the judges upon a re-hearing, reversed many of the judgments; but many lives had been taken away. All that I speak with, much wonder that any man, much less a man of such abilities, learning and experience as Mr. Stoughton, should take up a persuasion, that the devil cannot assume the likeness of an innocent, to afflict another person. In my opinion, it is a persuasion utterly destitute of any solid reason to render it so much as probable, and besides, contradictory to many instances of facts in history. If you think good, you may acquaint Mr. Stoughton and the other judges with what I write." Letter from London to Increase Mather, 9 January, 1692–3.

'I suppose the Long Parliament must be intended by the great reformation Parliament, for in 1644, 1645 and 1646, one Matthew Hopkins went from place to place to find out witches. Mr. Baxter says a great number were hanged by his discovery, and that Mr. Calamy went along with the judges to hear the confessions, and to see that there was no fraud or wrong done.[6] Hopkins searched for teats, set some upon stools or tables cross-legged, and kept them twenty-four hours without meat or drink, within which time it was said their imps would come and suck; others he tried by swimming [*floating*] them, and at length raised the indignation of certain gentlemen, who caused him to be seized, and his hands and feet being tied, to be thrown into the water, where fortunately for him he was proved to be a witch or wizard himself, by his swimming or floating upon the water. The country was cleared of him, and some lamented that the experiment had not been made sooner.' Hutchinson.]

A Trial of Witches

'This opinion at first, was generally received. Some of the most religious women who were accused, when they saw the appearance of distress and torture in their accusers, and heard their solemn declarations, that they saw the shapes or spectres of the accused afflicting them, persuaded themselves they were witches, and that the devil, somehow or other, although they could not remember how or when, had taken possession of their evil hearts, and obtained some sort of assent to his afflicting in their shapes; and thereupon they thought they might be justified in confessing themselves guilty.

'It seems, at this day, with some people, perhaps but few, to be the question whether the accused or the afflicted were under a preternatural or diabolical possession, rather than whether the afflicted were under bodily distempers, or altogether guilty of fraud and imposture. As many of the original examinations have fallen into my hands, it may be of service to represent this affair in a more full and impartial light than it has yet appeared to the world.

'In February 1692, a daughter and a niece of Mr. Parris, the minister of Salem village, girls of ten or eleven years of age, and two other girls in the neighbourhood, made the same sort of complaints as Goodwin's children had made, two or three years before.

> ['Douglass in his *Summary*[7] says, "In Salem and its neighbourhood, enthusiasm and other nervous disorders seem to be endemical; it was the seat of the New England witchcraft, A.D. 1692." I question whether he had any other foundation for this remark than merely this scene of witchcraft, which must be considered as the distemper of the country in general, rather than of any particular town or county, and had Mr. Parris's family lived in any other part of the province, perhaps the neighbourhood would have been as much infected; and no impression ought to be made to the disadvantage of a town the most ancient, and at this day the second in rank within the province, and upon other accounts justly respectable.' Hutchinson.]

'The physicians, having no other way of accounting for the disorder, pronounced them bewitched. An Indian woman, who was brought into the country from New Spain, and then lived with Mr. Parris, tried some experiments which she pretended to be used to, in her own country, in order to find out the witch. This coming to the children's knowledge, they cried out upon the poor Indian, as appearing to them, pinching, and pricking and tormenting them; and fell into fits. Tituba, the Indian, acknowledged that she had learned how to find out a witch, but denied that she was one herself. Several private fasts were kept at the minister's house and several, more public, by the whole village, and then a general fast through the colony, to seek to God to rebuke Satan, &c. So much notice taken of the children, together with the pity and compassion, expressed by those who visited them, not only tended to confirm them in their design but to draw others into the like. Accordingly, the number of the complainants soon increased, and among them there were two or three women and some girls old enough for witnesses. These had their fits too, and, when in them, cried out, not only against Tituba, but against Sarah Osborn, a melancholy distracted old woman, and Sarah Good, another old woman who was bedrid. Tituba, at length, confessed herself a witch, and that the two old women were her confederates; and they were all committed to prison; and Tituba upon search, was found to have scars upon her back which were called the devil's mark; but might as well have been supposed those of her Spanish master. This commitment was on the 1st of March. About three weeks after, two other women, of good characters and church members, Corey and Nurse, were complained of and brought upon their examination; when these children fell into fits, and the mother of one of them, and wife of Thomas Putman, joined with the children and complained of Nurse as tormenting her; and made most terrible shrieks, to the amazement of all the neighbourhood. The old women denied everything; but were sent to prison, and such was the infatuation, that a child of Sarah Good, about four or five years old, was committed also, being charged with biting some of the afflicted who showed the print of small teeth on their arms. On 3rd April Mr. Parris took for his text, "Have not I chosen you twelve, and one of you is a devil." Sarah Cloyse, supposing it to be occasioned by Nurse's case who was her sister, went out of meeting. She was, presently after, complained of for a witch, examined and committed. Elizabeth Proctor was charged about the same time: her husband, as every good husband would have done, accompanied her to her examination, but it cost the poor man his life. Some of the afflicted cried out upon him also, and they were both committed to prison.

'Instead of suspecting and sifting the witnesses, and suffering

A Trial of Witches

them to be cross-examined, the authority, to say no more, were imprudent in making use of leading questions, and thereby putting words into their mouths or suffering others to do it. Mr. Parris was over-officious; most of the examinations, although in the presence of one or more of the magistrates, were taken by him. The following examinations, of several of the accused, may serve as specimens, they being generally made in the same manner.

'At a court held at Salem 11th April 1692, by the honoured Thomas Danforth, Deputy Governor.

Q. John; who hurt you?

> ['This was Tituba's husband, who seems to have been a cunning fellow, and to avoid being accused joined with the afflicted.' Hutchinson.]

A. Goody Procter first, and then Goody Cloyse.
Q. What did she do to you?
A. She brought the book to me.
Q. John! tell the truth, who hurts you? Have you been hurt?
A. The first, was a gentlewoman I saw.
Q. Who next?
A. Goody Cloyse.
Q. But who hurt you next?
A. Goody Proctor.
Q. What did she do to you?
A. She choked me, and brought me the book.
Q. How oft did she come to torment you?
A. A good many times, she and Goody Cloyse.
Q. Do they come to you in the night as well as the day?
A. They come most in the day.
Q. Who?
A. Goody Cloyse and Goody Proctor.
Q. Where did she take hold of you?
A. Upon my throat, to stop my breath.
Q. Do you know Goody Cloyse and Goody Proctor?
A. Yes, here is Goody Cloyse.
(*Cloyse*) When did I hurt thee?
A. A great many times.
(*Cloyse*) Oh! you are a grievous liar.
Q. What did this Goody Cloyse do to you?
A. She pinched and bit me till the blood came.

A Trial of Witches

Q. How long since this woman came and hurt you?
A. Yesterday, at meeting.
Q. At any time before?
A. Yes a great many times.
Q. Mary Walcot! Who hurts you?
A. Goody Cloyse.
Q. What did she do to you?
A. She hurt me.
Q. Did she bring the book?
A. Yes.
Q. What was you do with it?
A. To touch it and be well.—(*Then she fell into a fit.*)
Q. Doth she come alone?
A. Sometimes alone, and sometimes in company with Goody Nurse and Goody Corey, and a great many I do not know.— (*Then she fell into a fit again.*)
Q. Abigail Williams; did you see a company at Mr. Parris's house eat and drink?
A. Yes, sir. That was their sacrament.
Q. How many were there?
A. About forty, and Goody Cloyse and Goody Good were their deacons.
Q. What was it?
A. They said it was our blood, and they had it twice that day.
Q. Mary Walcot! Have you seen a white man?
A. Yes sir, a great many times.
Q. What sort of man was he?
A. A fine grave man, and when he came he made all the witches to tremble.
Abigail Williams confirmed the same, and that they had such a sight at Deacon Ingersoll's.
Q. Who was at Deacon Ingersoll's then?
A. Goody Cloyse, Goody Nurse, Goody Corey, and Goody Good. —(*Then Sarah Cloyse asked for water, and sat down as one seized with a dying fainting fit; and several of the afflicted fell into fits, and some of them cried out, "Oh! Her spirit is gone to prison to her sister Nurse."*)
Q. Elizabeth Proctor! You understand whereof you are charged, viz. to be guilty of sundry acts of witchcraft; what say you to it? Speak the truth, and so you that are afflicted, you must

A Trial of Witches

speak the truth, as you will answer it before God another day. Mary Walcot! Doth this woman hurt you?
A. I never saw her so as to be hurt by her.
Q. Mary Lewis! does she hurt you?—(*Her mouth was stopped.*)
Q. Ann Putman! Does she hurt you?—(*She could not speak.*)
Q. Abigail Williams! Does she hurt you?—(*Her hand was thrust in her own mouth.*)
Q. John! Does she hurt you?
A. This is the woman that came in her shift and choked me.
Q. Did she ever bring the book?
A. Yes, sir.
Q. What to do?
A. To write.
Q. What, this woman?
A. Yes, sir.
Q. Are you sure of it?
A. Yes, sir.
Again Abigail Williams and Ann Putman were spoke to by the Court, but neither of them could make any answer, by reason of dumbness or other fits.
Q. What do you say Goody Proctor to these things?
A. I take God in heaven to be my witness, that I know nothing of it, no more than the child unborn.
Q. Ann Putman! Doth this woman hurt you?
A. Yes sir, a great many times.—(*Then the accused looked upon them and they fell into fits.*)
Q. She does not bring the book to you, does she?
A. Yes sir, often, and saith she hath made her maid set her hand to it.
Q. Abigail Williams! Does this woman hurt you?
A. Yes sir, often.
Q. Does she bring the book to you?
A. Yes.
Q. What would she have you do with it?
A. To write in it and I shall be well. Did not you (*said Abigail*), tell me, that your maid had written?
(*Proctor*) Dear child, it is not so. There is another judgment, dear child.
Then Abigail and Ann had fits. By and by they cried out, "Look you, there is Goody Proctor upon the beam." By and by, both of them cried

out of Goodman Proctor himself and said he was a wizard. Immediately, many, if not all of the bewitched, had grievous fits.
Q. Ann Putman! Who hurt you?
A. Goodman Proctor and his wife too.
Afterwards some of the afflicted cried, "There is Proctor going to take up Mrs. Pope's feet." And her feet were immediately taken up.
Q. What do you say Goodman Proctor to these things?
A. I know not. I am innocent.
Abigail Williams cried out, "There is Goodman Proctor going to Mrs. Pope", and immediately, said Pope fell into a fit.
Q. You see the devil will deceive you; the children could see what you was going to do before the woman was hurt. I would advise you to repentance, for the devil is bringing you out.
Abigail Williams cried out again, "There is Goodman Proctor going to hurt Goody Bibber;" and immediately Goody Bibber fell into a fit. There was the like of Mary Walcot, and divers others. Benjamin Gould gave in his testimony, that he had seen Goodman Corey and his wife, Proctor and his wife, Goody Close, Goody Nurse, and Goody Griggs in his chamber last Thursday night. Elizabeth Hubbard was in a trance during the whole examination. During the examination of Elizabeth Proctor, Abigail Williams and Ann Putman, both made offer to strike at said Proctor, but when Abigail's hand came near it opened, whereas it was made up into a fist before, and came down exceeding lightly, as it drew near to said Proctor, and at length with open and extended fingers, touched Proctor's hood very lightly. Immediately Abigail cried out her fingers, her fingers, her fingers burned, and Ann Putman took on most grievously of her head, and sunk down.

'"Salem, April 11, 1692. Mr. Samuel Parris was desired by the Honourable Thomas Danforth, Deputy-Governor, and the Council, to take in writing the aforesaid Examinations, and accordingly took and delivered them in; and upon hearing the same, and seeing what was then seen, together with the charge of the afflicted persons, were by the advice of the Council all committed by us,

John Hawthorne,
John Corwin,   Assistants."

'No wonder the whole country was in a consternation, when persons, of sober lives and unblemished characters, were committed to prison upon such sort of evidence. Nobody was safe. The most effectual way to prevent an accusation, was to become an accuser; and accordingly the number of the afflicted increased every day, and the number of the accused in proportion, who in general persisted in their innocency; but, being strongly urged to give glory to God by their confession, and intimation being given that this was the only way to save their lives, and their friends urging them to it, some were brought to own their guilt. The first confession upon the files, is of Deliverance Hobbs, 11 May 1692, being in prison. She owned everything she was required to do. The confessions multiplied the witches, new companions were always mentioned, who were immediately sent for and examined. Thus more than an hundred women, many of them of fair characters and of the most reputable families, in the town of Salem, Beverly, Andover, Billerica, &c. were apprehended, examined, and, generally committed to prison. The confessions being much of the same tenor, one or two may serve for specimens.

'The Examination and Confession (8 September 1692) of Mary Osgood, wife of Captain Osgood of Andover, taken before John Hawthorne and other their Majesties' justices.

'She confesses, that about eleven years ago, when she was in a melancholy state and condition, she used to walk abroad in her orchard and upon a certain time, she saw the appearance of a cat, at the end of the house, which yet she thought was a real cat. However, at that time, it diverted her from praying to God, and instead thereof she prayed to the devil; about which time she made a covenant with the devil, who as a black man came to her and presented her a book; upon which she laid her finger and that left a red spot: and that upon her signing, the devil told her he was her God, and that she should serve and worship him, and, she believes, she consented to it. She says further, that about two years ago, she was carried through the air, in company with Deacon Frye's wife, Ebenezer Baker's wife and Goody Tyler, to Five-Mile pond, where she was baptised by the devil, who dipped her face in the water and made her renounce her former baptism, and told her she must be his, soul and body for ever, and that she must serve him, which she promised to do. She says, the renouncing her first baptism was after her dipping, and that she was transported back again through the air, in company with the forenamed persons, in the same manner as she went, and believes they were carried upon a pole.—

Q. How many persons were upon the pole?
A. As I said before.
Viz. *four persons and no more but whom she had named above.—She confesses she has afflicted three persons, John Sawdy, Martha Sprague and Rose Foster, and that she did it by pinching her bedclothes, and giving consent the devil should do it in her shape, and that the devil could not do it without her consent.—She confesses the afflicting persons in the court, by the glance of her eye. She says, as she was coming down to Salem to be examined, she and the rest of the company with her stopped at Mr. Phillips's to refresh themselves, and the afflicted persons, being behind them upon the road, came up just as she was mounting again and were then afflicted, and cried out upon her, so that she was forced to stay until they were all past, and said she only looked that way towards them.—*
Q. Do you know the devil can take the shape of an innocent person and afflict?
A. I believe he cannot.
Q. Who taught you this way of witchcraft?
A. Satan, *and that he promised her abundance of satisfaction and quietness in her future state, but never performed anything; and that she has lived more miserably and more discontented since, than ever before. She confesses further, that she herself, in company with Goody Parker, Goody Tyler and Goody Dane, had a meeting at Moses Tyler's house, last Monday night, to afflict, and that she and Goody Dane carried the shape of Mr. Dane the minister, between them, to make persons believe that Mr. Dane afflicted.—*
Q. What hindered you from accomplishing what you intended?
A. The Lord would not suffer it so to be, that the devil should afflict in an innocent person's shape.—
Q. Have you been at any other witch meetings?
A. I know nothing thereof, as I shall answer in the presence of God and His people. *But said, that the black man stood before her, and told her, that what she had confessed was a lie; notwithstanding, she said that what she had confessed was true, and thereto put her hand. Her husband being present was asked, if he judged his wife to be any way discomposed. He answered, that having lived with her so long, he doth not judge her to be any ways discomposed, but has cause to believe what she has said is true. When Mistress Osgood was first called, she afflicted Martha Sprague and Rose Foster, by the glance of her eyes, and recovered them out of their fits by the touch of her hand. Mary*

A Trial of Witches

Lacey and Betty Johnson and Hannah Post saw Mistress Osgood afflicting Sprague and Foster. The said Hannah Post and Mary Lacey and Betty Johnson, jr. and Rose Foster and Mary Richardson were afflicted by Mistress Osgood, in the time of their examination, and recovered by her touching of their hands.

'I underwritten, being appointed by authority, to take this examination, do testify upon oath, taken in court, that this is a true copy of the substance of it, to the best of my knowledge, 5 January 1693. The within Mary Osgood was examined before their Majesties' justices of the peace in Salem.

(Attest.) John Higginson, Just. Pac.

'A miserable negro woman, charged by some of the girls with afflicting them, confessed, but was cunning enough to bring the greatest share of the guilt upon her mistress.

'Salem, Monday 4 July 1692. The examination of Candy, a Negro Woman, before Bartholomew Gidney and John Hawthorne, Esqrs. Mr. Nicholas Noyes also present.

Q. Candy! are you a witch?
A. Candy no witch in her country. Candy's mother no witch. Candy no witch. Barbados. This country, mistress give Candy witch.—
Q. Did your mistress make you a witch in this country?
A. Yes, in this country mistress give Candy witch.—
Q. What did your mistress do to make you a witch?
A. Mistress bring book and pen and ink, make Candy write in it.—
Q. What did you write in it?
She took a pen and ink and upon a book or paper made a mark.—
Q. How did you afflict or hurt these folks, where are the puppets you did it with?—
She asked to go out of the room and she would show or tell; upon which she had liberty, one going with her, and she presently brought in two clouts, one with two knots tied in it, the other one; which being seen by Mary Warren, Deliverance Hobbs and Abigail Hobbs, they were greatly affrighted and fell into violent fits, and all of them said that the black man and Mrs. Hawkes and the negro stood by the puppets or rags and pinched them, and then they were afflicted, and when the knots were untied yet they continued as aforesaid. A bit of

A Trial of Witches

one of the rags being set on fire, the afflicted all said they were burned, and cried out dreadfully. The rags being put into water, two of the forenamed persons were in dreadful fits, almost choked, and the other was violently running down to the river, but was stopped.

(Attest.) John Hawthorne, Just. Peace.

'Mrs. Hawkes, the mistress, had no other way to save her life but to confess also.

'Mr. Hale, the minister of Beverly, who has the character of an impartial relator, acknowledges that the confessors, generally, went off from their confessions; some saying they remembered nothing of what they had said, others that they had belied themselves, &c. but he thinks, if the times had been calm, the condition of the confessors might have called for a *melius inquirendum* [*an authorization for a fuller inquiry*]; and thinks it remarkable that children and grandchildren should confirm their parents' and grandparents' confession, instancing in the case of Goody Foster, her daughter Mary Lacey, and grand-daughter Mary Lacey, jr. and that other children should accuse their own parents, as in the case of Richard Carrier, a lad of eighteen years of age. These confessions are preserved, and a few extracts from them will show they were forced from them, through fear of losing their lives if they refused, and their fear, in some, was so great as to disorder their brains, and they scarce knew what they said.

'21 July 1692. Before Major Gidney, Mr. Hawthorne, Mr. Corwin and Captain Higginson.

> *Q.* Goody Foster! You remember we have three times spoken with you, and do you now remember what you then confessed to us?—You have been engaged in very great wickedness, and some have been left to hardness of heart to deny; but it seems that God will give you more favour than others, inasmuch as you relent. But your daughter here hath confessed some things that you did not tell us of. Your daughter was with you and Goody Carrier, when you did ride upon the stick.
> *A.* I did not know it.
> *Q.* How long have you known your daughter to be engaged?
> *A.* I cannot tell, nor have I any knowledge of it at all.
> *Q.* Did you see your daughter at the meeting?
> *A.* No.

A Trial of Witches

Q. Your daughter said she was at the witches' meeting, and that you yourself stood at a distance off and did not partake at that meeting; and you said so also; give us a relation from the beginning until now.

A. I know none of their names that were there, but only Goody Carrier.

Q. Would you know their faces if you saw them?

A. I cannot tell.

Q. Were there not two companies in the field at the same time?

A. I remember no more.—(*Mary Warren, one of the afflicted, said that Goody Carrier's shape told her, that Goody Foster had made her daughter a witch.*)

Q. Do not you acknowledge that you did so about thirteen years ago?

A. No, and I know no more of my daughter's being a witch than what day I shall die upon.

Q. Are you willing your daughter should make a full and free confession?

A. Yes.

Q. Are you willing to do so too?

A. Yes.

Q. You cannot expect peace of conscience without a free confession.

A. If I knew anything more, I would speak it to the utmost.—

Goody Lacey, the daughter, called in, began thus; "Oh! mother! how do you do? We have left Christ, and the devil hath got hold of us. How shall I get rid of this evil one? I desire God to break my rocky heart that I may get the victory this time."

Q. Goody Foster! you cannot get rid of this snare, your heart and mouth is not open.

A. I did not see the devil, I was praying to the Lord.

Q. What Lord?

A. To God.

Q. What God do witches pray to?

A. I cannot tell, the Lord help me.

Q. Goody Lacey! Had you no discourse with your mother when riding?

A. No, I think I had not a word.

Q. Who rid foremost on that stick to the village?

A. I suppose my mother.

A Trial of Witches

Goody Foster said, that Goody Carrier was foremost.
Q. Goody Lacey! How many years ago since they were baptised?
A. Three or four years ago, I suppose.
Q. Who baptised them?
A. The old serpent.
Q. How did he do it?
A. He dipped their heads in the water, saying, they were his, and that he had power over them.
Q. Where was this?
A. At Fall's river.
Q. How many were baptised that day?
A. Some of the chief; I think there were six baptised.
Q. Name them.
A. I think they were of the higher powers.

['It was time to stop.' Hutchinson.]

Mary Lacey, the grand-daughter, was brought in, and Mary Warren fell into a violent fit.
Q. How dare you come in here, and bring the devil with you, to afflict these poor creatures?
Lacey laid her hand on Warren's arm, and she recovered from her fit.
Q. You are here accused of practising witchcraft upon Goody Ballard, which way do you do it?
A. I cannot tell. Where is my mother that made me a witch, and I knew it not?
Q. Can you look upon that maid Mary Warren, and not hurt her? Look upon her in a friendly way.
She, trying so to do, struck her down with her eyes.
Q. Do you acknowledge now you are a witch?
A. Yes.
Q. How long have you been a witch?
A. Not above a week.
Q. Did the devil appear to you?
A. Yes.
Q. In what shape?
A. In the shape of a horse.
Q. What did he say to you?
A. He bid me not to be afraid of anything, and he would not bring me out, but he has proved a liar from the beginning.
Q. When was this?

A Trial of Witches

A. I know not; above a week.
Q. Did you set your hand to the book?
A. No.
Q. Did he bid you worship him?
A. Yes, he bid me also afflict persons.
Q. You are now in the way to obtain mercy if you will confess and repent. (*She said, "The Lord help me."*)
Q. Do not you desire to be saved by Christ?
A. Yes.
Q. Then you must confess freely what you know in this matter.
She then proceeded. "I was in bed and the devil came to me and bid me obey him and I should want for nothing, and he would not bring me out."
Q. But how long ago?
A. A little more than a year.
Q. Was that the first time?
A. Yes.
Q. How long was you gone from your father, when you ran away?
A. Two days.
Q. Where had you your food?
A. At John Stone's.
Q. Did the devil, appear to you then, when you was abroad?
A. No, but he put such thoughts in my mind as not to obey my parents.
Q. Who did the devil bid you afflict?
A. Timothy Swan. Richard Carrier comes often a-nights and has me to afflict persons.
Q. Where do ye go?
A. To Goody Ballard's sometimes.
Q. How many of you were there at a time?
A. Richard Carrier and his mother, and my mother and grandmother.
Upon reading over the confession so far, Goody Lacey, the mother, owned this last particular.
Q. How many more witches are there in Andover?
A. I know no more, but Richard Carrier.

'Carrier, at first, denied all, but was followed until he was brought to accuse his mother, much in the same manner with Foster's daughter and grand-daughter.

'It is urged by the writers of that day, as a principal part of the evidence against Mr. Burroughs, the minister, that seven or eight of the confessors witnessed against him. It will appear from the examinations, that the confession was drawn from the examinants by the Court.

Q. Mary Lacey! was there not a man also among you at your meeting?
A. None but the devil.
Q. What shape was the devil in then?
A. He was a black man, and had a high crowned hat.
Q. Your mother and your grandmother say, there was a minister there. How many men did you see there?
A. I saw none but Richard Carrier.
Q. Did you see none else?
A. There was a minister there, and I think he is now in prison.
Q. Were there not two ministers there?

['Mr. Dane, one of the ministers of Andover, then near fourscore, seems to have been in danger. He is tenderly touched in several of the examinations, which might be owing to a fair character, and he may be one of the persons accused, who caused a discouragement to further prosecutions. Deliverance Dane being asked why she and the rest brought in Mr. Dane as afflicting persons, she answered, it was Satan's subtlety, for he told her he would put a sham upon all these things, and make people believe that he did afflict. She said Mrs. Osgood and she gave their consent the devil should bring Mr. Dane's shape to afflict. Being asked again if Mrs. Osgood and she acted this business, she said yes. Mr. Dane was much beholden to this woman.' Hutchinson.]

A. Cannot tell.
Q. Was there not one Mr. Burroughs there?
A. Yes.

'Carrier's Examination is in this manner; the questions are omitted. "We met in a green which was the minister's pasture. We were in two companies at last. I think there was a few men with them. I heard Sarah Good talk of a minister or two. One of them was he that has been at the Eastward, his name is Burroughs, and is a little man. I remember not the other's name."

A Trial of Witches

'Margaret Jacobs had been brought to accuse herself, and then to charge Burroughs, the minister, and her own grandfather; but, struck with horror, chose to lose her own life, rather than persist in her confession; and begged forgiveness of Burroughs before his execution, who is said to have freely forgiven her; and recanted all she had said against her grandfather, but in vain as to his life. Her own life was saved by a disorder in her head, which prevented her trial at the first court; but before the next court, she made a formal recantation of all she had confessed and delivered it to the judges.

' "The humble Declaration of Margaret Jacobs unto the honoured Court now sitting at Salem, showeth,

' "That whereas your poor and humble declarant being closely confined here in Salem gaol for the crime of witchcraft, which crime thanks be to the Lord I am altogether ignorant of as will appear at the great day of judgment: May it please the honoured Court, I was cried out upon by some of the possessed persons, as afflicting them; whereupon I was brought to my examination, which persons at the sight of me fell down, which did very much startle and affright me. The Lord above knows I knew nothing in the least measure, how or who afflicted them; they told me, without doubt I did, or else they would not fall down at me; they told me, if I would not confess I should be put down into the dungeon and would be hanged, but if I would confess I should have my life; the which did so affright me, with my own vile wicked heart, to save my life; made me make the like confession I did, which confession, may it please the honoured Court, is altogether false and untrue. The very first night after I had made confession, I was in such horror of conscience that I could not sleep for fear the devil should carry me away for telling such horrid lies. I was, may it please the honoured Court, sworn to my confession, as I understand since, but then, at that time, was ignorant of it, not knowing what an oath did mean. The Lord, I hope, in whom I trust, out of the abundance of His mercy, will forgive me my false forswearing myself. What I said was altogether false against my grandfather and Mr. Burroughs which I did to save my life and to have my liberty; but the Lord charging it to my conscience made me in so much horror that I could not contain myself before I had denied my confession, which I did though I saw nothing but death before me choosing rather death with a quiet conscience, than to live in such horror, which I could not suffer. Where, upon my denying my confession, I was committed to close prison, where I have enjoyed more felicity in spirit, a thousand times, than I did before in my enlargement.

' "And now, may it please your honours, your declarant, having in part given your honours a description of my condition, do leave it to your honours' pious and judicious discretions, to take pity and compassion on my young and tender years, to act and do with me, as the Lord above and your honours shall see good, having no friend, but the Lord, to plead my cause for me; not being guilty in the least measure of the crime of witchcraft, nor any other sin that deserves death from man; and your poor and humble declarant shall for ever pray, as she is bound in duty, for your honours' happiness in this life and eternal felicity in the world to come. So prays your honours' declarant.

Margaret Jacobs."

'The Recantation of several persons in Andover will show in what manner they were brought to their confessions:

' "We whose names are under-written, inhabitants of Andover; when as that horrible and tremendous judgment beginning at Salem village in the year 1692, by some called witchcraft, first breaking forth at Mr. Parris's house, several young persons, being seemingly afflicted, did accuse several persons for afflicting them, and many there believing it so to be, we being informed that, if a person was sick, the afflicted person could tell what or who was the cause of that sickness: Joseph Ballard, of Andover, his wife being sick at the same time, he either from himself or by the advice of others, fetched two of the persons, called the afflicted persons, from Salem village to Andover, which was the beginning of that dreadful calamity that befell us in Andover, believing the said accusations to be true, sent for the said persons to come together to the meeting house in Andover, the afflicted persons being there. After Mr. Barnard had been at prayer, we were blindfolded, and our hands were laid upon the afflicted persons, they being in their fits and falling into their fits at our coming into their presence, as they said; and some led us and laid our hands upon them, and then they said they were well, and that we were guilty of afflicting them: whereupon, we were all seized, as prisoners, by a warrant from the justice of the peace and forthwith carried to Salem. And, by reason of that sudden surprisal, we knowing ourselves altogether innocent of that crime, we were all exceedingly astonished and amazed, and consternated and affrighted even out of our reason; and our nearest and dearest relations, seeing us in that dreadful condition, and knowing our great danger, apprehended there was no other way to save our lives, as the case was then circumstanced, but by our confessing ourselves to be such and such persons as the afflicted represented us to be, they, out of tenderness and pity, persuaded us to confess what we did confess. And indeed that confession, that it is said we made, was no other than what was suggested to us by some gentlemen, they telling us that we were witches, and they knew it, and we knew it, which made us to think that it was so; and our understandings, our reason, our faculties, almost gone, we were not capable of judging of our condition; as also the hard measures they used with us rendered us incapable of making our defence, but said anything and everything which they desired, and most of what we said was but, in effect, a consenting to what they said. Some time after, when we were better composed, they telling us what we had confessed, we did profess that we were innocent and ignorant of such things; and we hearing that Samuel Wardwell had renounced his confession, and quickly after condemned and executed, some of us were told we were going after Wardwell.

' "Mary Osgood, Deliverance Dane, Sarah Wilson, Mary Tiler, Abigail Barker, Hannah Tiler."

' The testimonial to these persons' characters by the principal inhabitants of Andover will outweigh the credulity of the justices who committed them or of the grand jury which found bills against them.

' "To the honoured Court of Assize held at Salem. The humble Address of several of the Inhabitants of Andover.

' "May it please this honoured Court, we being very sensible of the great sufferings our neighbours have been long under in prison, and charitably judging that many of them are clear of that great transgression which hath been laid to their charge, have thought it our duty to endeavour their vindication so far as our testimony for them will avail. The persons in whose behalf we are desired and concerned to speak something at present are Mrs. Mary Osgood, Eunice Frye, Deliverance Dane, Sarah Wilson and Abigail Barker, who are women of whom we can truly give this character and commendation, that they have not only lived among us so inoffensively as not to give the least occasion to any that know them to suspect them of witchcraft, but by their sober godly and exemplary conversation have obtained a good report in the place, where they have been well esteemed and approved in the church of which they are members.

' "We were surprised to hear that persons of known integrity and piety were accused of so horrid a crime, not considering, then, that the most innocent were liable to be so misrepresented and abused. When these women were accused by some afflicted persons of the neighbourhood, their relations and others, though they had so good grounds of charity that they should not have thought any evil of them yet, through a misrepresentation of the truth of that evidence that was so much credited and improved against people, took great pains to persuade them to own what they were, by the afflicted, charged with, and, indeed, did unreasonably urge them to confess themselves guilty, as some of us who were then present can testify. But these good women did very much assert their innocency, yet some of them said they were not without fear lest Satan had some way ensnared them, because there was that evidence against them which then was by many thought to be a certain indication and discovery of witchcraft, yet they seriously professed they knew nothing by themselves of that nature. Nevertheless, by the unwearied solicitations of those that privately discoursed them both at home and at Salem, they were at length persuaded publicly to own what they were charged with, and so submit to that guilt which we still hope and believe they are clear of. And, it is probable, the fear of what the event might be and the encouragement that, it is said, was suggested to them, that confessing was the only way to obtain favour, might be too powerful a temptation for timorous women to withstand, in the hurry and distraction that we have heard they were then in. Had what they said against themselves proceeded from conviction of the fact, we should have had nothing to have said for them, but we are induced to think that it did not, because they did soon privately retract what they had said, as we are informed, and, while they were in prison, they declared to such as they had confidence to speak freely and plainly to, that they were not guilty of what they had owned, and that what they had said against themselves was the greatest grief and burden they laboured under: now, though we cannot but judge it a thing very sinful for innocent persons to own a crime they are not guilty of, yet, considering the well-ordered conversation of those women while they lived among us,

A Trial of Witches

and what they now seriously and constantly affirm in a more composed frame, we cannot but in charity judge them innocent of the great transgression that hath been imputed to them. As for the rest of our neighbours, who are under the like circumstances with these that have been named, we can truly say of them that, while they lived among us, we have had no cause to judge them such persons as, of late, they have been represented and reported to be, nor do we know that any of their neighbours had any just grounds to suspect them of that evil that they are now charged with.

Dudley Bradstreet	Francis Dane, jr.
Francis Dane, sr.	George Abbot
Thomas Barnard	William Chandler, jr.
Thomas Chandler, sr.	John Chandler
John Barker	Joseph Robinson
Henry Ingolls, sr.	Thomas Johnson
William Chandler, sr.	Thomas Johnson, jr.
Samuel Martin	Andrew Peters
Stephen Parker	Mary Peters
Samuel Ingolls	Elizabeth Rite
Ephraim Stevens	William Peters
Daniel Poore	Samuel Peters
John Ingolls	Walter Wright
Henry Ingolls, jr.	Hooker Osgood
John Frie, sr.	Benjamin Stevens
James Frie	Ann Bradstreet
John Aslebee	Joanna Dane
Samuel Holt	Elizabeth Stevens
John Abbot, sr.	Elizabeth Barnard
Samuel Blanchard	Phoebe Robinson
William Ballard	Hannah Chandler
Thomas Hooper	Hannah Dane
John Hooper	Bridget Chandler
William Abbot	Mary Johnson
James Russell	Robert Russell
Oliver Holt	Mary Russell
John Presson"	

'Among the confessing witches I find Dorothy Falkener, a child of ten years, Abigail Falkener of eight, and Sarah Carrier between seven and eight.

A Trial of Witches

'Sarah Carrier's Confession, Aug. 11th, 1692.

'It was asked Sarah Carrier by the magistrates or justices, John Hawthorne Esq. and others:

Q. How long hast thou been a witch?
A. Ever since I was six years old.
Q. How old are you now?
A. Near eight years old, brother Richard says I shall be eight years old in November next.
Q. Who made you a witch?
A. My mother, she made me set my hand to a book.
Q. How did you set your hand to it?
A. I touched it with my fingers and the book was red, the paper of it was white.—(*She said she had never seen the black man; the place where she did it was in Andrew Foster's pasture and Elizabeth Johnson, jr. was there. Being asked who was there beside, she answered her Aunt Toothaker and her cousin. Being asked when it was, she said, when she was baptised.*)
Q. What did they promise to give you?
A. A black dog.
Q. Did the dog ever come to you?
A. No.
Q. But you said you saw a cat once. What did that say to you?
A. It said it would tear me in pieces if I would not set my hand to the book.—(*She said her mother baptised her and the devil or black man was not there as she saw, and her mother said when she baptised her, "Thou art mine for ever and ever and amen."*)
Q. How did you afflict folks?
A. I pinched them—(*And she said she had no puppets, but she went to them that she afflicted. Being asked whether she went in her body or her spirit, she said in her spirit. She said her mother carried her thither to afflict.*)
Q. How did your mother carry you when she was in prison?
A. She came like a black cat.
Q. How did you know that it was your mother?
A. The cat told me so that she was my mother.—(*She said she afflicted Phelp's child last Saturday, and Elizabeth Johnson joined with her to do it. She had a wooden spear, about as long as her finger, of Elizabeth Johnson, and she had it of the devil. She would not own that she had ever been at the witch meeting at the village. This is the substance.*)

(Attest.) Simon Willard.

A Trial of Witches

'This poor child's mother then lay under sentence of death, the mother of the other two children was in prison, and soon after tried and condemned, but upon her confession reprieved and finally pardoned.

'I meet with but one person in near an hundred whose examinations are upon file, that was dismissed after having been once charged, for which he might thank one of the girls who would not agree with the rest of the accusation.

'The Examination of Nehemiah Abbot, at a court at Salem village, by John Hawthorne and Jonathan Corwin Esqrs. 22 April 1692.

Q. What say you, are you guilty of witchcraft, of which you are suspected, or not?

A. No sir, I say before God, before whom I stand, that I know nothing of witchcraft.

Q. Who is this man?—(*Ann Putman named him. Mary Walcot said she had seen his shape.*)

Q. What do you say to this?

A. I never did hurt them.

Q. Who hurt you Ann Putman?

A. That man.

(*Abbot*) I never hurt her. (*Ann Putman said, "He is upon the beam."*)

Q. Just such a discovery of the person carried out, and she confessed; and if you would find mercy of God, you must confess.

A. If I should confess this, I must confess what is false.

Q. Tell how far have you gone, who hurts you?

A. I do not know, I am absolutely free.

Q. As you say, God knows. If you will confess the truth, we desire nothing else that you may not hide your guilt, if you are guilty, and therefore confess if so.

A. I speak before God that I am clear from this accusation.

Q. What, in all respects?

A. Yes in all respects.

Q. Doth this man hurt you?

Their mouths were stopped.

Q. You hear several accuse you, though one cannot open her mouth.

A. I am altogether free. (*"Charge him not unless it be he." "This is the man," say some, and some say "He is very like him."*)

Q. How did you know his name?

A. He did not tell me himself, but other witches told me.

Ann Putman said, "It is the same man," and then she was taken with a fit.

Q. Mary Walcot, is this the man?

A. He is like him, I cannot say it is he.

Mercy Lewis said "It is not the man." They all agreed, the man had a bunch [swelling] on his eyes. Ann Putman, in a fit said, "Be you the man? Ay, do you say you be the man? Did you put a mist before my eyes?" Then he was sent forth till several others were examined. When he was brought in again, by reason of much people and many in the windows so that the accusers could not have a clear view of him, he was ordered to be abroad and the accusers to go forth to him and view him in the light, which they did, and in the presence of the magistrates and many others discoursed quietly with him, one and all acquitting him, but yet said he was like that man, but he had not the wen they saw in his apparition. Note, he was a hilly-faced man, and stood shaded by reason of his own hair, so that for a time he seemed to some bystanders and observers, to be considerably like the person the afflicted did describe.

'Mr. Samuel Parris, being desired to take in writing the examination of Nehemiah Abbot, hath delivered it as aforesaid, and upon hearing the same did see cause to dismiss him.

John Hawthorne,
Jonathan Corwin, Assistants.

'We see, from the preceding examinations and confessions, the method of proceeding preparatory to the trial of the accused persons.

'For three or four months, the afflicted generally confined themselves to their own neighbourhood, in their accusations. In the examinations there is, sometimes, mention made of strangers, whose shapes or spectres were unknown to the afflicted. The first accused, in any other county, was Mrs. Cary, wife of Mr. Nathaniel Cary, a principal inhabitant of the town of Charlestown. He, as soon as he heard of it, carried his wife to Salem village, supposing she would not be known to the afflicted. They happened to arrive, just as the justices were going into the meeting house, where they held their court, to examine prisoners. All the prisoners which were brought in, were accused, and the girls fell into fits as usual; but Mrs. Cary came in and sat without any notice, except that one or two of the afflicted came to her and asked her name. After the examination, her husband went to the tavern, intending there to discourse with one of the girls, who he heard had accused his wife. John, the

A Trial of Witches

Indian who pretended to be one of the afflicted, was a servant in the house. Two of the girls were soon brought in, and instead of giving any opportunity of discoursing with them, they tumbled about the floor, crying out, "Cary, Cary," and a warrant came to apprehend her; the Indian joining with the two girls in the charge. No bail could be admitted, nor was it to any purpose to make any defence, and she was ordered to the prison in Boston; but, upon the request of her husband was removed to Cambridge gaol, where she was kept in irons. Afterwards when the trials came on at Salem, her husband went there to see how they were managed, and he thought the only chance his wife had for her life, was by an escape, which, by some means or other, he effected, and fled with her to New York, where Governor Fletcher entertained them very courteously.—They petitioned, I suppose before the escape, that she might be tried in the county where she lived. If the Court thought they were held to try the fact in the county where it was committed, there seems to have been room for an argument, her body being in Middlesex at the same time that her spectre and the body of the afflicted persons were in Essex.

'Mrs. Cary was committed about the middle of May. Towards the end of the month, Captain John Alden of Boston was accused, who was thereupon sent down to Salem. He had been many years commander of a sloop in the colony service, employed for supplying the forts east with provisions and stores; and although, upon his first appearing, the justices allowed that he always had the character of an honest man, yet one of them Gidney, soon after, let him know he then saw reason to think otherwise of him. Alden, in his account, says that the accuser first pointed to another man and said nothing, but that the man who held her stooped down to her ear and then she cried out "Alden, Alden!" All were ordered into the street and a ring made, and then she cried out, "There stands Alden a bold fellow with his hat on, sells powder and shot to the Indians, lies with the squaws and has papooses, &c." He was immediately taken into custody of the Marshal, and required to deliver up his sword. A further examination was had in the meeting house, and his hands were held open by the officer, that he might not pinch the afflicted, who were struck down at the sight of him, and made their usual cries; all which, the justices deemed sufficient grounds for committing him to gaol, where he lay fifteen weeks, and then he was prevailed on by his friends to make his escape, and to absent himself until the consternation should abate and the people recover the use of their reason.

'Although the number of prisoners had been increasing from February until the beginning of June, yet there had been no trials. The charter was expected from day to day, and the new constitution of government to take place.[8] Soon after its arrival, Commissioners of Oyer and Terminer were appointed for the trial of witchcrafts. By the charter, the general assembly are to constitute courts of justice, and the Governor with the advice of Council is to nominate and appoint judges, Commissioners of Oyer and Terminer, &c. but whether the Governor, with advice of Council can constitute a court of Oyer and Terminer, without authority for that purpose derived from the general assembly, has been made a question; however, this, the most important court to the life of the subject which ever was held in the province, was constituted in no other manner. It was opened at Salem, the first week in June. Only one of the accused, Bridget Bishop, alias Oliver, was then brought to trial. She had been charged with witchcraft twenty years before. The accuser, upon his death bed, confessed his own guilt in the accusation; but an old woman, once charged with being a witch, is never afterwards wholly free from the accusation, and she being, besides, of a fractious temper, all the losses the neighbours met with in their cattle and poultry, and accidents in oversetting their carts, &c. were attributed to her spite against them, and now suffered to be testified against her. This evidence, together with the testimony of the afflicted, and of the confessors, what they had heard from the spectres and seen of her spectre, and an excrescence, called a teat, found upon her body, were deemed by court and jury plenary proof, and she was convicted, and on the 10th of June executed. The further trials were put off to the adjournment, the 30th of June. The Governor and Council thought proper, in the meantime, to take the opinion of several of the principal ministers upon the state of things as they then stood. This was an old charter practice. They gave their opinion as follows.

> ['I fancy this must be what Douglass had heard something of and calls by mistake "the address of many of the very popular but very weak ministers or clergy to Sir W[*illiam*] P[*hips*] a very weak Governor, with thanks for what was already done, and exhorting him to proceed." '
> Hutchinson.]

A Trial of Witches

'"The Return of several Ministers, consulted by His Excellency and the Hon. Council upon the present Witchcraft in Salem village.

Boston, June 15th, 1692.

'"1. The afflicted state of our poor neighbours that are now suffering by molestations from the invisible world, we apprehend so deplorable, that we think their condition calls for the utmost help of all persons in their several capacities.

'"2. We cannot but, with all thankfulness, acknowledge the success which the merciful God has given to the sedulous and assiduous endeavours of our honourable rulers to defeat the abominable witchcrafts which have been committed in the country, humbly praying, that the discovery of those mysterious and mischievous wickednesses may be perfected.

'"3. We judge that in the prosecution of these and all such witchcrafts, there is need of a very critical and exquisite caution, lest by too much credulity for things received only upon the devil's authority, there be a door opened for a long train of miserable consequences, and Satan get an advantage over us; for we should not be ignorant of his devices.

'"4. As, in complaints upon witchcrafts, there may be matters of inquiry which do not amount unto matters of presumption, and there may be matters of presumption which yet may not be matters of conviction, so it is necessary, that all proceedings, thereabout, be managed with an exceeding tenderness towards those that may be complained of, especially if they have been persons formerly of an unblemished reputation.

'"5. When the first inquiry is made into the circumstances of such as may lie under the just suspicion of witchcrafts, we could wish that there may be admitted as little as possible of such noise, company and openness, as may too hastily expose them that are examined, and that there may be nothing used as a test for the trial of the suspected, the lawfulness whereof may be doubted by the people of God; but that the directions given by such judicious writers, as Perkins and Bernard, may be observed.[9]

'"6. Presumptions whereupon persons may be committed, and, much more, convictions whereupon persons may be condemned, as guilty of witchcrafts, ought certainly to be more considerable than barely the accused person's being represented by a spectre unto the afflicted; inasmuch as it is an undoubted and a notorious thing, that a demon may, by God's permission, appear, even to ill purposes, in the shape of an innocent, yea and a virtuous man. Nor can we esteem alterations made in the sufferers, by a look or touch of the accused, to be an infallible evidence of guilt, but frequently liable to be abused by the devil's legerdemain.

'"7. We know not whether some remarkable affronts given the devils, by our disbelieving those testimonies whose whole force and strength is from them alone, may not put a period unto the progress of the dreadful calamity begun upon us, in the accusation of so many persons, whereof some, we hope, are yet clear from the great transgression laid to their charge.

'"8. Nevertheless, we cannot but humbly recommend, unto the government, the speedy and vigorous prosecutions, of such as have rendered themselves obnoxious, according to the directions given in the laws of God and the wholesome statutes of the English nation for the detection of witchcrafts."

'The judges seem to have paid more regard to the last article of this return, than to several which precede it; for the prosecutions were carried on with all possible vigour and without that exquisite caution which is proposed.

'At the first trial, there was no colony or provincial law against witchcraft in force. The statute of James the First[10] must therefore have been considered as in force in the province, witchcraft not being an offence at common law. Before the adjournment, the old colony law, which makes witchcraft a capital offence, was revived, with the other local laws, as they were called, and made a law of the province.

'At the adjournment, 30 June, five women were brought upon trial, Sarah Good, Rebekah Nurse, Susannah Martin, Elizabeth How, and Sarah Wilder.

'There was no difficulty with any but Nurse. She was a member of the church and of a good character, and, as to her, the jury brought in their verdict not guilty; upon which the accusers made a great clamour, and the Court expressed their dissatisfaction with the verdict, which caused some of the jury to desire to go out again; and then they brought her in guilty. This was a hard case, and can scarcely be said to be the execution of law and justice in mercy.

[A part of the oath the king takes at his coronation, 'which judges should have written on their hearts.' Foster's Crown Law.]

A Trial of Witches

In a capital case, the Court often refuses a verdict of guilty, but, rarely, if ever, sends a jury out again, upon one of not guilty. It does not indeed appear, that in this case the jury was ordered out again; but the dissatisfaction expressed by the Court seems to have been in such a manner as to have the same effect. The certificate given by the foreman of the jury, to satisfy the relations of the woman, shows how the fact was.

4 July 1692.

'"I Thomas Fisk, the subscriber hereof, being one of them that were of the jury last week at Salem court, upon the trial of Rebekah Nurse, &c. being desired, by some of the relations, to give a reason why the jury brought her in guilty, after the verdict not guilty; I do hereby give my reasons to be as follows,

'"When the verdict not guilty was given, the honoured Court was pleased to object against it, saying to them, that they think they let slip the words which the prisoner at the bar spake against herself, which were spoken in reply to Goodwife Hobbs and her daughter, who had been faulty in setting their hands to the devil's book, as they had confessed formerly; the words were 'What! Do these persons give in evidence against me now? They used to come among us.' After the honoured Court had manifested their dissatisfaction of the verdict, several of the jury declared themselves desirous to go out again, and thereupon the honoured Court gave leave; but when we came to consider the case, I could not tell how to take her words as an evidence against her, till she had any further opportunity to put her sense upon them, if she would take it; and then going into court, I mentioned the words aforesaid, which by one of the Court were affirmed to have been spoken by her, she being then at the bar, but made no reply nor interpretation of them; whereupon these words were to me a principal evidence against her.

Thomas Fisk."

'Nurse, being informed of the use which had been made of her words, gave in a declaration to the Court, that "when she said Hobbs and her daughter were of her company, she meant no more than that they were prisoners as well as herself; and that, being hard of hearing, she did not know what the foreman of the jury said;" but her declaration had no effect.

'Mr. Noyes, the minister of Salem, a zealous prosecutor, excommunicated the poor old woman and delivered her to Satan, to whom he supposed she had formally given herself up many years before; but her life and conversation had been such, that the remembrance thereof, in a short time after, wiped off all the reproach occasioned by the civil or ecclesiastical sentence against her.

'It is said, that at the trial of Sarah Good, one of the afflicted persons fell into a fit, and after recovery, cried out, that the prisoner had stabbed her and broke her knife in doing it; and a piece of the knife was found upon the afflicted person; but a young man declared that the day before, he broke that very knife and threw away the piece, this afflicted person being then present. The Court took so much notice as to bid her tell no more lies, but went on to improve her as a witness against other prisoners.

> ['This story is related by Calef, who, by his narrative, gave great offence, having censured the proceedings, at a time when in general the country did not see the error they had been in; but in his account of facts which can be evidenced by records, and other original writings, he appears to have been a fair relator.'[11] Hutchinson.]

Something happened, not unlike to this, in a trial before Sir Matthew Hale. The afflicted children, in their fits would shriek out upon the least touch from Rose Cullender, one of the witches, but remained quite insensible when anybody else touched them. Lest there should be any fraud, Lord Cornwallis, Sir Edmund Bacon, Serjeant Keeling and other gentlemen attended one of the girls; whilst she was in her fits, at another part of the hall, and one of the witches was brought, and an apron was put before the girl's eyes; but instead of the witch's hand, another person's hand was taken to touch the girl, who thereupon shrieked out as she used to do. The gentlemen returned and declared to the Court they believed the whole was an imposture. Notwithstanding this, the witch was found guilty, and the judge and all the Court were fully satisfied with the verdict, and awarded sentence accordingly.

'Susannah Martin had been suspected ever since 1669, so that many witch stories were reported of her and given in evidence against her. One of these women, being told at her execution by the minister Mr. Noyes, that he knew she was a witch, and therefore advised her to confess, she replied, that he lied, and that she was no more a witch than he was a wizard; and if he took away her life God would give him blood to drink.

A Trial of Witches

['Calef.—They have a tradition among the people of Salem that a peculiar circumstance attended the death of this gentleman, he having been choked with blood, which makes them suppose her, if not a witch, a Pythonissa,[12] at least in this instance.' Hutchinson.]

'At the trial of another of them, it is said, that, one of the afflicted cried out in court upon Mr. Willard, a minister of Boston, and that she was immediately sent out of court; and it was given out that she was mistaken in the person.

[Calef.]

There was one Willard then in prison for witchcraft.

'At the next adjournment, 5 August, George Burroughs, John Procter and Elizabeth his wife, John Willard, George Jacobs and Martha Carrier were all brought upon trial, and condemned and all executed upon the 19th of August, except Elizabeth Procter, who escaped by pleading her belly.

'Burroughs had been a preacher, several years before this, at Salem village, where there had been some misunderstanding between him and the people.

['The confessing witches were examined concerning him.— "Richard Carrier affirmed to the jury that he saw Mr. George Burroughs at the witch meeting at the village, and saw him administer the sacrament. Mary Lacey, sr., and her daughter Mary affirmed that Mr. George Burroughs was at the witch meetings and witch sacraments, and that she knows Mr. Burroughs to be of the company of witches. 3 August 1692."' Hutchinson.]

Afterwards he became a preacher at Wells in the province of Maine. We will be a little more particular in our account of his trial.

['Among the sufferers discovered in England by Matthew Hopkins in 1645, there was one Mr. Lewis, whom Mr. Baxter calls an old reading parson, and says that he confessed he had two imps, and that he sent one to sink a ship which he saw on the coast, and that afterwards he saw the ship sink. Dr. Hutchinson, in his observations upon the Suffolk witches, says, Mr. Lewis was an ancient clergyman, near fourscore, who read Queen Elizabeth's

A Trial of Witches

homilies instead of sermons, but being what was then called a malignant parson, he was more easily convicted; that upon his trial he asserted his innocency, and at his execution read the service for burial himself; that the confession Mr. Baxter mentions was from the evidence of persons at his trial, and as Hopkins had swam him several times till he was near drowning, such confession, or any other, was not matter of great wonder.' Hutchinson.]

The indictment was as follows:

'"Anno Regis et Reginae, &c. quarto.

'"*Essex ss.* The jurors for our Sovereign Lord and Lady the King and Queen, present, that George Burroughs, late of Falmouth in the province of Massachusetts Bay, clerk, the 9th day of May, in the 4th year of the reign of our Sovereign Lord and Lady William and Mary, by the Grace of God of England, Scotland, France and Ireland, King and Queen, Defenders of the Faith, &c. and divers other days and times, as well before as after, certain detestable arts called witchcrafts and sorceries, wickedly and feloniously hath used, practised and exercised, at and within the town of Salem, in the county of Essex aforesaid, in upon and against one Mary Walcot of Salem village, in the county of Essex, single woman; by which said wicked arts, the said Mary Walcot, the 9th day of May, in the 4th year above said, and divers other days and times, as well before as after, was and is tortured, afflicted, pined, consumed, wasted and tormented, against the peace of our Sovereign Lord and Lady the King and Queen, and against the form of the statute in that case made and provided. Endorsed Billa vera."[13] Three other bills were found against him for witchcrafts upon other persons, to all which he pleaded not guilty, and put himself upon trial, &c.

'The afflicted persons, and the confessing witches were first examined; for although, by the advice of the elders, their evidence was not conclusive, yet some presumption arose from it, and with other circumstances to corroborate it, the proof might be sufficient to convict. One circumstance was, that, being a little man, he had performed feats beyond the strength of a giant, viz. had held out a gun of seven feet barrel with one hand, and had carried a barrel full of cider from a canoe to the shore. Upon his urging, that an Indian, who was present, held out the gun also, and the witnesses

46

not remembering that any Indian was there, it was said the Indian, must have been the black man or the devil, who the witnesses swore looks like an Indian. Other evidence was given of his harsh treatment of his wives, having been twice married, and of his pretending to them that he knew what had been said to them in his absence, and his persuading them to give it under their hands in writing, and to swear to it, that they would not reveal his secrets; and it was further said they had privately complained to the neighbours that their house was haunted with spirits. And a brother of one of his wives swore, that going out after strawberries, upon their return, he went into the bushes on foot, and though they rode a quick pace, yet when they came near home, to their astonishment, they found him with them, and that he fell to chiding his wife for talking to her brother about him, and said he knew their thoughts, which the brother said was more than the devil knew; to which Burroughs replied, that his God told him. Against this evidence he urged, that a man was with him, to show that another walked as fast as he did; and this was immediately determined to be the black man also. And, upon the whole, he was confounded and used many twistings and turnings, which I think we cannot wonder at. At his execution, he concluded his dying prayer with the Lord's prayer; probably to convince some of the spectators of his innocence, for it was the received opinion, that a true witch could not say the Lord's prayer without blundering, and in many of the examinations it was used as a test, and several of the old women not saying it right, this was improved against them.

['She was bid to say the Lord's prayer. When she came to "forgive us our trespasses as we forgive them that trespass against us," she said, "so do I". No other mistake, in saying the prayer, remarkable.' A woman's examination, 21 September 1692. Hutchinson.]

'September the 9th, Martha Corey,* Mary Esty,* Alice Parker,* Ann Pudeater,* Dorcas Hoar, and Mary Bradbury were tried, and September 17th, Margaret Scott,* Wilmot Read,* Samuel Wardwell,* Mary Parker,* Abigail Falkener, Rebecca Eames, Mary Lacey, Ann Foster and Abigail Hobbs, and all received sentence of death. Those marked * were executed the 22nd following.

'Mary Esty, who was sister to Nurse, gave into the Court a petition; in which she says, she does not ask her own life, although

A Trial of Witches

she is conscious of her innocence, but prays them before they condemn any more, to examine the confessing witches more strictly; for she is sure they have belied themselves and others, which will appear in the world to which she is going, if it should not in this world.

'Those who were condemned and not executed, I suppose all confessed their guilt. I have seen the confessions of several of them. Wardwell also confessed, but he recanted and suffered. His own wife, as well as his daughter, accused him and saved themselves.

> ['The daughter upon a second inquiry denied that she knew her father and mother to be witches; the wife was not asked a second time.' Hutchinson.]

There are many instances among the examinations, of children accusing their parents, and some of parents accusing their children. This is the only instance of a wife or husband, accusing one the other, and surely this instance ought not to have been suffered. I shudder while I am relating it. Besides this irregularity, there were others in the course of these trials. The facts laid in the indictments were, witchcrafts upon particular persons, there was no evidence of these facts, but what was called spectral evidence, which, in the opinion of the ministers, was insufficient; some of the other evidence was of facts ten or twenty years before, which had no relation to those with which they were charged; and some of them no relation to the crime of witchcraft. Evidence is not admitted, even against the general character of persons upon trial, unless to encounter other evidence brought in favour of it; much less ought their whole lives to be arraigned without giving sufficient time for defence.

> ['Against many of the women there was likewise given in evidence the return of a jury of one man, a doctor, and eight women appointed to examine their bodies for teats and other devil's marks. The search was curious enough, but the return is too indelicate to appear in this relation. Some said the credulity was such that a flea bite would pass well enough for a teat or the devil's mark.' Hutchinson.]

'Giles Corey was the only person, beside those already named, who suffered. He, seeing the fate of all who had put themselves upon trial, refused to plead; but the judges, who had not been careful enough in observing the law in favour of the prisoners, determined to do it against this unhappy man, and he had judgment of *peine fort et dure* for standing mute, and was pressed to death; the only instance which ever was, either before this time or since, in New England. In all ages of the world, superstitious credulity has produced greater cruelty than is practised among the Hottentots, or other nations, whose belief of a deity is called in question.

'This Court of Oyer and Terminer, happy for the country, sat no more. Nineteen persons had been executed, all asserting their innocence; but this was not enough to open the eyes of the people in general. The gaol at Salem was filled with prisoners, and many had been removed to other gaols; some were admitted to bail, all reserved for trial, a law having passed constituting a supreme standing court, with jurisdiction in capital, as well as all other criminal cases. The general court also showed their zeal against witchcraft, by a law passed in the words of the statute of James the First, but this law was disallowed by the King. If the Court was of opinion that the statute extended here, I see no necessity of a provincial act exactly in the same words; if the statute did not extend here, I know not by what law the first that was tried could be sentenced to death.

'The time, by law, for holding the court at Salem, was not until January. This gave opportunity for consideration; and this alone might have been sufficient for a change of opinions and measures, but another reason has been given for it. Ordinarily, persons of the lowest rank in life have had the misfortune to be charged with witchcrafts; and although many such had suffered, yet there remained in prison a number of women, of as reputable families as any in the towns where they lived, and several persons, of still superior rank, were hinted at by the pretended bewitched, or by the confessing witches. Some had been publicly named. Dudley Bradstreet, a justice of peace, who had been appointed one of President Dudley's Council, and who was son to the worthy old Governor, then living, found it necessary to abscond. Having been remiss in prosecuting, he had been charged by some of the afflicted as a confederate. His brother, John Bradstreet, was forced to fly also. Calef says it was intimated that Sir William Phips's lady was among the accused. It is certain, that one who pretended to be bewitched at Boston, where the infection was beginning to spread, charged the Secretary of the colony of Connecticut.

A Trial of Witches

['As to what you mention, concerning that poor creature in your town that is afflicted, and mentioned my name to yourself and son, I return you hearty thanks for your intimation about it, and for your charity therein mentioned, and I have great cause to bless God, who, of His mercy hitherto, hath not left me to fall into such an horrid evil.' Extract of a letter from Secretary Allen to Increase Mather, Hartford, 18 March, 1693.]

'Mrs. Hale, wife to the minister of Beverly, was accused also; which caused her husband to alter his judgment and to be less active in prosecutions than he had been.

'At the court in January, the grand jury found bills against about fifty for witchcraft, one or two men, the rest women; but, upon trial, they were all acquitted, except three of the worst characters, and those the Governor reprieved for the King's mercy. All that were not brought upon trial he ordered to be discharged.

[It is said, the Governor's lady, when Sir William was absent, saved one poor woman from trial. 'In Sir William's absence, his lady, I suppose upon account of her name's being Mary, (William and Mary) was solicited for a favour in behalf of a woman committed by one of the judges, on accusation of witchcraft, by a formal warrant under his hand and seal, and in close prison for trial the next assizes, then not far off. The good lady, *propria virtute*, granted and signed a warrant for the said woman's discharge, which was obeyed by the keeper, and the woman lives still for ought I know. Truly, I did not believe this story till I saw a copy of the mittimus and discharge, under the keeper's hand, attested a true copy, for which discovery the keeper was discharged from his trust and put out of his employment, as he himself told me.' MS. letter.]

Such a gaol delivery was made this court, as has never been known at any other time in New England.

'Several persons had been charged and imprisoned in the County of Middlesex also, and at the first court at Charlestown they were brought to trial, but the jury acquitted them all. Some of the Court were dissatisfied. The juries changed sooner than the judges. However, it was not long before one, at least, of the judges of the first

A Trial of Witches

Court of Oyer and Terminer was sensible of his error. Mr. Sewell, at a public fast, gave in to the minister a bill, acknowledging his error in the late proceedings, and desiring to humble himself in the sight of God and his people. It is said that, the Chief Justice, Mr. Stoughton, being informed of this action of one of his brethren, observed for himself that, when he sat in judgment, he had the fear of God before his eyes and gave his opinion according to the best of his understanding; and although it might appear afterwards, that he had been in an error, yet he saw no necessity of a public acknowledgment of it.

'One of the ministers, who, in the time of it, was fully convinced that the complaining persons were no impostures, and who vindicated his own conduct and that of the Court, in a narrative he published, remarks, not long after, in his diary, that many were of opinion that innocent blood had been shed. None of the pretended afflicted were ever brought upon trial for their fraud, some of them proved profligate persons, abandoned to all vice, others passed their days in obscurity or contempt.

'The opinion which prevailed in New England, for many years after this tragedy, that there was something preternatural in it, and that it was not all the effect of fraud and imposture, proceeded from the reluctance in human nature to reject errors once imbibed. As the principal actors went off the stage, this opinion has gradually lessened, and perhaps it is owing to a respect to the memory of their immediate ancestors, that many do not yet seem to be fully convinced. There are a great number of persons who are willing to suppose the accusers to have been under bodily disorders which affected their imaginations. This is kind and charitable, but seems to be winking the truth out of sight. A little attention must force conviction that the whole was a scene of fraud and imposture, began by young girls, who at first perhaps thought of nothing more than being pitied and indulged, and continued by adult persons, who were afraid of being accused themselves. The one and the other, rather than confess their fraud, suffered the lives of so many innocents to be taken away, through the credulity of judges and juries.'

['The general court, about twenty years after, upon the petitions of the relations of those who had been executed, and of several persons who had been charged and fled, and whose goods had been seized, made grants for and in consideration of the losses sustained; but the petitioners alleged, that they bore no proportion to the real damage. Philip English, a merchant in Salem, received 300*l*.—He computed his damages at 1500*l*.—Inquiry was made by a committee, and they professed to report such sums as each petitioner had suffered.' Hutchinson.][14]

The following Reports are from Lord Fountainhall's *Decisions*, &c.: 'Criminal Court. 10 and 11 September 1678.

'Eight or ten witches, all (except one or two) poor miserable like women were panelled, some of them were brought out of Sir Robert Hepburn of Keith's lands, others out of Ormiston, Crighton, and Pancaitland parishes. The first of them were delated [*informed against*] by these two who were burnt in Salt-Preston in May 1678, and they divulged and named the rest, as also put forth seven in the Lonehead of Leswade; and if they had been permitted were ready to file, by their delation, sundry gentlewomen and others of fashion; but the justices discharged them, thinking it either the product of malice, or melancholy, or the devil's deception, in representing such persons as present at their field-meetings who truly were not there. Yet this was cried out on as a prelimiting them from discovering these enemies of mankind. However, they were permitted to name Mr. Gideon Penman, who had been minister at Crighton, and for sundry acts of uncleanness and other crimes was deprived. Two or three of the witches constantly affirmed that he was present at their meetings with the devil; and that when the devil called for him, he asked, "Where is Mr. Gideon, my chaplain?" and that ordinarily Mr. Gideon was in the rear in all their dances, and beat up these that were slow. He denied all, and was liberate upon caution. They declared and confessed the first thing the devil caused them to do was to renounce their baptism; and by laying their hand on the top of their head, and the other on the sole of their foot, to renounce all betwixt the two to his service: that one of them was at the time with child in fornication, and in her resignation she excepted the child, at which the devil was very angry. That he lay frequently with them, and kissed them, but was cold, and his breath was like a damp air; that he cruelly beat them when they had done the evil he had enjoined them; for that he was (said they) a most wicked and barbarous master. That he adventured to give them the communion or holy sacrament. I remember in 1670 we heard that the devil appeared in the shape of a minister, in the copper mines of Sweden, and attempted the same villainous apery: the bread was like wafers, the drink was sometimes blood, and other times black moss-water. That he preached and most blasphemously mocked them, if they offered to trust in God who left them miserable in the world, and neither He nor His Son Jesus Christ ever appeared to them when they called on them, as he had, who would not cheat them. That sometimes he transformed them into bees, ravens, and crows, and they flew to such and such remote places; which was impossible for the devil to do, to rarify the substance of their body into so small a matter. And some thought he might take away their spirit and convey it to these places, leaving the body behind, but this were to give him the power of the resurrection of the dead; for death is nothing but the removal of the soul from the body, which being once done it is not in his power to reunite them. So that all he deludes them in is by representing such and such ideas, shapes and objects to their imagination and fancy when asleep, and in our sleep we will have very lively conceptions of things, only in these diabolic transports their sleep is so deep that no pinching will awake them. Their confessions made many intelligent sober persons stumble much what faith was to be adhibite to them. See at the end of February 1677, a large discourse about witchcraft, on the occasion of bewitching of Pollock Maxwell, and Janet Douglas the discoverer of it; Joseph Mead's story of the devil's apeing God in conveying the Tartars to Mexico, and Camerarii *Meditat. Histor. centur.* 1. c. 70.[15] There is a story told of one who in King James the Sixth's time was prosecuted as a witch, because a Scotchman being troubled with a disease in Italy, and craving a magician's help and cure for it, he was told he needed not have come so far from home, for there was one in Scotland could cure it, and gave him his marks. After some years, being returned, on the bridge of Earn, he met one to whom all the marks did quadrate, to whom having imparted the case, he cured him by application of some simple herbs. This coming abroad he is accused of necromancy, and compact with Satan, and found guilty, though he alleged that the cure was natural, and he would teach any of them to do as much; and that the devil's naming him could not make him guilty, else it should be in his power to ruin and destroy the most innocent and godly persons. As for the encounter betwixt Mr. Williamson schoolmaster at Couper, (who has wrote a grammar,) and the Rosicrucians, I never trusted it till I heard it from his own son, who is present minister of Kirkaldie. He tells, that a stranger came to Couper, and called for him; after they had drank a little, and the reckoning came to be paid, he whistled for spirits; one in the shape of a boy came, and gave him gold in abundance; no servant was seen riding with him to the town, nor enter with him into the inn: he caused his spirits against next day bring him noble Greek wine from the Pope's cellar, and tell the freshest news then at Rome; then trysted Mr. Williamson at London, who met the same man in a coach near to London bridge, and who called on him by his name; he marvelled to see any know him there; at last he found it was his Rosicrucian. He pointed to a tavern, and desired Mr. Williamson to do him the favour to dine with him at that house; whither he came about twelve o'clock, and found him and many others of good fashion there, and a most splendid and magnificent table, furnished with all the varieties of delicate meats, where they are all served by spirits. At dinner they debated on the excellency of being attended by spirits; and after dinner they proposed to him, to assume him into their society, and make him participant of their happy life: but among the other conditions and qualifications requisite this was one that they demanded, his abstracting his spirit from all materiality, and abandoning and renouncing his baptismal engagements. Being amazed at this proposal he falls a-praying, whereat they all disappear and leave him alone. Then he began to forethink what would become him if he were left to pay that vast reckoning, not having as much on him as would defray it. He calls the boy, and asks what was become of these gentlemen, and what was to pay? He answered there was nothing to pay, for they had done it, and were gone about their affairs in the city. Some said he was left in a jacks [*privy*], but this relation his son affirmed to be truth. As for appearances, by which the devil has actuated dead bodies, and made them move; see of Cornelius Agrippa and many others, some very odd stories recorded by Delrio, in his *Disquisitiones Magicae*,[16] though Gabriel Naudaeus in his *Apology*,[17] endeavours to wash Agrippa's face very clean, and to justify him and the rest from the imputation of magic. There was one or two of these women that denied, and so were set at liberty; nine of them upon their confession (and so seemed very rational and penitent) were sentenced to be strangled, and then burnt, which was shortly after executed upon five of them between

A Trial of Witches

Leith and Edinburgh, and the other four were burnt at Painstonmuir within their own parish where they had lived. The Secret Council gave a commission to Sir John Nicolson, John Clerk of Pennycuik, John Johnston of Polton, and Mr. John Preston, advocate, to judge these seven who were defamed for witches in the Lonehead of Leswade.

'At a Secret Council, Catherine Liddel exhibited a complaint against —— Rutherford baron baillie to Morison of Prestongrange, and against David Cowan in Tranent, bearing that they had seized upon her an innocent woman, and defamed her as a witch, and detained her under restraint as a prisoner; and that the said Cowan had pricked her with long pins, in sundry places of her body, and bled her and tortured her most cruelly. The defences were, that she was delated by other witches, and that "*mala fama laborabat*" [*a bad reputation worked against her*], and was thereupon apprehended, and yet so kindly used as not to be thrust into any public prison, but kept in a private house; that she and her son-in-law consented that she might be searched, "et sic volenti seu consentienti non fit injuria neque dolus" [*being thus by will and consent, did no injustice or crime*], it being desired for the manifestation and vindication of her innocency. As for the pricker, 1mo, He learned his trade from Kincaid, a famed pricker. 2do, He never came unsent for, because he was either called by sheriffs, magistrates of boroughs, ministers or baillies of baronies, so what he did was "auctore praetore" [*by magisterial authority*]; and so "velle non creditur qui obsequitur imperio domini, et non est in dolo qui judici obtemperat" [*he is not thought to be responsible who follows his master's command, and he is not guilty who obeys a judge*]. 3tio, The trade was not improbat or condemned by any law among us; and so not being prohibitum it was "de genere permissorum" [*permitted*]. 4to, All divines and lawyers who write on witchcraft, as Perkins, Delrio, &c. acknowledge there are such marks, called by them, "stigmata sagarum" [*witches' marks*], why then may there not be an art for discerning and distinguishing them from other marks in the body. 5to, "Error communis facit jus" [*universal errors become law*]. The council may restrain that way of trial for the future, but must pardon bygones. Answered, 1mo, Denies consent. 2do, None can validly consent to their own torture, for "nemo est dominus suorum membrorum" [*no one is absolute master of his own limbs*]. As for the pricker, he was a cheat, and abused the people for gain; and the Chancellor remembered that he had caused imprison that Kincaid the pricker in Kinross, for abusing the country there. The Lords of Privy Council first declared the woman innocent, and restored her to her good name and fame, and ordained it to be publicly intimate the next Sunday in her parish church: they reproved Rutherford the baron baillie for his rashness, and discharged him to proceed so hereafter; and found that no inferior judge, much less a baron baillie, had power to apprehend, or incarcerate, or detain any of the King's lieges under restraint, upon the pretence of their being delated or suspected as witches, but that they must immediately intimate it with the first occasion, either to the Lords of Privy Council, or to the Lords of Justiciary, and obtain their warrant for the taking of them: As also "found they might not use any torture by pricking, or by withholding them from sleep, &c. but reserved all that to themselves, and the justices, and those who acted by commissions from them." And as a mark of their displeasure against the pricker, they commanded him to prison, there to lie during their pleasure.

'6 November 1678. Criminal Court. Three witches brought in from Falla parish were condemned at the criminal court to be burnt, upon their judicial confessions.'

Hawkins in his Chapter of Witchcraft (*Pleas of the Crown* book 1, c.4) distributes offenders of this nature into three kinds; first, conjurers who by force of certain magic words endeavoured to raise the devil, and compel him to execute their commands; secondly, witches, who by way of friendly conference are said to bargain with an evil spirit to do what they desire of him; thirdly, sorcerers or charmers, who by the use of certain superstitious forms of words, or by means of images, or other odd representations of persons or things, &c. are said to produce strange effects above the ordinary course of nature.

A Trial of Witches

At the Assizes and general Gaol Delivery, held at Bury St. Edmunds for the County of Suffolk, the 10th day of March, in the 16th year of the reign of our Sovereign Lord King Charles II, before Matthew Hale, knt. Lord Chief Baron of his Majesty's Court of Exchequer; Rose Cullender and Amy Duny, widows, both of Lowestoft in the County aforesaid, were severally indicted for bewitching Elizabeth and Ann

A Trial of Witches

Durent, Jane Bocking, Susan Chandler, William Durent, Elizabeth and Deborah Pacy: and the said Cullender and Duny, being arraigned upon the said indictments, pleaded not guilty: and afterwards upon a long evidence, were found guilty, and thereupon had judgment to die for the same.

To the Reader

This trial of witches hath lain a long time in a private gentleman's hands in the country, it being given to him by the person that took it in the court for his own satisfaction; but it came lately to my hands, and having perused it, I found it a very remarkable thing, and fit to be published; especially in these times, wherein things of this nature are so much controverted, and that by persons of much learning on both sides. I thought that so exact a relation of this trial would probably give more satisfaction to a great many persons, by reason that it is pure matter of fact, and that evidently demonstrated; than the arguments and reasons of other very learned men, that probably may not be so intelligible to all readers; especially, this being held before a judge, whom for his integrity, learning, and law, hardly any age either before or since could parallel; who not only took a great deal of pains, and spent much time in this trial himself; but had the assistance and opinion of several other very eminent and learned persons: so that this being the most perfect narrative of anything of this nature hitherto extant, made me unwilling to deprive the world of the benefit of it; which is the sole motive that induced me to publish it.[18]

The evidence whereupon these persons were convicted of witchcraft, stands upon divers particular circumstances.

1. Three of the parties above-named, viz. Anne Durent, Susan Chandler, and Elizabeth Pacy were brought to Bury to the assizes and were in a reasonable good condition; but that morning they came into the hall to give instructions for the drawing of their bills of indictments, the three persons fell into strange and violent fits, shrieking out in a most sad manner, so that they could not in any wise give any instruction in the court who were the cause of their distemper. And although they did after some certain space recover out of their fits, yet they were every one of them struck dumb, so that none of them could speak neither at that time, nor during the assizes until the conviction of the supposed witches.

As concerning William Durent, being an infant, his mother

A Trial of Witches

Dorothy Durent sworn and examined deposed in open court, that about the 10th of March, nono Caroli Secundi [*1657*], she having a special occasion to go from home, and having none in her house to take care of her said child (it then sucking) desired Amy Duny her neighbour, to look to her child during her absence, for which she promised her to give her a penny; but the said Dorothy Durent desired the said Amy not to suckle her child, and laid a great charge upon her not to do it. Upon which it was asked by the Court, why she did give that direction, she being an old woman and not capable of giving suck? It was answered by the said Dorothy Durent, that she very well knew that she did not give suck, but that for some years before, she had gone under the reputation of a witch, which was one cause made her give her the caution. Another was, that it was customary with old women, that if they did look after a suckling child, and nothing would please it but the breast, they did use to please the child, to give it the breast, and it did please the child, but it sucked nothing but wind, which did the child hurt. Nevertheless after the departure of this deponent, the said Amy did suckle the child; and after the return of the said Dorothy, the said Amy did acquaint her, that she had given suck to the child contrary to her command. Whereupon the deponent was very angry with the said Amy for the same; at which the said Amy was much discontented, and used many high expressions and threatening speeches towards her; telling her, that she had as good to have done otherwise than to have found fault with her, and so departed out of her house; and that very night her son fell into strange fits of swounding, and was held in such terrible manner, that she was much affrighted therewith, and so continued for divers weeks. And the said examinant farther said, that she being exceedingly troubled at her child's distemper did go to a certain person named Dr. Jacob, who lived at Yarmouth, who had the reputation in the country, to help children that were bewitched; who advised her to hang up the child's blanket in the chimney-corner all day, and at night when she put the child to bed, to put it into the said blanket, and if she found anything in it, she should not be afraid, but to throw it into the fire. And this deponent did according to his direction; and at night when she took down the blanket with an intent to put her child therein, there fell out of the same a great toad, which ran up and down the hearth, and she having a young youth only with her in the house, desired him to catch the toad, and

A Trial of Witches

throw it into the fire, which the youth did accordingly, and held it there with the tongs; and as soon as it was in the fire it made a great and horrible noise, and after a space there was a flashing in the fire like gunpowder, making a noise like the discharge of a pistol, and thereupon the toad was no more seen nor heard. It was asked by the Court, if that after the noise and flashing, there was not the substance of the toad to be seen to consume in the fire? And it was answered by the said Dorothy Durent, that after the flashing and noise, there was no more seen than if there had been none there. The next day there came a young woman a kinswoman of the said Amy, and a neighbour of this deponent, and told this deponent, that her aunt (meaning the said Amy) was in a most lamentable condition, having her face all scorched with and that she was sitting alone in her house, in her smock without any fire. And thereupon this deponent went into the house of the said Amy Duny to see her, and found her in the same condition as was related to her; for her face, her legs, and thighs, which this deponent saw, seemed very much scorched and burnt with fire, at which this deponent seemed much to wonder. And asked the said Amy how she came into that sad condition? and the said Amy replied, she might thank her for it, for that she this deponent was the cause thereof, but that she should live to see some of her children dead, and she upon crutches. And this deponent farther saith, that after the burning of the said toad, her child recovered, and was well again, and was living at the time of the assizes. And this deponent farther saith, that about the 6th of March, 11 Charles II [*1659*], her daughter Elizabeth Durent, being about the age of ten years, was taken in like manner as her first child was, and in her fits complained much of Amy Duny, and said, that she did appear to her, and afflict her in such manner as the former. And she this deponent going to the apothecary's for something for her said child, when she did return to her own house, she found the said Amy Duny there, and asked her what she did do there, and her answer was, that she came to see her child, and to give it some water. But she this deponent was very angry with her, and thrust her forth of her doors, and when she went out of doors, she said, 'You need not be so angry, for your child will not live long': and this was on a Saturday, and the child died on the Monday following. The cause of whose death this deponent verily believeth was occasioned by the witchcraft of the said Amy Duny: for that the said Amy hath been long reputed to be a witch, and a person of very evil behaviour, whose kindred and relations have been many of them accused for witchcraft, and some of them have been condemned.

The said deponent further saith, that not long after the death of her daughter, Elizabeth Durent, she this deponent was taken with a lameness in both her legs, from the knees downward, that she was fain to go upon crutches and that she had no other use of them but only to bear a little upon them till she did remove her crutches, and so continued till the time of the assizes, that the witch came to be tried, and was there upon her crutches; the Court asked her, that at the time she was taken with this lameness, if it were with her according to the custom of women? Her answer was, that it was so, and that she never had any stoppages of those things, but when she was with child.

This is the substance of her evidence to this indictment.

There was one thing very remarkable, that after she had gone upon crutches for upwards of three years, and went upon them at the time of the assizes in the court when she gave her evidence, and upon the jury's bringing in their verdict, by which the said Amy Duny was found guilty; to the great admiration of all persons, the said Dorothy Durent was restored to the use of her limbs, and went home without making use of her crutches.

2. As concerning Elizabeth, and Deborah Pacy, the first of the age of eleven years, the other of the age of nine years or thereabouts: as to the elder, she was brought into the court at the time of the instructions given to draw up the indictments, and afterwards at the time of trial of the said prisoners, but could not speak one word all the time, and for the most part she remained as one wholly senseless, as one in a deep sleep, and could move no part of her body, and all the motion of life that appeared in her was, that as she lay upon cushions in the court upon her back, her stomach and belly, by the drawing of her breath, would arise to a great height: and after the said Elizabeth had lain a long time on the table in the court, she came a little to herself and sat up, but could neither see nor speak, but was sensible of what was said to her, and after a while she laid her head on the bar of the court with a cushion under it, and her hand and her apron upon that, and there she lay a good space of time: and, by the direction of the judge, Amy Duny was privately brought to Elizabeth Pacy, and she touched her hand; whereupon the child without so much as seeing her, for her eyes were closed all the while, suddenly leaped up, and catched Amy Duny by the hand,

A Trial of Witches

and afterwards by the face; and with her nails scratched her till blood came, and would by no means leave her till she was taken from her, and afterwards the child would still be pressing towards her, and making signs of anger conceived against her.

Deborah the youngest daughter was held in such extreme manner, that her parents wholly despaired of her life, and therefore could not bring her to the assizes.

The evidence which was given concerning these two children was to this effect:

Samuel Pacy a merchant of Lowestoft aforesaid, (a man who carried himself with much soberness during the trial, from whom proceeded no words either of passion or malice, though his children were so greatly afflicted,) sworn and examined, deposeth, that his youngest daughter Deborah, upon Thursday the 10th of October last, was suddenly taken with a lameness in her legs, so that she could not stand, neither had she any strength in her limbs to support her, and so she continued until the 17th day of the same month, which day being fair and sunshiny, the child desired to be carried on the east part of the house to be set upon the bank which looketh upon the sea; and whilst she was sitting there, Amy Duny came to this deponent's house to buy some herrings, but being denied she went away discontented, and presently returned again, and was denied, and likewise the third time and was denied as at first; and at her last going away, she went away grumbling; but what she said was not perfectly understood. But at the very same instant of time, the said child was taken with most violent fits, feeling most extreme pain in her stomach, like the pricking of pins, and shrieking out in a most dreadful manner like unto a whelp; and not like unto a sensible creature. And in this extremity the child continued to the great grief of the parents until the 30th of the same month. During this time this deponent sent for one Dr. Feavor, a doctor of physic, to take his advice concerning his child's distemper; the doctor being come, he saw the child in those fits, but could not conjecture, as he then told this deponent, and afterwards affirmed in open court, at this trial, what might be the cause of the child's affliction. And this deponent farther saith, that by reason of the circumstances aforesaid, and in regard Amy Duny is a woman of an ill fame, and commonly reported to be a witch and sorceress, and for that the said child in her fits would cry out of Amy Duny as the cause of her malady, and that she did affright her with apparitions of her person (as the child in the intervals of her fits related) he

A Trial of Witches

this deponent did suspect the said Amy Duny for a witch, and charged her with the injury and wrong to his child, and caused her to be set in the stocks on the 28th of the same October: and during the time of her continuance there, one Alice Letteridge and Jane Buxton demanding of her, as they also affirmed in court upon their oaths, what should be the reason of Mr. Pacy's child's distemper, telling her, that she was suspected to be the cause thereof: She replied, 'Mr. Pacy keeps a great stir about his child, but let him stay until he hath done as much by his children, as I have done by mine.' And being further examined, what she had done to her children, she answered, that she had been fain to open her child's mouth with a tap to give it victuals.

And the said deponent further deposeth, that within two days after speaking of the said words, being the 30th of October, the eldest daughter Elizabeth, fell into extreme fits, insomuch, that they could not open her mouth to give her breath, to preserve her life, without the help of a tap which they were enforced to use; and the younger child was in the like manner afflicted, so that they used the same also for her relief.

And further the said children being grievously afflicted would severally complain in their extremity, and also in the intervals, that Amy Duny (together with one other woman whose person and clothes they described) did thus afflict them, their apparitions appearing before them, to their great terror and affrightment: and sometimes they would cry out, saying, 'There stands Amy Duny, and there Rose Cullender;' the other person troubling them.

Their fits were various, sometimes they would be lame on one side of their bodies, sometimes on the other: sometimes a soreness over their whole bodies, so as they could endure none to touch them: at other times they would be restored to the perfect use of their limbs, and deprived of their hearing; at other times of their sight, at other times of their speech; sometimes by the space of one day, sometimes for two; and once they were wholly deprived of their speech for eight days together and then restored to their speech again. At other times they would fall into swoonings, and upon the recovery to their speech they would cough extremely, and bring up much phlegm, and with the same crooked pins, and one time a twopenny nail with a very broad head, which pins (amounting to forty or more) together with the twopenny nail, were produced in court, with the affirmation of the said deponent, that he was present when the said nail was vomited up, and also most of the pins. Commonly at the end of every fit they would cast up a pin, and sometimes they would have four or five fits in one day.

In this manner the said children continued with this deponent for the space of two months, during which time in their intervals this deponent would cause them to read some chapters in the New Testament. Whereupon this deponent several times observed, that they would read till they came to the name of Lord, or Jesus, or Christ; and then before they could pronounce either of the said words they would suddenly fall into their fits. But when they came to the name of Satan, or devil, they would clap their fingers upon the book, crying out, 'This bites, but makes me speak right well.'

At such time as they be recovered out of their fits (occasioned as this deponent conceives upon their naming of Lord, or Jesus, or Christ,) this deponent hath demanded of them, what is the cause they cannot pronounce those words. They reply and say, that Amy Duny saith, I must not use that name.

And farther, the said children after their fits were past, would tell, how that Amy Duny, and Rose Cullender would appear before them holding their fists at them, threatening, that if they related either what they saw or heard, that they would torment them ten times more than ever they did before.

In their fits they would cry out, 'There stands Amy Duny, or Rose Cullender'; and sometimes in one place and sometimes in another, running with great violence to the place where they fancied them to stand, striking at them as if they were present; they would appear to them sometimes spinning, and sometimes reeling, or in other postures, deriding or threatening them.

And this deponent farther said, that his children being thus tormented by all the space aforesaid, and finding no hopes of amendment, he sent them to his sister's house, one Margaret Arnold, who lived at Yarmouth, to make trial whether the change of the air might do them any good. And how, and in what manner they were afterwards held, he this deponent refers himself to the testimony of his said sister.

Margaret Arnold, sworn and examined, saith, that the said Elizabeth and Deborah Pacy came to her house about the 30th of November last, her brother acquainted her, that he thought they were bewitched, for that they vomited pins; and farther informed her of the several passages which occurred at his own house. This deponent said, that she gave no credit to that which was related to her, conceiving possibly the children might use some deceit in putting pins in their mouths themselves. Wherefore this deponent unpinned all their clothes, and left not so much as one pin upon them, but sewed all the clothes they wore, instead of pinning them. But this deponent saith, that notwithstanding all this care and circumspection of hers, the children afterwards raised at several times at least thirty pins in her presence, and had most fierce and violent fits upon them.

The children would in their fits cry out against Rose Cullender and Amy Duny, affirming that they saw them; and they threatened to torment them ten times more, if they complained of them. At some times the children only would see things run up and down the house in the appearance of mice; and one of them suddenly snapped one with the tongs, and threw it in the fire, and it screeched out like a rat.

At another time, the younger child being out of her fits went out of doors to take a little fresh air, and presently a little thing like a bee flew upon her face, and would have gone into her mouth, whereupon the child ran in all haste to the door to get into the house again, screeking out in a most terrible manner, whereupon this deponent made haste to come to her, but before she could get to her, the child fell into her swooning fit, and at last with much pain, straining herself, she vomited up a twopenny nail with a broad head; and after that the child had raised up the nail she came to her understanding; and being demanded by this deponent, how she came by this nail, she answered, that the bee brought this nail and forced it into her mouth.

And at other times, the elder child declared unto this deponent, that during the time of her fits, she saw flies come unto her and bring with them in their mouths crooked pins; and after the child had thus declared the same, she fell again into violent fits, and afterwards raised several pins.

At another time, the said elder child declared unto this deponent, and sitting by the fire suddenly started up and said, she saw a mouse, and she crept under the table looking after it, and at length, she put something in her apron, saying, she had caught it; and immediately she ran to the fire and threw it in, and there did appear upon it to this deponent like the flashing of gunpowder, though she confessed she saw nothing in the child's hand.

A Trial of Witches

At another time the said child being speechless, but otherwise, of perfect understanding, ran round about the house holding her apron, crying 'Hush, hush,' as if there had been some poultry in the house; but this deponent could perceive nothing: but at last she saw the child stoop as if she had catched at something, and put it into her apron, and afterwards made as if she had thrown it into the fire: but this deponent could not discover anything: but the child afterwards being restored to her speech, she this deponent demanded of her what she saw at the time she used such a posture? Who answered, that she saw a duck.

At another time, the younger daughter being recovered out of her fits, declared, that Amy Duny had been with her, and that she tempted her to drown herself, and to cut her throat, or otherwise to destroy herself.

At another time in their fits they both of them cried out upon Rose Cullender and Amy Duny, complaining against them; 'Why do not you come yourselves, but send your imps to torment us?'

These several passages, as most remarkable, the said deponent did particularly set down as they daily happened, and for the reasons aforesaid, she doth verily believe in her conscience, that the children were bewitched, and by the said Amy Duny, and Rose Cullender; though at first she could hardly be induced to believe it.

As concerning Ann Durent, one other of the parties supposed to be bewitched, present in court:

Edmund Durent her father sworn and examined; said, that he also lived in the said town of Lowestoft and that the said Rose Cullender, about the latter end of November last, came into this deponent's house to buy some herrings of his wife, but being denied by her, the said Rose returned in a discontented manner; and upon the 1st of December after, his daughter Ann Durent was very sorely afflicted in her stomach, and felt great pain, like the pricking of pins, and then fell into swooning fits, and after the recovery from her fits, she declared, that she had seen the apparition of the said Rose, who threatened to torment her. In this manner she continued from the 1st of December, until this present time of trial; having likewise vomited up divers pins (produced here in court). This maid was present in court, but could not speak to declare her knowledge, but fell into most violent fits when she was brought before Rose Cullender.

Ann Baldwin sworn and examined, deposeth the same thing as touching the bewitching of the said Ann Durent.

A Trial of Witches

As concerning Jane Bocking, who was so weak, she could not be brought to the assizes:

Diana Bocking sworn and examined, deposed, that she lived in the same town of Lowestoft, and that her said daughter having been formerly afflicted with swooning fits recovered well of them, and so continued for a certain time; and upon the 1st of February last, she was taken also with great pain in her stomach, like pricking with pins; and afterwards fell into swooning fits, and so continued till the deponent's coming to the assizes, having during the same time taken little or no food, but daily vomiting crooked pins; and upon Sunday last raised seven pins. And whilst her fits were upon her she would spread forth her arms with her hands open, and use postures as if she catched at something, and would instantly close her hands again; which being immediately forced open, they found several pins diversely crooked, but could neither see nor perceive how or in what manner they were conveyed thither. At another time, the same Jane being in another of her fits, talked as if she were discoursing with some persons in the room, (though she would give no answer nor seem to take notice of any person then present) and would in like manner cast abroad her arms, saying, 'I will not have it, I will not have it'; and at last she said, 'Then I will have it,' and so waving her arm with her hand open, she would presently close the same, which instantly forced open, they found in it a lath-nail. In her fits she would frequently complain of Rose Cullender and Amy Duny, saying, that now she saw Rose Cullender standing at the bed's feet, and another time at the bed's head, and so in other places. At last she was stricken dumb and could not speak one word, though her fits were not upon her, and so she continued for some days, and at last her speech came to her again, and she desired her mother to get her some meat; and being demanded the reason why she could not speak in so long time? She answered, that Amy Duny would not suffer her to speak. This lath-nail, and divers of the pins, were produced in court.

As concerning Susan Chandler, one other of the parties supposed to be bewitched and present in court:

Mary Chandler, mother of the said Susan, sworn and examined, deposed and said, that about the beginning of February last past, the said Rose Cullender and Amy Duny were charged by Mr. Samuel Pacy for bewitching of his daughters. And a warrant being granted at the request of the said Mr. Pacy, by Sir Edmund Bacon,

A Trial of Witches

baronet, one of the justices of the peace for the County of Suffolk, to bring them before him, and they being brought before him were examined, and confessed nothing. He gave order that they should be searched; whereupon this deponent with five others were appointed to do the same: and coming to the house of Rose Cullender, they did acquaint her with what they were come about, and asked whether she was contented that they should search her? She did not oppose it, whereupon they began at her head, and so stripped her naked, and in the lower part of her belly they found a thing like a teat of an inch long, they questioned her about it, and she said, that she had got a strain by carrying of water which caused that excrescence. But upon narrower search, they found in her privy parts three more excrescences or teats, but smaller than the former. This deponent farther saith, that in the long teat at the end thereof there was a little hole, and it appeared unto them as if it had been lately sucked, and upon the straining of it there issued out white milky matter.

And this deponent farther saith, that her said daughter, being of the age of eighteen years, was then in service in the said town of Lowestoft, and rising up early the next morning to wash, this Rose Cullender appeared to her, and took her by the hand, whereat she was much affrighted, and went forthwith to her mother, being in the same town, and acquainted her with what she had seen; but being extremely terrified, she fell extreme sick, much grieved at her stomach; and that night after, being in bed with another young woman, she suddenly shrieked out, and fell into such extreme fits as if she were distracted, crying against Rose Cullender; saying, she would come to bed to her. She continued in this manner beating and wearing herself, insomuch, that this deponent was glad to get help to attend her. In her intervals she would declare, that some time she saw Rose Cullender, at another time with a great dog with her. She also vomited up divers crooked pins; and sometimes she was stricken with blindness, and at another time she was dumb, and so she appeared to be in court when the trial of the prisoners was; for she was not able to speak her knowledge; but being brought into the court at the trial, she suddenly fell into her fits, and being carried out of the court again, within the space of half an hour she came to herself and recovered her speech, and thereupon was immediately brought into the court, and asked by the court whether she was in condition to take an oath, and to give evidence, she said she could. But when she was sworn, and asked what she could say against

A Trial of Witches

either of the prisoners, before she could make any answer, she fell into her fits, shrieking out in a miserable manner, crying 'Burn her, burn her,' which were all the words she could speak.

Robert Chandler father of the said Susan gave in the same evidence, that his wife Mary Chandler had given; only as to the searching of Rose Cullender as aforesaid.

This was the sum and substance of the evidence which was given against the prisoners concerning the bewitching of the children before mentioned. At the hearing this evidence there were divers known persons as Mr. Serjeant Keeling, Mr. Serjeant Earl, and Mr. Serjeant Barnard, present. Mr. Serjeant Keeling seemed much unsatisfied with it, and thought it not sufficient to convict the prisoners: for admitting that the children were in truth bewitched, yet said he, it can never be applied to the prisoners, upon the imagination only of the parties afflicted; for if that might be allowed, no person whatsoever can be in safety, for perhaps they might fancy another person, who might altogether be innocent in such matters.

There was also Dr. [*Thomas*] Browne of Norwich, a person of great knowledge; who after this evidence given, and upon view of the three persons in court, was desired to give his opinion, what he did conceive of them: and he was clearly of opinion, that the persons were bewitched; and said, that in Denmark there had been lately a great discovery of witches, who used the very same way of afflicting persons, by conveying pins into them, and crooked as these pins were, with needles and nails. And his opinion was, that the devil in such cases did work upon the bodies of men and women, upon a natural foundation, that is to stir up, and excite such humours superabounding in their bodies to a great excess, whereby he did in an extraordinary manner afflict them with such distempers as their bodies were most subject to, as particularly appeared in these children; for he conceived, that these swooning fits were natural, and nothing else but that they call the mother, but only heightened to a great excess by the subtlety of the devil, cooperating with the malice of these which we term witches, at whose instance he doth these villainies.

Besides the particulars above-mentioned touching the said persons bewitched, there were many other things objected against them for a further proof and manifestation that the said children were bewitched.

As first, during the time of the trial, there were some experiments made with the persons afflicted, by bringing the persons to touch them; and it was observed, that when they were in the midst of their fits, to all men's apprehension wholly deprived of all sense and understanding, closing their fists in such manner, as that the strongest man in the court could not force them open; yet by the least touch of one of these supposed witches, Rose Cullender by name, they would suddenly shriek out opening their hands, which accident would not happen by the touch of any other person.

And lest they might privately see when they were touched, by the said Rose Cullender, they were blinded with their own aprons, and the touching took the same effect as before.

There was an ingenious person that objected, there might be a great fallacy in this experiment, and there ought not to be any stress put upon this to convict the parties, for the children might counterfeit this their distemper, and perceiving what was done to them, they might in such manner suddenly alter the motion and gesture of their bodies, on purpose to induce persons to believe that they were not natural, but wrought strangely by the touch of the prisoners.

Wherefore to avoid this scruple it was privately desired by the judge, that the Lord Cornwallis, Sir Edmund Bacon, and Mr. Serjeant Keeling, and some other gentlemen there in court, would attend one of the distempered persons in the farther part of the hall, whilst she was in her fits, and then to send for one of the witches, to try what would then happen, which they did accordingly: and Amy Duny was conveyed from the bar and brought to the maid. They put an apron before her eyes, and then one other person touched her hand, which produced the same effect as the touch of the witch did in the court. Whereupon the gentlemen returned, openly protesting, that they did believe the whole transaction of this business was a mere imposture.

This put the Court and all persons into a stand. But at length Mr. Pacy did declare, that possibly the maid might be deceived by a suspicion that the witch touched her when she did not. For he had observed divers times that although they could not speak, but were deprived of the use of their tongues and limbs, that their understandings were perfect, for that they have related divers things, which have been when they were in their fits, after they were recovered out of them. This saying of Mr. Pacy was found to be true afterwards, when his daughter was fully recovered, as she afterwards was, as shall in due time be related. For she was asked whether she did hear and understand anything that was done and acted in the court during the time that she lay as one deprived of her understanding. And she said she did. And by the opinions of some, this experiment, which others would have a fallacy, was rather a confirmation that the parties were really bewitched than otherwise, for, say they, it is not possible that any should counterfeit such distempers, being accompanied with such various circumstances, much less children, and for so long time, and yet undiscovered by their parents and relations. For no man can suppose that they should all conspire together, being out of several families and, as they affirm, no way related one to the other, and scarce of familiar acquaintance, to do an act of this nature whereby no benefit or advantage could redound to any of the parties, but a guilty conscience for perjuring themselves in taking the lives of two poor simple women away, and there appears no malice in the case. For the prisoners themselves did scarce so much as object it. Wherefore, say they, it is very evident that the parties were bewitched, and that when they apprehend or understand by any means that the persons who have done them this wrong are near, or touch them, then their spirits being more than ordinarily moved with rage and anger at them being present, they do use more violent gestures of their bodies, and extend forth their hands, as desirous to lay hold upon them; which at other times not having the same occasion, the instance there falls not out the same.

Secondly, one *John Soam* of Lowestoft aforesaid, yeoman, a sufficient person, deposeth that not long since, in harvest time he had three carts which brought home his harvest, and as they were going into the field to load, one of the carts wrenched the window of Rose Cullender's house, whereupon she came out in a great rage and threatened this deponent for doing that wrong, so they passed along into the fields and loaded all the three carts, the other two carts returned safe home, and back again, twice loaded that day afterwards; but as to this cart which touched Rose Cullender's house, after it was loaded it was overturned twice or thrice that day, and after that they had loaded it again the second or third time, as they brought it through the gate which leadeth out of the field into the town, the cart stuck so fast in the gate's head that they could not possibly get it through, but were enforced to cut down the post of the gate to make the cart pass through, although they could not perceive

A Trial of Witches

that the cart did on either side touch the gateposts. And this deponent further saith, that after they had got it through the gateway, they did with much difficulty get it home into the yard. But for all that they could do, they could not get the cart near unto the place where they should unload the corn, but were fain to unload it at a great distance from the place, and when they began to unload they found much difficulty therein, it being so hard a labour that they were tired that first came; and when others came to assist them, their noses burst forth a-bleeding. So they were fain to desist and leave it until the next morning, and then they unloaded it without any difficulty at all.

Robert Sherringham also deposeth against Rose Cullender that about two years since, passing along the street with his cart and horses the axletree of his cart touched her house, and broke down some part of it, at which she was very much displeased, threatening him that his horses should suffer for it. And so it happened, for all those horses, being four in number, died within a short time after. Since that time he hath had great losses by the sudden dying of his other cattle. So soon as his sows pigged, the pigs would leap and caper, and immediately fall down and die. Also, not long after, he was taken with a lameness in his limbs that he could neither go nor stand for some days. After all this, he was very much vexed with great number of lice of an extraordinary bigness, and although he many times shifted himself, yet he was not anything the better, but would swarm again with them. So that in the conclusion he was forced to burn all his clothes, being two suits of apparel, and then was clean from them.

As concerning Amy Duny, one *Richard Spencer* deposeth that about the 1st of September last he heard her say at his house that the devil would not let her rest until she were revenged on one Cornelius Sandeswell's wife.

Ann Sandeswell, wife unto the above-said Cornelius, deposed that about seven or eight years since, she having bought a certain number of geese, meeting with Amy Duny, she told her if she did not fetch her geese home they would all be destroyed, which in a few days after it came to pass.

Afterwards the said Amy became tenant to this deponent's husband for a house, who told her that if she looked not well to such a chimney in her house that the same would fall. Whereupon this deponent replied that it was a new one; but not minding much her words, at that time they parted. But in a short time the chimney fell down, according as the said Amy had said.

Also this deponent farther saith, that her brother being a fisherman, and using to go into the Northern Seas, she desired him to send her a firkin of fish, which he did accordingly; and she having notice that the said firkin was brought into Lowestoft road, she desired a boatman to bring it ashore with the other goods they were to bring; and she going down to meet the boatman to receive her fish, desired the said Amy to go along with her to help her home with it. Amy replied, she would go when she had it. And thereupon this deponent went to the shore without her, and demanded of the boatman the firkin, they told her, that they could not keep it in the boat from falling into the sea, and they thought it was gone to the devil, for they never saw the like before. And being demanded by this deponent, whether any other goods in the boat were likewise lost as well as hers, they answered not any.

This was the substance of the whole evidence given against the prisoners at the bar; who being demanded, what they had to say for themselves, they replied, nothing material to anything that was proved against them. Whereupon, the judge in giving his direction to the jury, told them, that he would not repeat the evidence unto them, lest by so doing he should wrong the evidence on the one side or on the other. Only this acquainted them, that they had two things to inquire after. First, whether or no these children were bewitched? Secondly, whether the prisoners at the bar were guilty of it?

That there were such creatures as witches he made no doubt at all; for first, the scriptures had affirmed so much. Secondly, the wisdom of all nations had provided laws against such persons, which is an argument of their confidence of such a crime. And such hath been the judgment of this Kingdom, as appears by that Act of Parliament which hath provided punishments proportionable to the quality of the offence. And desired them, strictly to observe their evidence; and desired the great God of heaven to direct their hearts in this weighty thing they had in hand. For to condemn the innocent, and to let the guilty go free, were both an abomination to the Lord.

With this short direction the jury departed from the bar, and within the space of half an hour returned, and brought them in both guilty upon the several indictments, which were thirteen in number, whereupon they stood indicted.

This was upon Thursday in the afternoon, 13 March 1665. The

next morning, the three children with their parents came to the Lord Chief Baron Hale's lodging, who all of them spake perfectly, and were as in good health as ever they were; only Susan Chandler, by reason of her very much affliction, did look very thin and wan. And their friends were asked at what time they were restored thus to their speech and health? And Mr. Pacy did affirm, that within less than half an hour after the witches were convicted, they were all of them restored, and slept well that night, feeling no pain; only Susan Chandler felt a pain like pricking of pins in her stomach.

After, they were all of them brought down to the court, but Ann Durent was so fearful to behold them, that she desired she might not see them. The other two continued in the court, and they affirmed in the face of the country, and before the witches themselves, what before hath been deposed by their friends and relations; the prisoners not much contradicting them. In conclusion, the judge and all the Court were fully satisfied with the verdict, and thereupon gave judgment against the witches that they should be hanged.

They were much urged to confess but would not.

That morning we departed for Cambridge, but no reprieve was granted. And they were executed on Monday the 17th of March following, but they confessed nothing.

Chapter Two

The Trial of John Huggins (1729)

The system of imprisonment for debt and the general state of the gaols had disturbed the parliamentary and public conscience for more than a century before Dickens published his *Pickwick Papers*. In the fiction of the eighteenth century, arrest for debt and its consequences had been described by Smollett in *Peregrine Pickle* and, most movingly of all, by Fielding in his last novel *Amelia*. Yet the reality was more remarkable and grotesque than any fiction might suggest. After his arrest, at the suit of one of his creditors, the debtor would normally be taken to a 'sponging house', a bailiff's house near the prison, where he might live under supervision until such money as he had left had, for the most part, been squeezed from him for his board and lodging. At this stage, he would be transferred from the sponging house to the harsher conditions of prison life. Prisons like the Fleet, in London, were run for profit by their Wardens and in the 1720s the office of Warden of the Fleet was considered profitable enough to be sold for as much as £5,000. There were statutory fees to be paid by prisoners on entry and discharge, though the inmates of the Fleet claimed that they were charged more than the law allowed. Table 1 shows two lists of fees, those due and those actually taken, according to *A True State of the Proceedings of the Prisoners in the Fleet Prison* (1729).[1]

Almost every account of English prisons in the eighteenth century emphasizes the means used to make them what the twentieth century might euphemistically describe as 'cost effective'. They were easy sources of profit when, for instance, the squalor and hopelessness of life in a debtors prison made gin so welcome a commodity. Despite an Act of Parliament forbidding its sale in prisons, there were, according to Dr William

Smith in his *State of the Gaols in London, Westminster, and the Borough of Southwark* (1776), no less than thirty gin shops in the King's Bench Prison. In this prison 120 gallons of gin were sold weekly as 'vinegar', 'gossip', 'crank', 'Mexico', or 'skyblue'.

Whatever the hazards of gin, the official indifference to poor ventilation and insanitary conditions brought the threat of gaol-fever to prisoners and warders alike. It killed judges and barristers at assizes and spread through the ranks of regiments in which ex-prisoners were serving. In 1750 two judges and a

Table 1

	Fees due £ s. d.	Fees taken £. s. d.
For Liberty of the House and Irons at first coming in	1 6 8	2 4 4
Chaplain	Nil	2 0
Entering the Name and Cause	4	Nil
Porter's Fee	1 0	1 0
Chamberlain's Fee	1 0	3 0
At first coming in	1 9 0	2 10 4
The Dismission Fee	7 4	12 6
Turnkey's Dismission	Nil	2 6
	1 16 4	3 5 4

lord mayor died of the disease in London. The English force sent north to deal with the Jacobite insurrection of 1745 suffered 200 'casualties' from gaol-fever in a single regiment. Later in the century, the army sent to fight the American rebels lost 2,000 men from the disease. There could hardly have been any conditions more favourable to the spread of the infection than those on board the transports where men were cooped up for the Atlantic crossing. There was no doubt as to the origin of the fever. As Smith remarked, turnkeys opening the wards or cells of prisons in the morning, 'are obliged to drink a glass of spirits to keep them from fainting, for the putrid steam or miasma is enough to knock them down'.[2] In 1777, almost half a century after the trial of Huggins, John Howard in *The State of the Prisons in England and Wales*, showed that conditions had still changed less than might have been hoped.[3]

> A cruel custom obtains in most of our Gaols, which is that of the prisoners demanding of a new comer GARNISH, FOOTING, or (as it is called in some London Gaols) CHUMMAGE. 'Pay or strip' are the fatal words. I say *fatal*, for they are so to some; who having no money are obliged to give up part of their scanty apparel; and if they have no bedding, or straw to sleep on, contract diseases, which I have known to prove mortal.

Howard visited the Fleet and describes what he found there, fifty years after the administration of Huggins and his associates.[4]

> The apartments for the Common-side Debtors are only part of the right wing of the Prison. Besides the cellar (which was intended for their kitchen, but is occupied with lumber, and shut up) there are four floors. On each floor is a room about twenty-four or twenty-five feet square, with a fire-place; and on the sides seven closets or cabins to sleep in. Such of the Prisoners as swear in Court or before a Commissioner that they are not worth five pounds, and cannot subsist without charity, have the donations which are sent to the Prison, and the begging-box, and grate. Of them there were at my last visit sixteen.

Bad though the situation might be in the 1770s, it was an improvement on the conditions of the prisoners at the time of the Huggins scandal in the 1720s. Huggins had obtained the office of Warden of the Fleet for himself and his son for £5,000 and was obliged, in turn, to make his living from the prisoners. On the Master's Side of the Fleet lived prisoners who could afford to rent their own accommodation, while on the Common Side lived those who could only pay a nominal sum. From such rent, from the sale of food and drink to the prisoners, and from the fees charged to prisoners arriving and leaving, the Warden derived his income. Prisoners who wished to enjoy the 'liberty of the rules', to move freely within the prison and to wear no irons, found fees payable for the privilege.

The Trial of John Huggins

By 1728 Huggins was an old man but his son showed no inclination to take on the office of Warden. The solution was for Huggins to allow his rights to be bought for £5,000 by his deputy, Thomas Bambridge, and by Dougal Cuthbert. At the same time, a number of prisoners had been released in consequence of the relief given them by the Insolvent Debtors Act of 1725, and partly through their stories the truth of rumours about the Fleet Prison was established. Means amounting to intimidation and torture had been used to extort money from prisoners. Men who were sick or diseased faced almost certain death. Even men in good health sickened and died, once they were confined in such places as the 'strong room'. On the other hand, those whom the Warden or his Deputy Warden chose to favour might be privately released from prison and allowed to go about their business. Whether Huggins himself was aware of the full extent of the corruption in the Fleet is uncertain. He blamed his underlings and it was pointed out that for a time there had been a curious situation in which the prisoners themselves ruled the prison through a 'Court of Inspectors', who were so powerful that no official dared to challenge them nor, on occasion, to enter the prison.

The scandal broke after Bambridge had taken over the Fleet. One of the prisoners, Robert Castell, died of smallpox, but Castell had a powerful friend in General James Oglethorpe, M.P. A Parliamentary inquiry was begun into the affairs of the Fleet, which resulted in charges of murder being brought against Huggins, Bambridge, Richard Corbett, and Thomas Acton, Deputy-Keeper of the Marshalsea. The trials were all held in 1729 and the verdict was, in every case, the same. Huggins was the first to be tried and his case represented something of a precedent so far as the others were concerned. Ultimately, the defendants began to turn against one another, Huggins prosecuting Bambridge, in consequence of which Bambridge spent some time as a prisoner in the Fleet

An Act of Parliament was passed, enabling the King to overrule the rights of Bambridge and grant the office of Warden to someone else. It is not known how long Huggins survived his trial, but Bambridge lived for another twenty years and is said to have committed suicide about the year 1750.

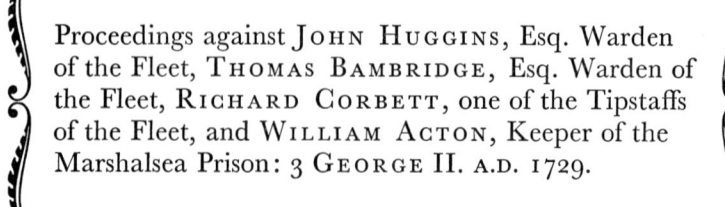

Proceedings against JOHN HUGGINS, Esq. Warden of the Fleet, THOMAS BAMBRIDGE, Esq. Warden of the Fleet, RICHARD CORBETT, one of the Tipstaffs of the Fleet, and WILLIAM ACTON, Keeper of the Marshalsea Prison: 3 GEORGE II. A.D. 1729.

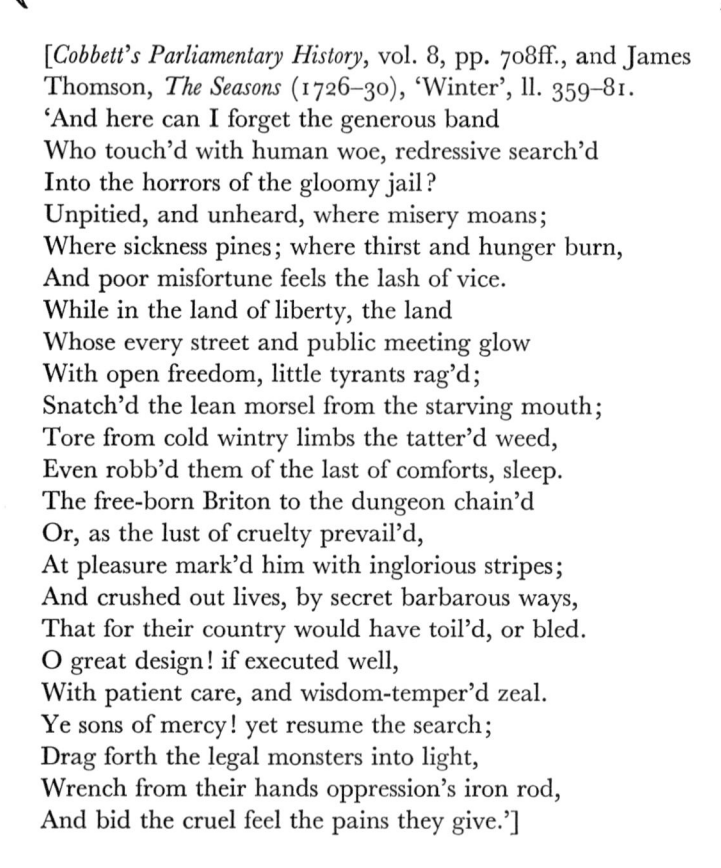

[*Cobbett's Parliamentary History*, vol. 8, pp. 708ff., and James Thomson, *The Seasons* (1726–30), 'Winter', ll. 359–81.
'And here can I forget the generous band
Who touch'd with human woe, redressive search'd
Into the horrors of the gloomy jail?
Unpitied, and unheard, where misery moans;
Where sickness pines; where thirst and hunger burn,
And poor misfortune feels the lash of vice.
While in the land of liberty, the land
Whose every street and public meeting glow
With open freedom, little tyrants rag'd;
Snatch'd the lean morsel from the starving mouth;
Tore from cold wintry limbs the tatter'd weed,
Even robb'd them of the last of comforts, sleep.
The free-born Briton to the dungeon chain'd
Or, as the lust of cruelty prevail'd,
At pleasure mark'd him with inglorious stripes;
And crushed out lives, by secret barbarous ways,
That for their country would have toil'd, or bled.
O great design! if executed well,
With patient care, and wisdom-temper'd zeal.
Ye sons of mercy! yet resume the search;
Drag forth the legal monsters into light,
Wrench from their hands oppression's iron rod,
And bid the cruel feel the pains they give.']

A REPORT FROM THE COMMITTEE OF THE HOUSE OF COMMONS APPOINTED TO INQUIRE INTO THE STATE OF THE GAOLS OF THIS KINGDOM, SO FAR AS RELATES TO THE CRUEL USAGE OF THE PRISONERS; WHICH OCCASIONED THE FOLLOWING TRIALS.
Jovis 20 Die Martii, 1729.

The Trial of John Huggins

Mr. Oglethorpe, from the Committee appointed to inquire into the State of the Gaols of this Kingdom, made a report of some progress which the Committee had made in their inquiry into the state of the Fleet prison, with the Resolutions of the Committee thereupon; and he read the report in his place, and afterwards delivered the same in at the table, viz.

The Committee find, that the Fleet prison is an ancient prison, and formerly used for the reception of prisoners committed by the council-table, then called the Court of the Star Chamber, which exercised unlimited authority, and inflicted heavier punishments than by any law were warranted.

And as that assumed authority was found to be an intolerable burden to the subject, and the means to introduce an arbitrary power and government, all jurisdiction, power, and authority belonging unto, or exercised in the same Court, or by any the judges, officers, or ministers thereof, were clearly and absolutely dissolved, taken away, and determined by an Act made in the 16th year of the reign of King Charles the First.[5]

And thereby the Committee apprehend all pretences of the Warden of the Fleet to take fees from archbishops, bishops, temporal peers, baronets, and others of lower degree, or to put them in irons, or exact fees for not doing so, were determined, and abolished.

That after the said Act took place, the Fleet prison became a prison for debtors, and for contempts of the Courts of Chancery, Exchequer, and Common Pleas only, and fell under the same regulations as other gaols of this Kingdom.

That by an act of the 22nd and 23rd of King Charles the Second, the future government of all prisons was vested in the lords chief justices, the chief baron, or any two of them, for the time being; and the justices of the peace in London, Middlesex, and Surrey; and the judges for the several circuits; and the justices of the peace, for the time being, in their several precincts.[6] And pursuant thereunto, several orders and regulations have been made, which the present Warden of the Fleet hath not regarded or complied with, but hath exercised an unwarrantable and arbitrary power, not only in extorting exorbitant fees, but in oppressing prisoners for debt, by loading them with irons, worse than if the Star Chamber was still subsisting, and contrary to the Great Charter, the foundation of the liberty of the subject, and in defiance and contempt thereof, as well as of other good laws of this kingdom.

It appears by a patent of the third year of Queen Elizabeth, recited in letters patents bearing date the 19th year of King Charles the Second that the Fleet prison was an ancient prison, called Prisona de le Fleet, alias the Queen's Gaol of the Fleet; and that certain constitutions were then established by agreement between Richard Tyrrel, Warden, and the prisoners of the Fleet, and a table of fees annexed, in which the fees to be paid by an archbishop, duke, marquis, earl, or other lord spiritual or temporal, are particularly mentioned, and the fine ascertained which they are to pay for the liberty of the house and irons; and that these constitutions and orders were confirmed by the said letters patent of King Charles the Second. Which letters patent grant the office of Warden of the Fleet, and of the Keeper of the Old Palace at Westminster, the shops in Westminster Hall, certain tenements adjoining to the Fleet, and other rents and profits belonging to the Warden, to Sir Jeremy Whichcot and his heirs for ever. And the said Sir Jeremy rebuilt the said prison at his own expense, as a consideration for the grant thereof. But the said prison, and the custody of the prisoners, being a freehold, and falling by descent or purchase into the hands of persons incapable of executing the office of Warden, was the occasion of great abuses, and frequent complaints to Parliament, till at length the patent was set aside.

And a patent for life was granted to Baldwyn Leighton, Esq. in consideration of his great pains and expenses in suing the former patentees to a forfeiture, and he soon dying, John Huggins, Esq. by giving 5,000*l.* to the late Lord Clarendon, did, by his interest, obtain a grant of the said office for his own and his son's life.

That it appeared to the Committee, that in the year 1725, one Mr. Arne, an upholder,[7] was carried into a stable which stood where the strong room on the master's side now is, and was there confined (being a place of cold restraint) till he died, and that he was in good state of health before he was confined to that room.

That the said John Huggins growing in years, and willing to retire from business, and his son not caring to take upon him so troublesome an office, he hath for several years been engaged in continual negotiations about the disposal of the said office, and in August last concluded a final treaty with Thomas Bambridge and Dougal Cuthbert, Esqrs. and for 5,000*l.* to be paid unto him, obliged himself to surrender the said patent for his and his son's life, and procure a new patent for the said Bambridge and Cuthbert,

The Trial of John Huggins

which the said Huggins did accordingly obtain, and Cuthbert paid in money, or gave good security to pay 2,500*l.* for one moiety of the said office of Warden; and Bambridge gave land and other security, which the said Huggins was then content with, for 2,500*l.* being for the other moiety of the said office.

That Mr. Huggins being examined touching an instrument signed by him in November 1724, appointing Richard Corbett, one of the five tipstaffs of or belonging to the Fleet prison, acknowledged that he had no power by virtue of any patent from the Crown to constitute such tipstaff, but that when he came to his office he found that such an officer had been so constituted, and he took that for a precedent to do the same.

That since the said Thomas Bambridge has acted as Warden, the books belonging to the office of the Warden have been very negligently kept, and the discharges not duly entered, to the great prejudice of many of His Majesty's subjects; and he hath not regularly taken charge of the prisoners committed to his care by his patent; and hath not, as he himself confesseth, ever had any authentic list of the prisoners in the rules delivered him, so he cannot have executed the trust of keeping his prisoners in safe custody, when he did not know who or where they were.

The Committee find that the said Thomas Bambridge, who for some years acted as Deputy-Warden of the Fleet, and is now actually Warden of that prison, hath himself been aiding and assisting in an escape: that he caused a private door to be made through the walls of the prison out of the yard where the dogs are, the key of which door was kept by himself, and he with his own hands opened the door and let out Boyce, the smuggler, charged at the King's suit with upwards of 30,000*l.*, who was afterwards seen at Islington, and hath been several times let out of the prison by Bambridge.

The Committee find that the said Bambridge hath by himself and his agents often refused to admit prisoners into the prison, though committed by due course of law: and in order to extort money from them, hath often, contrary to an act of the 22nd and 23rd of King Charles II, without their free and voluntary consent, caused them to be carried away from the prison gate unto a public victualling or drinking-house, commonly called a sponging-house, belonging to him the said Bambridge as Warden, and rented of him by Corbett his tipstaff, and hath there kept them at exorbitant charges, and forced them to call for more liquor than they were inclined to, and to spend more than they were able to afford, to the defrauding of their creditors, and the distressing of their families, whose substance they are compelled there to consume; and for the more effectual making them stretch their poor remains of credit, and to squeeze out of them the charity of their friends, each prisoner is better or worse treated according to his expenses, some being allowed a handsome room and bed to themselves, some stowed in garrets, three in one bed, and some put in irons.

That these houses were further used by the said Bambridge, as a terror for extorting money from the prisoners, who on security given have the liberty of the rules; of which Mr. Robert Castell was an unhappy instance, a man born to a competent estate, but being unfortunately plunged in debt, was thrown into prison. He was first sent (according to custom) to Corbett's, from whence he by presents to Bambridge redeemed himself, and, giving security, obtained the liberty of the rules; notwithstanding which he had frequently presents, as they are called, extracted from him by Bambridge, and was menaced, on refusal, to be sent back to Corbett's again.

The said Bambridge having thus unlawfully extorted large sums of money from him in a very short time, Castell grew weary of being made such a wretched property, and resolving not to injure farther his family or his creditors for the sake of so small a liberty, he refused to submit to further exactions; upon which the said Bambridge ordered him to be recommitted to Corbett's, where the small-pox then raged, though Castell acquainted him with his not having had that distemper, and that he dreaded it so much, that the putting him into a house where it was would occasion his death, which, if it happened before he could settle his affairs, would be a great prejudice to his creditors, and would expose his family to destruction; and therefore he earnestly desired that he might either be sent to another house, or even into the gaol itself, as a favour. The melancholy case of this poor gentleman moved the very agents of the said Bambridge to compassion, so that they also used their utmost endeavours to dissuade him from sending this unhappy prisoner to that infected house. But Bambridge forced him thither, where he (as he feared he should) caught the small-pox, and in a few days died thereof, justly charging the said Bambridge with his death; and unhappily leaving all his affairs in the greatest confusion, and a numerous family of small children in the utmost distress.

The Trial of John Huggins

It appeared to the Committee, that the letting-out of the Fleet tenements to victuallers, for the reception of prisoners, hath been but of late practised, and that the first of them let for this purpose was to Mary Whitwood, who still continues tenant of the same, and that her rent has from 32*l.* per annum been increased to 60*l.* and a certain number of prisoners stipulated to be made a prey of, to enable her to pay so great a rent; and that she, to procure the benefit of having such a number of prisoners sent to her house, hath, over and above the increased rent, been obliged to make a present to the said Bambridge of forty guineas, as also of a toy, (as it is called) being the model of a Chinese ship, made of amber, set in silver, for which fourscore broad-pieces[8] had been offered her.

This is the first method of extorting money from the unhappy prisoners; and when they can no longer bear the misery and expense of a sponging-house, before they can obtain the privilege of being admitted into the prison, they are obliged to comply with such exorbitant fees as the said Bambridge thinks fit to demand, which, if they do not, they are sure, under various pretences, of being turned down to the common side, if not put in irons and dungeons; and this has been done to those who were willing and offered to pay the fees established by the regulation made by the judges of the Common Pleas in Trinity Term 1727, which ought to have been hung up in some public place in the prison, to which the prisoners might have free access, but was secreted by the said James Barnes, pursuant to orders of the said Bambridge; which table of fees seems to be unreasonable, because it obliges men who are committed for not being able to pay their debts, to pay such sums of money as their circumstances render them altogether unable to comply with.

And, notwithstanding the payment of such large fees, in order to extort further sums from the unfortunate prisoners, the said Bambridge unjustly pretends he has a right, as Warden, to exercise an unlimited power of changing prisoners from room to room; of turning them into the common side, though they have paid the master's side fee; and inflicting arbitrary punishments by locking them down in unwholesome dungeons, and loading them with torturing irons; some instances of which follow: viz.

Jacob Mendez Solas, a Portuguese, was, as far as it appeared to the Committee, one of the first prisoners for debt that ever was loaded with irons in the Fleet. The said Bambridge one day called him into the gatehouse of the prison, called the Lodge, where he caused him to be seized, fettered, and carried to Corbett's the sponging-house, and there kept for upwards of a week, and when brought back into the prison, Bambridge caused him to be turned into the dungeon, called the strong room of the master's side.

This place is a vault like those in which the dead are interred, and wherein the bodies of persons dying in the said prison are usually deposited, till the coroner's inquest hath passed upon them; it has no chimney nor fireplace, nor any light but what comes over the door, or through a hole of about eight inches square. It is neither paved nor boarded; and the rough bricks appear both on the sides and top, being neither wainscotted nor plastered. What adds to the dampness and stench of the place is, its being built over the common sewer, and adjoining to the sink and dunghill where all the nastiness of the prison is cast. In this miserable place the poor wretch was kept by the said Bambridge, manacled and shackled for near two months. At length, on receiving five guineas from Mr. Kemp, a friend of Solas's, Bambridge released the prisoner from his cruel confinement. But though his chains were taken off, his terror still remained, and the unhappy man was prevailed upon by that terror, not only to labour *gratis* for the said Bambridge, but to swear also at random all that he hath required of him: and the Committee themselves saw an instance of the deep impression his sufferings had made upon him; for on his surmising, from something said, that Bambridge was to return again, as Warden of the Fleet, he fainted, and the blood started out of his mouth and nose.

Captain John Mackpheadris, who was bred a merchant, is another melancholy instance of the cruel use the said Bambridge hath made of his assumed authority. Mackpheadris was a considerable trader, and in a very flourishing condition until the year 1720, when being bound for large sums to the Crown, for a person afterwards ruined by the misfortunes of that year, he was undone. In June, 1727, he was a prisoner in the Fleet, and although he had before paid his commitment-fee, the like fee was extorted from him a second time, and he having furnished a room, Bambridge demanded an extravagant price for it, which he refused to pay; and urged, that it was unlawful for the Warden to demand extravagant rents, and offered to pay what was legally due. Notwithstanding which, the said Bambridge, assisted by the said James Barnes and other accomplices, broke open his room, and took away several things of great value, amongst others, the King's extent in aid of the prisoner

The Trial of John Huggins

(which was to have been returned in a few days, in order to procure the debt to the Crown, and the prisoner's enlargement,) which Bambridge still detains. Not content with this, Bambridge locked the prisoner out of his room, and forced him to lie in the open yard, called the Bare. He sat quietly under his wrongs, and getting some poor materials, built a little hut to protect himself as well as he could, from the injuries of the weather. The said Bambridge seeing his unconcernedness, said, 'Damn him! He is easy. I will put him into the strong room before to-morrow;' and ordered Barnes to pull down his little hut, which was done accordingly. The poor prisoner being in an ill state of health, and the night rainy, was put to great distress. Some time after this he was, about eleven o'clock at night, assaulted by Bambridge, with several other persons his accomplices, in a violent manner; and Bambridge, though the prisoner was unarmed, attacked him with his sword, but by good fortune was prevented from killing him; and several other prisoners coming out upon the noise, they carried Mackpheadris for safety into another gentleman's room. Soon after which Bambridge coming with one Savage, and several others, broke open the door, and Bambridge strove with his sword to kill the prisoner: but he again got away, and hid himself in another room. Next morning the said Bambridge entered the prison with a detachment of soldiers, and ordered the prisoner to be dragged to the Lodge, and ironed with great irons; on which he desiring to know for what cause, and by what authority he was to be so cruelly used. Bambridge replied, it was by his own authority, and damn him he would do it, and have his life. The prisoner desired he might be carried before a magistrate, that he might know his crime before he was punished; but Bambridge refused, and put irons upon his legs which were too little, so that in forcing them on, his legs were like to have been broken; and the torture was impossible to be endured. Upon which the prisoner complaining of the grievous pain and straitness of the irons, Bambridge answered that he did it on purpose to torture him. On which the prisoner replying, that by the law of England no man ought to be tortured, Bambridge declared, that he would do it first, and answer for it afterwards; and caused him to be dragged away to the dungeon, where he lay without a bed, loaded with irons so close riveted that they kept him in continual torture, and mortified his legs. After long application his irons were changed, and a surgeon directed to dress his legs, but his lameness is not, nor ever can be cured. He was kept in this miserable condition for three weeks, by which his sight is greatly prejudiced, and in danger of being lost.

The prisoner, upon this usage, petitioned the judges, and after several meetings, and a full hearing, the judges reprimanded Mr. Huggins and Bambridge, and declared, that a gaoler could not answer the ironing of a man before he was found guilty of a crime; but it being out of term, they could not give the prisoner any relief or satisfaction.

Notwithstanding this opinion of the judges, the said Bambridge continued to keep the prisoner in irons till he had paid him six guineas; and to prevent the prisoner's recovering damages for the cruel treatment of him, Bambridge indicted him and his principal witnesses at the Old Bailey, before they knew anything of the matter; and to support that indictment, he had recourse to subornation, and turned two of his servants out of places which they had bought, because they would not swear falsely that the prisoner had struck the said Bambridge, which words he had inserted in affidavits ready prepared for signing, and which they knew to be false. As soon as they were apprised of it, they applied to the Lord Mayor, who ordered the grand jury down to the Fleet, where they found that Bambridge was the aggressor. But the bill against the prisoners being already found, the second inquiry was too late.

The prisoners being no longer able to bear the charges of prosecution, which had already cost 100*l.* and being softened by promises, and terrified by threats, submitted to plead guilty, on a solemn assurance and agreement made with Bambridge before witnesses, of having but one shilling fine laid upon them; but so soon as they had pleaded guilty, Bambridge took advantage of it, and has continued harassing them and their securities ever since.

The desire of gain urged the said Bambridge to the preceding instances of cruelty; but a more diabolical passion, that of malice, animated him to oppress Captain David Sinclair in the following manner:

At the end of June or beginning of July last, the said Bambridge declared to the said James Barnes, one of the agents of his cruelties, that he would have Sinclair's blood; and he took the opportunity of the first festival day, which was on the 1st of August following, when he thought Captain Sinclair might, by celebrating the memory of the late King, be warmed with liquor so far as to give him some excuse for the cruelties which he intended to inflict upon him. But in some measure he was disappointed; for Captain Sinclair was perfectly sober, when the said Bambridge rushed into his room with a dark lantern in his hand, assisted by his accomplices James Barnes and William Pindar, and supported by his usual guard, armed with muskets and bayonets, and without any provocation given, run his lantern into Captain Sinclair's face, seized him by the collar, and told him he must come along with him. Captain Sinclair, though surprised, asked for what, and by what authority he so treated him. Upon which Barnes and the rest seized Captain Sinclair, who still desiring to know by what authority they so abused him, Bambridge grossly insulted him, and struck him with his cane on the head and shoulders, whilst he was held fast by Pindar and Barnes. Such base and scandalous usage of this gentleman, who had in the late wars always signalised himself with the greatest courage, gallantry and honour, in the service of his country upon many the most brave and desperate occasions, must be most shocking and intolerable. Yet Captain Sinclair bore it with patience, refusing only to go out of his room unless he was forced. Whereupon the said Bambridge threatened to run his cane down his throat, and ordered his guard to stab him with their bayonets, or drag him down to the said dungeon, called the strong room; the latter of which they did, and Bambridge kept him confined in that damp and loathsome place, till he had lost the use of his limbs and memory, neither of which has he perfectly recovered to this day. Many aggravating cruelties were used to make his confinement more terrible; and when Bambridge found he was in danger of immediate death, he removed him, for fear of his dying in duress, and caused him to be carried in a dying condition from that dungeon to a room where there was no bed or furniture; and so unmercifully prevented his friends having any access to him, that he was four days without the least sustenance.

It appeared to the Committee by the evidence of a surgeon and others, who were prisoners in the house, that when Captain Sinclair was forced into that loathsome dungeon he was in perfect health.

Captain Sinclair applied for remedy at law against the said cruelties of Bambridge, and had procured a *habeas corpus* for his witnesses to be brought before the sessions of Oyer and Terminer, when the said Bambridge, by colour of his assumed authority as Warden, took the said writs of *habeas corpus* from the officer whose duty it was to make a return of them, and commanded him to keep out of the way, whilst he himself went to the Old Bailey, and immediately indicted Captain Sinclair and such of his witnesses as he knew he could not deter by threats, or prevail with by promises to go from the truth.

Captain Sinclair had temper enough to bear patiently almost insupportable injuries, and to reserve himself for a proper occasion, when justice should be done him by the laws of the realm.

But the said Bambridge has forced others by wrongs and injuries beyond human bearing, to endeavour the avenging injuries and oppressions which they could no longer endure.

And it appeared to the Committee, that the said Bambridge, in order to avoid the punishment due to these crimes, hath committed greater, and hath not only denied admittance to the solicitors, who might procure justice to the injured prisoners, and in open defiance to the law, disobeyed the King's writs, but hath also seduced some by indulging them in riot, and terrified others with fear of duress, to swear to and subscribe such false affidavits as he thought fit to prepare for them, on several occasions; in all which wrongs and oppressions John Everett also acted as one of the said Bambridge's wicked accomplices.

That the said Bambridge being asked by the Committee, by what authority he pretended to put prisoners into dungeons and irons, answered, that he did it by his own authority as Warden, to preserve the quiet and safety of the custody of the prison.

But it appeared to the Committee by the examinations of many witnesses, that before the time when Gybbon and the said Bambridge acted as Deputy-Wardens under Mr. Huggins, the quiet and safety of the custody were very well preserved without the use of irons or dungeons.

That the two dungeons, called the strong room on the master's side, and the strong room on the common side, were both built within these few years; and that the old method of punishing drunken and disorderly persons was putting them in the stocks; and the punishment of those who had escaped, or attempted to escape, was putting them upon a tub at the gate of the prison, by way of public shame, or securing them without irons, in their proper rooms for some days.

And that the said dungeons were built in defiance of, and contrary to the declaration of the Lord King, when Lord Chief Justice of the Common Pleas; who, upon an application made to him on behalf of the prisoners of the Fleet, when Mr. Huggins and —— Gybbon urged that there was danger of prisoners escaping, declared, that they might raise their walls higher, but that there should be no prison within a prison.

That upon the strictest inquiry, the Committee could not find that any prisoner in the Fleet for debt had been put in irons before the said Mr. Huggins had the office of Warden.

That it is not the only design of the said Thomas Bambridge to extort money from his prisoners, if they survive his inhuman treatment, but he seems to have a farther view, in case it causes death, of possessing himself of their effects. One remarkable proof of which the Committee think proper here to insert, viz.

Mr. John Holder, a Spanish merchant, was a prisoner in the Fleet, and had a room which he fitted up with his own furniture, and had with him all his books, accounts and writings, and other effects, to the value of about 30,000*l*. which he declared by affidavit, upon the following occasion:

The said Thomas Bambridge, by force, turned the said Mr. Holder over to the common side, and took possession of his room, in which all his effects were.

Mr. Holder remonstrated strongly against this usage, and Bambridge refusing to restore him to his room, or possession of his effects, he made a proper affidavit in order to apply to the judges for relief, and declared that he feared his effects might be embezzled whilst he was thus unjustly forced from them, and that he feared Bambridge's cruel treatment of him would be the cause of his death. The miseries of the common side, which he dreaded, had such an effect upon him (being a man of an advanced age, and accustomed to live in ease and plenty,) that it threw him into such a fit of sickness as made his life despaired of, and in his illness he often declared, that the villain Bambridge would be the occasion of his death. Which proved true; for Bambridge finding Mr. Holder like to die in the duress which he had put him into, for his own sake, to avoid the punishment inflicted by law upon gaolers who so inhumanly destroy their prisoners, permitted him to be carried back to his room, where in a few days he died of the said sickness, contracted by the said forcible removal of him to the common side by Bambridge, as aforesaid.

Mr. Holder by his last will appointed Major Wilson and Mr. John Pigott trustees for his son, a youth of about thirteen years of age, who had accompanied him in the time of his confinement.

The Trial of John Huggins

This young gentleman, after his father's death, locked up his effects in several trunks and boxes, and delivered the keys thereof to Mr. Pigott as his trustee, who locked up the room and took the key with him: but the said Thomas Bambridge caused the said room to be broke open by Thomas King, another of his accomplices, and caused the said effects to be seized, after that he, Bambridge, had forced Mr. Pigott out of the prison, though a prisoner in execution and locked down Major Wilson the other trustee, in the dungeon, to prevent their taking any inventory in behalf of the heir-at-law, then an orphan.

These evil practices of letting out prisoners, extorting exorbitant fees, suffering escapes, and exercising all sorts of inhumanity for gain, may in a great measure be imputed to the venality of the Warden's office; for the Warden who buys the privilege of punishing others, does consequently sell his forbearance at high rates, and repair his own charge and loss at the wretched expense of the ease and quiet of the miserable objects in his custody.

Upon the whole matter the Committee came to the following Resolutions, viz.

Resolved, that it appears to this Committee, that Thomas Bambridge, the acting Warden of the prison of the Fleet, hath wilfully permitted several debtors to the Crown in great sums of money, as well as debtors to divers of His Majesty's subjects, to escape; hath been guilty of the most notorious breaches of his trust, great extortions, and the highest crimes and misdemeanours in the execution of his said office; and hath arbitrarily and unlawfully loaded with irons, put into dungeons, and destroyed prisoners for debt under his charge, treating them in the most barbarous and cruel manner, in high violation and contempt of the laws of this Kingdom.

Resolved, that it appears to this Committee, that John Huggins, Esq. late Warden of the prison of the Fleet, did, during the time of his wardenship, wilfully permit many considerable debtors in his custody to escape, and was notoriously guilty of great breaches of his trust, extortions, cruelties, and other high crimes and misdemeanours in the execution of his said office, to the great oppression and ruin of many of the subjects of this Kingdom.

The Resolutions of the Committee being severally read a second time, were, upon the question severally put thereupon, agreed unto by the House, and are as follows, viz.

Resolved, *nem. con.* that Thomas Bambridge, the acting Warden of the prison of the Fleet, hath wilfully permitted several debtors to the Crown in great sums of money, as well as debtors to divers of his Majesty's subjects, to escape; hath been guilty of the most notorious breaches of his trust, great extortions, and the highest crimes and misdemeanours in the execution of his said office; and hath arbitrarily and unlawfully loaded with irons, put into dungeons, and destroyed prisoners for debt under his charge, treating them in the most barbarous and cruel manner, in high violation and contempt of the laws of this Kingdom.

Resolved, *nem. con.* that John Huggins, Esq. late Warden of the prison of the Fleet, did, during the time of his wardenship, wilfully permit many considerable debtors, in his custody, to escape; and was notoriously guilty of great breaches of his trust, extortions, cruelties, and other high crimes and misdemeanours in the execution of his said office, to the great oppression and ruin of many of the subjects of this Kingdom.

Resolved, that it appears to this House, that James Barnes was an agent of, and an accomplice with the said Thomas Bambridge in the commission of his said crimes.

Resolved, that it appears to this House, that William Pindar was an agent of, and an accomplice with the said Thomas Bambridge in the commission of his said crimes.

Resolved, that it appears to this House, that John Everett was an agent of, and an accomplice with the said Thomas Bambridge in the commission of his said crimes.

Resolved, that it appears to this House, that Thomas King was an agent of, and an accomplice with the said Thomas Bambridge in the commission of his said crimes.

Resolved, *nem. con.* that an humble address be presented to His Majesty that he will be graciously pleased to direct his Attorney-General forthwith to prosecute, in the most effectual manner, the said Thomas Bambridge for his said crimes.

Resolved, *nem. con.* that an humble address be presented to His Majesty that he will be graciously pleased to direct his Attorney-General forthwith to prosecute, in the most effectual manner, the said John Huggins for his said crimes.

Resolved, that an humble address be presented to His Majesty that he will be graciously pleased to direct his Attorney-General forthwith to prosecute, in the most effectual manner, the said James

Barnes, William Pindar, John Everett, and Thomas King, for their said crimes.

Ordered, that the said Thomas Bambridge be committed close prisoner to His Majesty's gaol of Newgate, and that Mr. Speaker do issue his warrants accordingly.

Ordered, that the said John Huggins, Esq. be committed close prisoner to His Majesty's gaol of Newgate, and that Mr. Speaker do issue his warrants accordingly.

Ordered, that the said James Barnes be committed close prisoner to His Majesty's gaol of Newgate, and that Mr. Speaker do issue his warrants accordingly.

Ordered, that the said William Pindar be committed close prisoner to His Majesty's gaol of Newgate, and that Mr. Speaker do issue his warrants accordingly.

Ordered, that the said John Everett be committed close prisoner to His Majesty's gaol of Newgate, and that Mr. Speaker do issue his warrants accordingly.

Ordered, that the said Thomas King be committed close prisoner to His Majesty's gaol of Newgate, and that Mr. Speaker do issue his warrants accordingly.

Ordered, *nem. con.* that leave be given to bring in a Bill to disable the said Thomas Bambridge to hold or execute the office of Warden of the prison of the Fleet, or to have or exercise any authority relating thereto; and that Mr. Oglethorpe, Mr. Earl, the Lord Percivall, and Mr. Hughes do prepare and bring in the same.

Ordered, *nem. con.* that leave be given to bring in a Bill for better regulating the prison of the Fleet, and for more effectual preventing and punishing arbitrary and illegal practices of the Warden of the said prison; and that Mr. Oglethorpe, Mr. Cornwall, Mr. Glanville, and Mr. Hughes do prepare and bring in the same.

Which Bills passed into a law.

They also inquired into the state and condition of the Marshalsea prison, and ordered a prosecution against William Acton for murder.

The Trial of JOHN HUGGINS, Esq., Warden of the Fleet Prison, for the Murder of Edward Arne, at the Sessions House in the Old Bailey, 21 May, before Mr. Justice Page, Mr. Baron Carter, and others His Majesty's Justices: 3 GEORGE II. A.D. 1729.

[These trials of Huggins, Bambridge, and Acton, were all taken in shorthand by Mr. Luke Kenn, (Clerk to the Committee appointed to inquire into the gaols of the Fleet, Marshalsea, &c.) who in his lifetime asked 200*l*. for the copy of them.]

Tuesday 20 May 1729
Proclamation was made for all persons concerned to attend.
Clerk of Arraigns. You good men that are empanelled to inquire, &c. answer to your names, and save your fines. John Huggins, hold up thy hand.
Which he did.
Clerk. Thou standest indicted by the name of John Huggins, Esq., Warden of the Fleet, &c. How sayest thou, John Huggins, art thou guilty of the felony and murder whereof thou standest indicted, or not guilty.
Huggins. Not guilty.
Clerk. How wilt thou be tried?
Huggins. By God and my country.
Clerk. God send thee a good deliverance.

Wednesday, 21 May
Proclamation was made for information.
Clerk. Thou the prisoner at the bar, these men that thou shalt hear called, and personally appear, are to pass between our Sovereign Lord the King and thee, upon the trial of thy life and death; therefore, if thou wilt challenge them, or any of them, thy time to speak is as they come to the book to be sworn, before they are sworn.

JURY
Philip Frushard,   Thomas Clayton,
John Fillebrown,   John Hoar,

The Trial of John Huggins

   Peter Sojourney, Martin Wardell,
   Thomas Gregg,   Richard Pitt,
   John Milward,   John Price,
   Daniel Town,   James King.

Clerk. John Huggins, hold up thy hand. (*Which he did.*) You of the jury look upon the prisoner. (*And was going on.*)

Huggins. My lord, the distance is too great to be heard: I desire I may come to the inner bar; for, my lord, when any inconvenience happens, it is the constant rule to admit the prisoner to come there: it was done in the case of Sanders and Clifton.

Mr. Justice Page. Whenever the Court conceives an inconvenience, it has been allowed: but I cannot allow it till then.

Clerk. You gentlemen of the jury look upon the prisoner; he stands indicted by the name of, &c.

Huggins. I must desire, my lord, to have the indictment read in Latin. (*Which was accordingly done.*)

Mr. Holland, (*Member of Parliament for Chippenham.*) My lord, and you gentlemen of the jury, I am counsel for the King; and this is an indictment against John Huggins, for aiding and abetting James Barnes in the murder of Edward Arne; that John Huggins was Warden, and one James Barnes was then his agent, who did in November, in the 11th year of his late Majesty, make an assault upon Edward Arne, and took Arne involuntarily, and confined him in the strong room (without the comfort of fire, close-stool, or other utensil), built near the place where excrements are thrown out, a place very unwholesome, and most dangerous to the health; that Arne fell sick in the said room, and languished till the 7th December, and then died; that Huggins, through his cruel disposition, being an oppressor of the prisoners, did, &c.

Serjeant Cheshire.[9] My lord, and you gentlemen of the jury, James Barnes, who stands indicted for the murder of Edward Arne, is fled from justice; and John Huggins the prisoner at the bar, also stands indicted for aiding and abetting in the said fact. He was then Warden of the Fleet, and had the custody and care of the prisoners then committed to his charge; therefore it will be necessary to let you know what bounds the law sets to gaolers, and to prisoners. The law sets fences to them both. The gaoler is to be protected in his duty, supported and

The Trial of John Huggins

maintained in it; and it is justifiable, if, in defence of himself, he destroys a man, and commits an act of felony. On the other hand, if by any unnecessary tyranny, or restraint, any of the prisoners come by an untimely death, it is murder in the gaoler; and this last is principally necessary for your attention.

Edward Arne, on the 12th of May, 1725, was committed upon mesne process;[10] he was a quiet, peaceable, and inoffensive man, and continued so till September in that year. The gentleman at the bar, not content with the same security that his predecessors had, took it in his head to make a strong room, which was built about three months before the death of Edward Arne; it was like a vault, built over the common sewer, near a laystall [*refuse heap*], where the filthy matter was lodged, nothing but bricks and mortar, not tiled or pointed; and in this condition, about September, one Barnes, servant of the defendant, came to the said Arne, as he was sitting in the cellar, rushed upon him, and took him away to the dungeon, a place where nobody had been put in before. In this said place of restraint he was confined, though he was in a quiet condition. There was no fire, nor fireplace, no light but through a hole over the door, and a little hole by the side, big enough to put a quart pot in at; there was not the want only of fire, or fireplace, but there was no chamber-pot, no convenience for the ease of nature, so that it must fall, and he converse with it. The place was so moist, that drops of wet ran down the wall. The man immediately lost his voice, his throat was swelled, and his clothes rotted with the dampness of the place, and the poor man, having a feather-bed, crept into it, and the feathers stuck close to him, and in this condition he lay; but one day, the door being open, he got out, and ran into the common hall; he looked, gentlemen, more like a feathered fowl, than an human creature. This was represented to Mr. Huggins, who generally lived in the country, and did not come to the gaol so often as he ought; but at one time, when he was at the prison, he saw the man, and the poor man just saw him, his eye fell, the door was closed, and he died. The Warden, gentlemen, had the door shut, and ordered him to be locked up, and he continued so locked up from September till the

20th of October; and it is wonderful to think, if he had not been a man of a very strong frame, how he could have continued there so long. It moved the compassion of his fellow-prisoners, who applied to have him released out of that place, but that not being done, a little care was taken to attend him. Gentlemen, at the time when Mr. Gybbon was deputy, some of the prisoners asked him, why he did not take care of Arne, for the man cannot speak. And answer was made by Barnes, 'Let him die and be damned'; and this was in the presence of the Warden. Gentlemen, I must observe to you, that for security of the lives of prisoners, the coroner's inquest ought to sit upon them, to see if any marks could be found to give an information of the cause of death, but this was not done: this is the substance of the evidence, which cannot be aggravated.

Attorney-General. (*Sir Philip Yorke, afterwards Earl of Hardwick and Lord Chancellor.*) My lord, and you gentlemen of the jury. I am of counsel for the King, and this prosecution is the effect of a useful, compassionate inquiry concerning the gaols, so it was found necessary to bring the cause before you, that gaolers may be punished, who have opportunity, and have endeavoured to oppress the unfortunate persons under their charge and power. It is necessary there should be gaols and prisons, and that persons should be under confinement; but not for gaolers to have it in their power to commit oppressions and cruelties, to the loss of the lives of His Majesty's subjects. If the evidence be true, which shall be offered to you, this will appear to be an instance of the utmost oppression, and the utmost cruelty. Mr. Huggins was Warden of the Fleet prison, and had the care and custody of the prisoners, and ought personally, or by his deputy, to take care of them, and so is answerable for them. Mr. Edward Arne came a prisoner in May 1725, and continued there till he died. At his first coming in, he lodged with one Robert Shaw; but some difference happening between them, he was turned out of that room, and lay in the common hall. This unhappy man was said to be disordered in his senses, which his oppression might reasonably occasion; he was an inoffensive, quiet man; but about this time, there was a new scheme of having a prison within a prison, which was the

The Trial of John Huggins

occasion of their committing oppressions upon the prisoners. This strong room was then erected in the manner of a vault, commonly called a dungeon; there was no window, no chimney; it was built with bare brick and mortar: upon what occasion it was built, the prisoner will give you an account, if he had any authority for building it. Gaolers are to take care of prisoners, but not to build dungeons to put them in. The walls were not dry, but very damp and unwholesome, as usually such places must be. While Arne was standing in the cellar inoffensively, Barnes, who was entrusted with the care of the prisoners, seized him and put him in this place, and he was there put without any manner of provision to sustain life; there was a little hole where you might put a little drink through, sometimes he had an opportunity of having some, and sometimes none. Under this restraint this person was kept, without any convenience to ease nature; the description is such that must move everybody to compassion. His bed was dragged in with him, and he ripped it open and crept into it to keep himself warm, and the feathers stuck to him by reason of his being besmeared with his own ordure, which he had not opportunity of doing out of the place. During the whole time whilst Arne was confined, Mr. Huggins, who was then Warden, came twice, though he ought to have come oftener, and his duty required him so to do; Mr. Huggins looked upon him there, and saw him lie in that condition, in the place built by his own order; but the prisoner, so far from giving him any relief, or removing him out of that confinement, ordered the door to be locked up in his presence, he being Warden, and by his authority. This affecting condition the poor man was in, and in the circumstance he was in, he ought to have relieved him. Several applications were made to Gybbon, and other the servants of the Warden, to desire this unhappy man to be released. Letters were sent to show his miserable condition, that he was not likely to live, and to desire that he might be put under a proper custody; but nothing was done. At that time even the prisoner saw him languish; his speech was lost, and then he languished, and continued in the dungeon till the time of his death; this will appear clearly by the evidence, that he died in duress, and that the distemper there contracted was the occasion of his death. The next consideration is, who, and what was the occasion of his death? It is the duty of the gaoler to have a coroner's inquest to inquire into the death of a prisoner for his own justification, who, by having the custody of, and the power over his prisoners, may destroy them; therefore, if there was no particular reason, why should it not have been done? Though he cannot pretend to show a particular order why he did not, when I consider, that nothing could be done but by his authority, nothing done but by his direction, that was his particular order.

If he who was the principal gaoler, who had the authority to confine him, and to discharge him from an improper confinement, who saw him there did not release him, but instead of that suffered him to be locked up, he is guilty of his death. In point of law, if a prisoner dies in duress of the gaoler by hard confinement, in a cruel manner, unnecessary to the gaoler's safe custody, it is death by law; if the gaoler is not answerable for the act, what needs the dead persons to be inquired after by a jury? Justice ought to be done, let it fall on whom it will; and I do not doubt, but the jury, for the sake of their oaths, will find him guilty.

Solicitor-General. (Hon. Mr. Talbot, afterwards a Peer and Lord Chancellor.)[11] We will call our evidence to prove the facts.

Call *Richard Longborn. (Who was sworn, as were all the rest that appeared.)*

He produced a copy of Mr. Huggins's patent, bearing the date the 22nd July, the 12th Queen Anne, which he proved to be a true copy, and such part of it was read as proved him to be Warden.

Huggins. My lord, I desire the *Habendum* may be read, by which I have a power to appoint a deputy or deputies for and during my natural life.

Mr. Justice Page. I don't know what use you will make of it; but you may call for it in your defence.

Robert Bigrave sworn.

Solicitor-General. Do you know the prisoner?

Bigrave. Very well.

Solicitor-General. How long have you known him?

Bigrave. I knew him when I was Clerk of the Papers, in April 1725.

Solicitor-General. Did he act?

The Trial of John Huggins

Bigrave. He was Warden, but did not act, Mr. Gybbon was deputy to Mr. Huggins.
Solicitor-General. Who constituted you Clerk of the Papers?—*Bigrave.* Mr. Huggins.
Solicitor-General. Were the securities taken in the name of Mr. Huggins?
Bigrave. The security bonds were taken, and returns made in the name of Mr. Huggins.
Huggins. My lord, I desire to come to the inner bar, for I can't hear.
Mr. Justice Page. You shall have all reasonable indulgence, and if you cannot hear you must be allowed to come. (*Which he accordingly did.*)
Solicitor-General. Mr. Bigrave, did Mr. Huggins continue Warden during the whole year 1725?
Bigrave. He did continue Warden during the whole year 1725, and returns were made in his name.
Solicitor-General. Do you know James Barnes?
Bigrave. Yes, he was servant to Mr. Gybbon, and was employed as watchman and runner, to take care that the prisoners did not escape.
Solicitor-General. Did he act in this capacity, whilst Mr. Huggins was principal Warden?
Bigrave. He did.
Solicitor-General. When did you come there?
Bigrave. In April 1725.
Solicitor-General. What do you know of the building the strong room?
Bigrave. When I came there, there was a stable which was converted into a strong room, but as to the time it was pulled down and rebuilt, I am not certain.
Solicitor-General. What sort of a place is it?
Bigrave. It is a place arched like a wine-vault, and built of brick and mortar.
Solicitor-General. What are the dimensions?
Bigrave. It is eight feet wide, and eleven feet long.
Solicitor-General. Had it any floor?
Bigrave. I did not see it had.
Solicitor-General. Did you see Mr. Arne in it?
Bigrave. I never saw anybody in it, till Captain Mackpheadris was put in it.

The Trial of John Huggins

Solicitor-General. Did the common sewer run under it?
Bigrave. I can't say whether the common sewer runs under it or not.
Solicitor-General. How near was the dunghill to it?
Bigrave. The dunghill was as nigh as to the other part of the Court.
Solicitor-General. Was there any fireplace or chimney?—*Bigrave.* No.
Solicitor-General. Was there any place to let the air or light in?
Bigrave. There was a hole in the side of the wall seven or eight inches square, and an opening of two foot over the door.
Solicitor-General. Did not you see Edward Arne confined in that place?
Bigrave. I remember Edward Arne, and I did hear he was confined there.
Solicitor-General. Whom was the place built by?
Bigrave. It was built by Mr. Gybbon; because I saw Mr. Gybbon give directions about it.
Solicitor-General. Do you know Daniel Hopkins?
Bigrave. I do.
Solicitor-General. Whose servant was he?
Bigrave. I esteemed him to be Gybbon's servant.
Solicitor-General. Did not he belong to Mr. Huggins?
Bigrave. He used to be clerk to Mr. Huggins.
Solicitor-General. Did you at any time, during the building the strong room, take any notice of it?
Bigrave. I can't say I did.
Solicitor-General. Was not James Barnes a runner to look after prisoners that had escaped?
Bigrave. Yes.
Solicitor-General. Were not the warrants given to him in Mr. Huggins's name?
Bigrave. They generally were.
Mr. Justice Page. What were the dimensions of this room?
Bigrave. The room is eight foot wide, eleven foot long, and nine foot high.
Attorney-General. Did not Hopkins from time to time acquaint Mr. Huggins with the transactions of the gaol?
Bigrave. He was Clerk of the Inquiries to the Warden of the Fleet.
Attorney-General. So he chose to be deputy to Mr. Gybbon?
Juryman. My Lord, I desire the witness may be asked if the room was boarded or floored?

The Trial of John Huggins

Bigrave. I did not observe it till Mackpheadris's time.
Attorney-General. How were the sides of it?
Bigrave. Brick and mortar.
Attorney-General. Were you not in the room till after Arne died?—
Bigrave. No.
Huggins. My lord, I shall follow the gentleman step by step, and desire Mr. Bigrave may be asked, if the bonds were not made up by Mr. Gybbon's direction, and he took the advantage of them?
Bigrave. He always did, and I filled up several by his order.
Huggins. Did he receive all the advantage and benefit of the office to his own use?
Bigrave. I took it so.
Attorney-General. Can you take upon you to say that Mr. Huggins had no part?
Bigrave. I can't say.
Huggins. Was not Gybbon appointed my deputy?
Bigrave. I found Mr. Gybbon deputy, when I came there, but can't say, whether he was appointed by writing or not.
Huggins. Did he pay no salary?
Bigrave. I heard he paid 400*l.* per annum and I always apprehended Mr. Gybbon had the whole account.
Huggins. I desire he may be asked, whether the bonds were not filled up by Mr. Gybbon?
Bigrave. Always.
Huggins. Returns of writs were made in my name; I desire he may be asked, whether he did not receive direction from Mr. Gybbon to make returns?
Bigrave. I did receive directions from him, for in 1727, I had some difficulty in making a return of a *Languidus*,[12] and then made returns in writing, and I received two rule fees, and 1*s.* out of each was due to the Warden, which I allowed and paid to Mr. Gybbon, and had a receipt under his hand for it.
Huggins. Were warrants in my name for prisoners escaping?
Bigrave. The warrants were generally left in the public office, and signed and sealed in blank, and they were filled up by Mr. Gybbon, and signed and sealed by Mr. Huggins.
Huggins. In whose name were the warrants returned?
Bigrave. The warrants were returned in the name of Mr. Huggins, but by the direction of Mr. Gybbon.

The Trial of John Huggins

Huggins. Was Barnes my servant or Mr. Gybbon's?
Bigrave. He was allowed to be a servant to Mr. Gybbon.
Mr. Justice Page. I will ask a question or two.
Huggins. I must beg leave, my lord, to ask one question more, and then will make some observations upon the evidence.
Mr. Justice Page. It is not proper to break in upon the evidence to make any observations now.
Huggins. This is the grand point.
Mr. Justice Page. Whether it is or no, that will come anon. If you insist upon making your remarks now you shall; but I think it will be to your prejudice, for by that you will be precluded from making your remarks upon the close of the evidence.
Huggins. My lord, I will then submit.
Mr. Justice Page. If you will ask Mr. Bigrave any more questions, you may proceed.
Huggins. Did you hear of any ill-usage from me to this man? (*Meaning Mr. Arne.*)
Bigrave. I remember Mr. Arne was there, though I knew no such man, and heard he was in the strong room.
Huggins. Did you hear of any alteration that was made in the strong room while Mr. Arne was there?
Bigrave. I never heard of any alteration during that time.
Huggins. Did not Gybbon keep two distinct offices in one and the same house?
Bigrave. In the year 1725 he did.
Attorney-General. Pray distinguish nicely as to Barnes, Huggins, and Gybbon, whether Barnes was not employed as watchman while Huggins was principal, and Gybbon Deputy-Warden?
Bigrave. He was.
Attorney-General. Who put you into your office?
Bigrave. Mr. Huggins put me into the place, and I made an agreement, and was to have 1*s*. paid me out of each day-rule.
Mr. Baron Carter. Who made the agreement?
Bigrave. I made the agreement with Mr. Huggins, and paid 700*l*. to Mr. Huggins and fifty guineas.
Mr. Baron Carter. Who put Mr. Barnes in?
Bigrave. Mr. Gybbon.
Mr. Baron Carter. How do you know?
Bigrave. I heard so.

1 *Witches Apprehended, Examined, and Executed* (1613). The frontispiece shows the 'examiners' swimming a suspected witch. If the suspect floated, she was guilty. If she sank, she was innocent.

2   *The Representations* (1729). This print was published in May 1729, shortly after the Report of the Committee of the House of Commons, which ordered the prosecutions of John Huggins and Thomas Bambridge, Wardens of the Fleet Prison, and of William Acton, Deputy-Keeper of the Marshalsea Prison, Southwark, for murder. The Fleet strong-room, where Arne died, appears top right.

The Trial of John Huggins

Call *Richard Bishop*.
Solicitor-General. What are you?
Bishop. I was tipstaff to Mr. Huggins, presently after Huggins came to his office, and paid him 200*l.* for it.
Solicitor-General. Who was deputy then?
Bishop. There was no Deputy-Warden, only Mr. Dickson, Clerk of the Papers.
Solicitor-General. When did Gybbon come there?
Bishop. In the year 1724.
Solicitor-General. What time did Arne become a prisoner?
Bishop. In 1724 or 1725, I brought him down from the judge's chambers, and put him at the Vine as usual.
Solicitor-General. Why did you not bring him into the prison?
Bishop. Because he thought to give security.
Solicitor-General. Was not that a sponging house?
Bishop. Yes.
Solicitor-General. How long did he continue there?
Bishop. About two months.
Solicitor-General. Where did he lie, when he went into the gaol?
Bishop. When he went into the gaol, I did not trouble myself about it.
Solicitor-General. Do you remember the building the strong room?
Bishop. I do remember its being built in 1725.
Solicitor-General. What sort of a place is it?
Bishop. I have seen the outside, but never saw the inside, I believe it is built over the common sewer, and but a little way from the dunghill; the ashes and dirt of the house is flung down there.
Solicitor-General. Did you see Mr. Arne there?
Bishop. I saw him once in the long room out of his clothes, before he was brought into the strong room, and I complained to Mr. Gybbon, and said he ought to be sent to Bethlehem, but he put him in the strong room.
Solicitor-General. Can you tell of any complaints made about Arne's being put there?
Bishop. I did apply to Mr. Gybbon, and said it was better to keep him in his own room, for if a wise man was put there it would make him mad; and it would have made me mad if I had been put there myself; and I heard Mr. Gybbon speak to Mr. Hopkins to acquaint Mr. Huggins, that as Mr. Taylor

was one of the governors of Bethlem, and Mr. Huggins's friend and acquaintance, he might easily get him in there.

Huggins. It was no part of the office of Warden of the Fleet; but I might, by a friendly office, use my interest with Mr. Taylor, and that would show me more a humane man, than one guilty of cruelty.

Solicitor-General. Did you see Mr. Huggins in the gaol, during the time Mr. Arne was in the strong room?

Bishop. I saw Mr. Huggins there several times, but can't say whether then or not when Mr. Arne was in the strong room.

Solicitor-General. Was he any way abusive?

Bishop. I never heard that Arne was any way abusive, or needed any such restraint.

Solicitor-General. What was James Barnes?

Bishop. He was to take up people that the Warden directed him to take up, and acted as watchman in the gaol, and was servant under the Warden.

Solicitor-General. What time was Arne put in the strong room?

Bishop. He came into the prison before the strong room was built.

Solicitor-General. Do you remember when it was built?

Bishop. It was built in 1725, I believe at the latter part of the summer season.

Solicitor-General. Do you remember the time while Arne was there? —*Bishop.* I do.

Solicitor-General. Was there anything of consequence done in the gaol, without the direction of Mr. Huggins?

Bishop. Nothing of consequence was done without his direction; but the common business of the gaol was done by Mr. Gybbon's direction.

Solicitor-General. Did you ever speak to Mr. Huggins in relation to Arne's confinement?

Bishop. I believe I might speak to Mr. Gybbon, and I believe I might speak to Mr. Huggins, for I frequently did speak to him about business.

Solicitor-General. What condition was Mr. Arne in, when brought to the Fleet?

Bishop. I think he was in his senses, he was inoffensive, and I think there was no occasion to confine him. I saw him several times walking about the yard, and if he had been confined to

The Trial of John Huggins

his own room anybody might have looked after him, even if it had been a child.

Solicitor-General. Had he any bed whilst in the strong room?

Bishop. I think he had no bed there, it was a dark place, I could not see into it.

Solicitor-General. Did Huggins use to come there after Gybbon was deputy?

Bishop. I saw Mr. Huggins there several times after Mr. Gybbon was Deputy-Warden, and Huggins used to give directions, during the time Gybbon was his deputy, and Hopkins used to bring orders to Mr. Gybbon from Mr. Huggins.

Solicitor-General. In what condition of health was Mr. Arne when he was brought in?

Bishop. He was in a good condition of health, and in his senses; and I believe, being put in the strong room in the Fleet, would have killed anybody, and that that forwarded Arne's death, and he would not have died so soon if he had not been there.

Huggins. When you spoke to Mr. Gybbon to apply to me to make interest to the governor of Bethlehem, whether it was *quatenus* [*as*] warden, or only as I was supposed to have acquaintance or interest?

Bishop. It was to apply to you as Warden.

Huggins. Were there not women prisoners and men's wives in the gaol?—*Bishop.* Yes.

Huggins. My lord, it was very unfit for a man to go naked about where there were women, and it was fit he should be confined somewhere. Whose servant was James Barnes?

Bishop. Mr. Gybbon's.

Mr. Justice Page. At the time when he ran about naked, was there no other room that he could have been put in?

Bishop. There certainly were other places where he might have been put.

Mr. Justice Page. How often have you seen him naked?

Bishop. I saw him naked but once.

Mr. Baron Carter. You said Gybbon gave some directions, and Huggins gave some directions; now during the time that Gybbon acted, did the prisoner, Mr. Huggins, give any directions as to the moving of prisoners?

Bishop. My lord, I never meddled with what was done in the inside of the prison, so can't inform you.

Call *Mr. John Cotton.*
Attorney-General. What officer are you belonging to the Fleet?—
Cotton. Clerk of the Papers.
Attorney-General. Pray see what time Arne was committed?
Cotton. He was committed the 12th of May, 1725, at the suit of John Martin and others upon mesne process.
Huggins. I desire he may see, when Barnes became a prisoner?—
Cotton. In Hilary, 1724.
Attorney-General. Is not Barnes still a prisoner, and what is become of him?
Cotton. He was a prisoner, and had the liberty of the gate; and when the order of the House of Commons came for taking him into custody, he ran away, and Corbett has endeavoured to find him out, but could not.
Attorney-General. Was Arne charged in execution?
Cotton. No, he was not.
Call *Mr. Thomas Farrington.*
Attorney-General. Did you know Edward Arne?
Farrington. I did, and the first time, that he came into the prison, it was between the 20th and 28th of June, 1725. He was some time at the Vine before.
Attorney-General. What state of health, was he in?
Farrington. When he came into the Fleet prison he was in a good state of health, and free from any sort of deliriousness, and I never saw him do anything amiss to man, woman, or child.
Attorney-General. Do you remember his being confined in the strong room?
Farrington. I do remember his being confined in September, and that he died in October.
Attorney-General. When was the first time you knew of his confinement?
Farrington. The first time I ever heard of his being confined, I heard he was carried into the strong room by Barnes, by the directions of Gybbon, Deputy-Warden to the prisoner at the bar, and he had lain before that in number 7, with Robert Shaw, and upon some difference, being turned out of that room, he then lay in the common hall, upon a bed of his own, which he laid upon part of a broken table-bedstead.
Attorney-General. When was the first time you saw Arne in the strong room?

The Trial of John Huggins

Farrington. I saw him the very day he was put in.

Attorney-General. What sort of a place is it?

Farrington. It is a room arched over like a vault, and had been new erected about six weeks, and the walls were very damp and wet. You might strike off the drops with your hand like the dew on the top of the grass in a morning. There was no wainscot nor plastering, there were some boards at the bottom, but whether entirely boarded I can't tell. It was a vault arched over, and when Arne was carried in not tiled; there was a window over the door three quarters of a yard long, and another on the side of the door seven or eight inches long, and four wide, and no fireplace, and the common sewer runs under it.

Attorney-General. Who supplied him with victuals?

Farrington. I saw Mr. Louden give him victuals.

Attorney-General. Who kept the key of the room?

Farrington. Barnes.

Attorney-General. From the time that Mr. Arne came into the prison, which was between the 20th and 28th of June, till he was put in the strong room, what state of health was he in?

Farrington. He continued in a good state of health, till a little before he was put in the strong room, and then he grew somewhat disordered; and from the time he was put in the strong room he altered every day, grew hoarse, and at last could not speak, and he grew weaker and weaker every day; about the beginning of October he lost his voice, he grew then delirious, and ripped open his bed, and crept into the feathers, and one day came to the chapel with excrement and feathers sticking about him like a magpie, being forced to ease nature in that place. And after that, I saw the prisoner at the bar, and Hopkins, looking into the strong room, the door being open, upon Arne, and Arne was lying in the bed ripped open, and covered much about as high as his navel.

Attorney-General. Did you hear Arne speak?

Farrington. He was very hoarse, and could not speak, but lifted up his eyes, and looked at Mr. Huggins.

Attorney-General. Did Huggins then see him?

Farrington. Mr. Huggins must see him, if he was not blind.

Attorney-General. Did you hear them speak?

Farrington. Mr. Huggins and Hopkins whispered, but I did not hear what they said; but Huggins shook his head, then Barnes shut the door, and Huggins and Hopkins were then going away.

Attorney-General. How long after was it before Arne died?—

Farrington. About fourteen days.

Attorney-General. Did you see Arne between this time of Huggins being there and his death?

Farrington. I saw him the morning before he died, and at that time he was so weak, he could not stir any way, but there lay gaping for life.

Attorney-General. What was the occasion of his lying in that languishing condition?

Farrington. Arne's confinement was the occasion. I was in the strong room three days myself with one Smith, my legs were so swelled that the small was as big as my thigh, and I never knew a day's sickness till that time, and if I had continued a week longer it would have killed me, and I was forced to buy paper to ease nature in, and fling it out of the window.

Attorney-General. What is the situation of that room?

Farrington. Its situation is at the furthest part of the prison northward, and there is a sewer under it, into which runs the water from the pump to carry off the excrements of the prison, which are emptied into it, and the dunghill was then about six yards from it.

Attorney-General. What distance is there between the strong room and the dunghill now?

Farrington. About eight yards, and all the nuisance of the house is flung there, and there are very bad smells.

Attorney-General. What was the occasion of the death of Arne?

Farrington. I think it was the strong room was the occasion of it, for it was enough to kill the strongest body.

Attorney-General. Did Arne die there?

Farrington. He did, and Mr. Huggins always said he had authority to put persons in the strong room, or irons, which I can prove under his hand. (*And was going to pull out a paper, which not being allowed as evidence, he desisted.*) I saw Mr. Huggins a second time walking upon the Bare with Gybbon and Levinz, between the hours of eleven and one, a week or a fortnight after which he was at the strong room.

Attorney-General. How long did Mr. Huggins stand looking upon Mr. Arne in the strong room?

The Trial of John Huggins

Farrington. About three, four, or five minutes, and he then stood looking at the door, as I now stand looking at the counsel.

Attorney-General. Was Arne let out of the strong room afterwards?

Farrington. I never heard that Arne was afterwards out of the strong room till he died.

Huggins. Did not you make some affidavits by way of complaint to the Court of Common Pleas?—*Farrington.* Yes.

Huggins. Please, my lord, to ask, whether or not Mr. Arne was mentioned in that complaint that he made?

Farrington. I never made but three affidavits, two of which I have in my hand in print, but don't remember Mr. Arne's being mentioned in either of them.

Huggins. My lord, the affidavits tend chiefly to the sending of coffins in.

Mr. Justice Page. If you intend to make any use of those affidavits they must be produced and read.

Mr. Richard Fulthorpe sworn.

Attorney-General. Did you know Edward Arne?

Fulthorpe. I did, I was a prisoner then myself, he was brought in the latter end of August; and I remember him a prisoner before he was confined in the strong room. I being in the cellar, one Barnes and two or three other servants of the Warden's took him by violence and carried him there.

Attorney-General. Had you been in his company, and had conversation with him?

Fulthorpe. I had several times.

Attorney-General. Was he disorderly?

Fulthorpe. He might be a little in liquor, but he did nothing to offend anyone, and gave no disturbance to the company. He was carried by Barnes into the strong room.

Attorney-General. What sort of a place is the strong room?

Fulthorpe. It is a place like a dungeon, with a hole on the side big enough to put in a full pot of beer.

Attorney-General. How big is the room?

Fulthorpe. The room is about half the bigness of the court where the counsel sit, and stands near the dunghill, and the sewer runs under it. I saw it opened.

Attorney-General. What was over the common sewer?

Fulthorpe. There were boards laid loose over.

The Trial of John Huggins

Attorney-General. What was between the common sewer and the boards?

Fulthorpe. Nothing. The walls were green. It was not tiled in, and had scarce been built above a week, and was as wet as anything could be.

Attorney-General. Who put Arne into the strong room?

Fulthorpe. Barnes and some others, then prisoners, who acted under the Warden, took him out of the cellar, put him in there, and locked him up.

Attorney-General. Did you see Mr. Huggins during the time Arne was there confined?

Fulthorpe. I saw Mr. Huggins twice there. I saw him at the strong room; he went along with Gybbon and Hopkins, and Mr. Huggins laid his hand upon the door, and looked in, the door being open.

Attorney-General. How long was he there?

Fulthorpe. A minute or two.

Attorney-General. Who was there besides?

Fulthorpe. Several belonging to the Fleet. I believe Barnes was there.

Attorney-General. How long before the death of Arne?—*Fulthorpe.* About a month.

Attorney-General. What condition was Arne in at the time he was put in there?

Fulthorpe. When he was put in there, he was a little out of the way when fuddled, but when sober as well as any man; when I came to the door, there used to be a smell enough to strike one down.

Attorney-General. How long was Arne in the strong room, before you saw him there?

Fulthorpe. I went the next morning, and at several other times.

Attorney-General. How long was Arne there?

Fulthorpe. About six weeks.

Attorney-General. What condition was he in when Huggins looked upon him?

Fulthorpe. He was very ill when Huggins looked upon him.

Attorney-General. What do you think was the occasion of his death?

Fulthorpe. The confinement and the dampness of the room gave him his death.

Attorney-General. Had Mr. Huggins spoke to have Arne taken out?

The Trial of John Huggins

Fulthorpe. He had not, for the door was shut, Mr. Huggins being then present.

Attorney-General. How came you to be there?

Fulthorpe. I wanted to speak to Mr. Huggins about business, for the payment of the bill drawn upon Huggins by one Lewis.

Attorney-General. How came Arne to cut his bed in pieces, and creep into the feathers?

Fulthorpe. It was occasioned by his confinement; there was no fire there, and I believe the confinement was the occasion of his death.

Huggins. How often did you know him let out?

Fulthorpe. Two or three times.

Huggins. How long were you a prisoner after?

Fulthorpe. I was discharged by the Act of Grace.

Attorney-General. How came you to be present at the time Mr. Huggins looked into the strong room?

Fulthorpe. I waited for an opportunity of speaking to him about a note.

Mr. Tudor Smith sworn.

Solicitor-General. Did you know Edward Arne?

Smith. I knew Mr. Arne very well, and that he was in the Fleet prison. I remember the time of his coming into the Fleet prison. I was with him in the sponging house, and then he was carried into the Fleet prison.

Solicitor-General. Where did he lie?

Smith. In the room of one Robert Shaw, and continued there about a fortnight or three weeks; but upon some quarrel was turned out.

Solicitor-General. When Arne came out of the room, was not his bed turned out with him?

Smith. It was; upon which, he then lay in the common hall for some time.

Solicitor-General. Did you see Arne carried to the strong room?

Smith. I was in the cellar, when he was carried to the strong room; Barnes took him away.

Solicitor-General. What was Barnes?

Smith. I apprehended him to be Mr. Huggins's servant.

Solicitor-General. What did you see done by Barnes?

Smith. I did see Barnes come, and take Arne by the collar, and he said, he must go along with him. Arne said, 'Where?' Barnes replied 'No matter where, you must go along with me:' and the next morning I saw Arne in the strong room.

Solicitor-General. What state of health was he in, when carried there?

Smith. He was in an ill state of health.

Solicitor-General. What sort of a room was it?

Smith. It was newly built, very damp, and a nauseous place. I knowing him before, was under more than common concern, and asked Arne how he did? And he said Barnes carried him there. I asked him if he had a bed? He said he had no bed; but the next day a bed was brought to him.

Solicitor-General. How long did he lie there?

Smith. A month or six weeks; I visited him often.

Solicitor-General. Was there any fireplace, any candle, or anything necessary to ease nature in?

Smith. There was no fireplace, no candle, nothing necessary to ease nature in, and he was forced to do all that nature required there; and many a time, when I carried drink, meat or ale to him, I have been forced to hold my nose.

Solicitor-General. What place was there to let in the air?

Smith. There was a place over the door with iron bars, three foot in length, and another hole on the side, about a foot and a half.

Attorney-General. Did you give any notice to Mr. Huggins of the condition this man was in?

Smith. Having been a prisoner some time, I applied for the benefit of the rules, and he received 12*l.* for the liberty of the rules, and Hopkins and Gybbon insisted upon ten guineas more; and I wrote four letters of the usage I received, having paid several sums of money; which I sent to Mr. Huggins by Robin the porter, and did in one of them, of the 5th of October, mention Mr. Arne's confinement.

Mr. Baron Carter. To what purpose was that letter?

Smith. It partly related to my own business, and I mentioned that the strong room was a place not fit for a Christian to be in, and Mr. Arne lay in a very miserable condition; and seeing him in such a condition, I gave him an old night-gown, being in a manner naked for want of covering, he had ripped open his bed, and got into the feathers.

The Trial of John Huggins

Mr. Baron Carter. Did you take any notice in the letter of his lying in the feathers?

Smith. I had wrote in the letter about seeing him in the feathers, and directed the letter to Mr. Huggins, at his house in St. Martin's Lane, and sent it by Robin the porter. I spoke to Mr. Hopkins.

Mr. Justice Page. That was not material.

Mr. Baron Carter. Did you ever see Mr. Huggins in the gaol?

Smith. I never did, but watched an opportunity of seeing him.

Mr. Baron Carter. What condition was Arne in?

Smith. It was a miserable scene; and I take it that it was the cause of his death; and that he perished by being in such a condition.

Huggins. I desire he may be asked, my lord, if ever I had come into the Fleet prison, he should have seen me?

Smith. I believe I should.

Huggins. Did you ever see me there?

Smith. I saw Mr. Huggins two or three times, at the time the protonotaries[13] were there.

Huggins. I desire he may be asked, my lord, if he received any answer from me to the letter?

Smith. I received no answer from Mr. Huggins.

Huggins. Did the letter contain other business?—*Smith.* It did.

Robert Saintclair, the porter, sworn.

Attorney-General. Is that the man, Robin?

Smith. It is the man I sent.

Attorney-General. Did you carry any letters for Mr. Smith?

Saintclair. I carried several letters, and brought answers back again to them; but by reason of the distance of the time, cannot remember the delivery of the letters, but gave the answers to Mr. Smith.

Attorney-General. Do you remember about what time?

Saintclair. I cannot say about what time.

Attorney-General. Did you carry any letters from Mr. Smith to Mr. Huggins?

Saintclair. I carried several letters to Mr. Huggins from Mr. Smith, and always returned an answer to whom I delivered them.

Huggins. My lord, I desire he may be asked, if he ever delivered a letter from Mr. Smith to me?

Saintclair. I cannot say I ever saw Mr. Huggins at his own house.

Thomas Paine sworn.
Attorney-General. Did you know Edward Arne?
Paine. I did, and remember his being put in the Fleet Prison.
Attorney-General. What state of health was he in when he came there?
Paine. He was in a good state of health. I was in company with him and Captain Bateman, who was at cards, and Arne was at play, and did not seem to be lunatic; and one James Barnes came into the room whilst I was in company drinking with them, and Arne was doing nothing disorderly, and Barnes forced him into the strong room, and I was then by.
Attorney-General. Who was Barnes?
Paine. Barnes was a prisoner, and was made a watchman by Gybbon, who gave him the liberty of the gate.
Attorney-General. What was his business?
Paine. He was a watchman.
Attorney-General. Whose servant did you look upon him to be?
Paine. I looked upon him to be a servant of Mr. Gybbon's.
Attorney-General. Did you ever see Mr. Huggins there?
Paine. I never saw Mr. Huggins there, but when the protonotaries were there.
Attorney-General. What sort of a place was it before it was made so?
Paine. It was a stable where the cocks and hens roosted.
Attorney-General. Did you see it after it was converted into a strong room, before Mr. Arne was put into it?
Paine. I did; and the walls were green; there was certainly a dampness.
Attorney-General. Was there any sewer ran under it?
Paine. I cannot say: but there was an ill smell came both from the necessary-house and from the dunghill.
Attorney-General. What condition was Arne in, after he was put in by Barnes?
Paine. Arne grew outrageous, and tore his clothes and bedding.
Attorney-General. What condition of health was Arne in?
Paine. I never talked to him but through the hole in the wall.
Attorney-General. How was he before he died?
Paine. I was discharged before he died.
Attorney-General. What kind of alteration was there in his voice?
Paine. He was a little hoarser, and I could not see him, but only as I talked to him through the hole.

The Trial of John Huggins

Attorney-General. Was it a fit place to confine a prisoner in?
Paine. It was not a fit place to confine prisoners in without danger of their lives.
Huggins. Was there a court of inspectors or governors of the Fleet?
Paine. There was such.
Huggins. Did they not ballot once a month?
Paine. We once balloted for steward and inspector.
Huggins. Did not the court of inspectors place Arne in the strong room?
Paine. The inspectors did not so much as visit the strong room.
Huggins. If any complaint had been made, was not the power vested in the court of inspectors to redress?
Mr. Justice Page. Mr. Huggins, that is not a proper question.
Huggins. My lord, I desire he may be asked then how long it was before Mr. Arne died that he left the prison?
Paine. I was discharged in September, about the 8th.
Huggins. The 8th of September, my lord, which was about six weeks before Mr. Arne died.
Mr. Justice Page. When was the strong room built?—*Paine.* In Mr. Gybbon's time.
Huggins. My lord, if Mr. Gybbon built the strong room, there is reason to believe he paid for it.
John Bouch sworn.
Attorney-General. Did you belong to the Fleet?
Bouch. I did, I was turnkey there.
Attorney-General. When was the strong room built?
Bouch. It was built in 1725, the latter end of the summer, by the direction of Mr. Huggins.
Attorney-General. During the time that you belonged there, did not Mr. Huggins come frequently?
Bouch. He came now and then, not very often.
Attorney-General. When was Arne put in the strong room?
Bouch. He was put in about August.
Attorney-General. Did you know him before he was carried there?
Bouch. I knew him very well, and never saw any ill offered by him.
Attorney-General. Whose order was he put in by?
Bouch. He was put in by the order of Mr. Gybbon and Mr. Huggins.
Attorney-General. Did he die in that place?
Bouch. He did.

Attorney-General. How long was he there?
Bouch. About a month or six weeks.
Attorney-General. Did you see Mr. Huggins there during the time Arne was in the strong room?
Bouch. I cannot say I did.
Attorney-General. Who was it overlooked the building the strong room?
Bouch. Mr. Huggins, when he came to the Lodge.
Attorney-General. Was he there when the building was a-raising?
Bouch. I cannot be certain, but I remember there was a direction of the Court of Common Pleas for Mr. Huggins to inspect the gaol, and that he came once a week after the order from the Court of Common Pleas.
Attorney-General. What was the condition of the room?
Bouch. The room was newly built and green.
Attorney-General. Did you carry any letter to Mr. Huggins relating to Mr. Arne?
Bouch. I did carry a letter from a friend of Mr. Arne's, and he was so weak then that he could not speak.
Attorney-General. Where did you carry it from?
Bouch. From the Fleet prison.
Attorney-General. What was it about?
Bouch. It was about getting Arne his liberty; a gentleman gave me the letter, and desired me to bring an answer as to Arne's having the liberty of the rules; and I went myself, and saw Mr. Huggins, and gave him the letter; he opened it, and said he would send an answer by Mr. Hopkins.
Attorney-General. When was this?
Bouch. It was in October, about a week before Arne died.
Attorney-General. Where did Arne die?
Bouch. He died in the strong room, I saw him two days before he died; he was just as if dead then, and very weak and ill.
Attorney-General. What kind of a place was the strong room?
Bouch. It was a very sickly place, because of the common sewer running under it.
Attorney-General. What message did Mr. Huggins send by Mr. Hopkins as to the letter?
Bouch. Mr. Huggins sent word by Daniel Hopkins, that he would inform Mr. Arne's friend what was to be done.
Attorney-General. Who was it built the strong room?

The Trial of John Huggins

Bouch. One Fry, a bricklayer, took directions from Mr. Huggins, at Mr. Huggins's own house, and I was present when Fry was there.

Attorney-General. Who paid for the building?

Bouch. I believe Mr. Huggins, for Fry was a master bricklayer, and I saw him there about business after the building was finished.

Attorney-General. How came you to be there?

Bouch. I went there then to get a place of Mr. Huggins.

Attorney-General. When were you turnkey?

Bouch. I was not turnkey till after Mr. Arne's death.

Attorney-General. Did you see him in the strong room?

Bouch. I saw him in the strong room twenty times, for I was then endeavouring to get to be turnkey.

Attorney-General. Whom had you the place from?

Bouch. From Mr. Huggins; and during the time I was endeavouring for it, I saw Mr. Arne in the strong room.

James Tucker sworn.

Attorney-General. Do you know the place that is called the strong room in the Fleet prison?

Tucker. I do, and was employed by the bricklayer and carpenter to make the iron-work.

Attorney-General. Whom did you make out your bill to?

Tucker. I made it out to Mr. Huggins, as debtor.

Attorney-General. Who paid you?

Tucker. I made the bill out in Mr. Huggins's name, and was paid by Pindar, and a receipt was given in full of that bill.

Mrs. Elizabeth Le Pointz sworn.

Attorney-General. Did you know Edward Arne?

Le Pointz. I did.

Attorney-General. Do you remember him a prisoner in the Fleet, and his confinement in the strong room?

Le Pointz. I do; he had been confined two or three days before I went to him; the first time I saw him sitting upon a bench, and the next time in his feather-bed, and he was covered therein, and his bed lay on the floor.

Attorney-General. What condition of health was he in?

Le Pointz. I never found him any way distempered, only disordered by the cold and dampness of the place.

Attorney-General. Was not his voice altered?

The Trial of John Huggins

Le Pointz. He had a shivering hoarseness upon him.
Attorney-General. How long did he continue there?
Le Pointz. He continued there seven weeks, or thereabouts.
Attorney-General. What condition was the place in?
Le Pointz. It was building in July, and I remember the finishing of it some time in August.
Attorney-General. When was Mr. Arne put in?
Le Pointz. He was put in as soon as it was finished.
Attorney-General. Do you believe that was the occasion of his death?
Le Pointz. It was impossible to be otherwise; for the building was so very green, that you might pull the mortar from the bricks with your fingers, and it was impossible anybody could be continued therein for seven weeks without being killed by the dampness of the place; and I verily believe that confinement was the occasion of Arne's death.
Attorney-General. Did you ever speak to anybody about his releasement?
Le Pointz. Whilst he was in this place, I met with Mr. Hopkins, and spoke to him to acquaint Mr. Huggins, that it was impossible but that Arne must perish, if continued in that place; and if he did not speak to Mr. Huggins, I would send to him myself. To which Hopkins replied, he would; and afterwards I met with him, and asked him, whether he had spoke? He told me he had spoke to Mr. Huggins, who said it was no business of his.
Mr. Justice Page. That cannot be given in evidence, for it is only hearsay.
Le Pointz. (*Standing up again.*) I saw Mr. Huggins upon the Bare, with one Levinz, a Quaker, then a prisoner in the house, and Mr. Gybbon, during the time Arne was in the strong room.
Serjeant Cheshire. Which way did he come upon the Bare?
Le Pointz. I cannot tell; there were then but two ways, one by the strong room, and the other through the house.
Serjeant Cheshire. Whereabouts is the strong room?
Le Pointz. The strong room was built near the Bare, and joins to the end of the house; and I saw them walking together; and that he could not well come in or out without coming near the strong room.
Serjeant Cheshire. What did you think was the occasion of his coming there?

3 *Louisa Calderon being Tortured by Order of General Picton*, a popular version of the crime from *The New Newgate Calendar* (1864).

4 *The Court of King's Bench* from Rudolf Ackermann's *Microcosm of London* (1808–10). The figures are the work of Thomas Rowlandson, while the architectural setting is by Auguste Charles Pugin, father of Augustus Welby Pugin.

The Trial of John Huggins

Le Pointz. To take a survey of the walls, which were then finished, for that I saw him look up at them.
Serjeant Cheshire. Did you know Mr. Huggins?
Le Pointz. I knew him very well.
Serjeant Cheshire. When was this?
Le Pointz. I take it to be some time in October, about fourteen days before Arne died: it was after the fire happened in Bell-Savage yard.
Thomas Levinz was called, and being a Quaker, refused to take an oath, and therefore could not be admitted an evidence.

['In the case of Bambridge the appellant's counsel called a Quaker; and insisted that this is a civil suit, in which he might be a witness. But the Chief Justice said, it was to this purpose a criminal proceeding, and therefore he could not be a witness. Strange's *Reports*, vol. II, p. 856.' *Former Edition.*]

Huggins. It is a great while ago since this matter happened; there is no notice taken by the course of the evidence how this matter has gone on, and therefore it was very difficult to answer particularly thereto. This I do solemnly affirm, that during the time Arne was there, I never heard of his name, that he died, or was in the strong room, till that I was in the Fleet to be examined: that I never was seen in the Fleet prison while Arne was in the strong room; and that no one of the King's witnesses has said, that I used any hard words about Mr. Arne. There was a suggestion of my getting Arne into Bethlehem, it was no part of my office as Warden of the Fleet, but I might by a friendly office use my interest with Mr. Taylor; and that would show me more a humane man, than one guilty of cruelty.

That some of the prisoners, who were witnesses, were discharged the prison the 7th of September, so it was not likely that they should be able to swear as to Arne's death, who did not die till October.

As to Gybbon being deputy, the first evidence to be produced will be the Act for insolvent debtors in 1725, to prove that Gybbon carried in a list pursuant to that Act; and delivered it as gaoler, and swore to it; and I must desire, that Mr. Tanner may read the clause in that Act of

The Trial of John Huggins

Parliament, where gaolers are directed to make out a list of prisoners.

Attorney-General. If you would prove Mr. Gybbon Warden, you must prove what consideration he gave, and what style he bore.

Mr. Justice Page. Did the commissioners in that act take notice who was Deputy-Warden or not? Let it be deputy, or how it would, they took no notice of that. It would be no evidence for the King.

Huggins. It will prove that Gybbon acted.

Mr. Justice Page. We shall see that when the Act of Parliament is read. I allow Gybbon did act in fact.

Attorney-General. If he has a mind to prove Mr. Gybbon deputy, he must prove it by his deputation.

Serjeant Cheshire. It is too early to offer this before the deputation lies before us; therefore I submit it, if it is not too soon to offer this in evidence.

Mr. Justice Page. I cannot direct the prisoner how he should proceed; whether this may be of advantage to him I cannot find. If he be charged from a particular fact that did arise by Gybbon, why should not Huggins, by the same rule of reason, justify himself by any other act done by Gybbon?

Then the clause in the Act of Insolvency in the year 1725, was ordered to be read.[14]

Mr. Justice Page. I do not see, upon reading of the Act, it affects anything that has been said. I take it that the officer acts, and makes returns, and the law does not say whether it is the Warden or the Deputy-Warden. Mr. Huggins, I dare to say you yourself will own it; and the use that you would make of it is to show, that he acted as Warden.

Huggins. Fulthorpe was discharged the 7th of September. I desire Mr. Tanner may produce the list, and that it may be read to show that.

Mr. Justice Page. If Fulthorpe's evidence was laid aside, yet there are witnesses enough to prove, that they saw you there. However, I must take notice of what Fulthorpe said. He said, that Arne was a peaceable man, and then gave a description of the room; and said, that the floor was covered with a few boards; and that he saw the prisoner twice in the Fleet, and that he was there at one time, and

The Trial of John Huggins

looked in at the door, and then the door was shut, and he went away. This defence seems but trifling.

Huggins. I intended it as to the credit of the witness.

Mr. Justice Page. The man has sworn honestly, and if it was struck out of the evidence it would not signify; and I must a little assist you, as no counsel is allowed but in cases of high treason. You were going to show the act of the deputy, without showing what authority was given to the deputy. If you have any instrument or agreement by which you constituted Gybbon deputy, you must produce it.

Huggins. My lord, I cannot produce it, because it is in the hands of the widow Gybbon, or some other person; and we are at this time in equity.

Mr. Justice Page. Affairs of this nature have always been done by indenture—as the Sheriffs of London to their Under Sheriff—and then you must have a counterpart.

Huggins. My lord, I never made any such indenture. I desire Mr. Tanner may be asked, who appeared as Warden upon the Insolvent Act?

Tanner. Mr. Gybbon, my lord.

Mr. Justice Page. Do you believe he was deputy or not?

Tanner. I looked upon Gybbon as a proper officer.

Mr. Justice Page. Who do you think was Warden?

Tanner. I cannot say who was Warden.

Mr. Justice Page. I thought you would not have equivocated. You are a good officer, but I shall never examine you as a witness.

John Jeffreys, Keeper of the Compter, sworn.

Huggins. Mr. Jeffreys, pray acquaint the Court, what agreement was made between Mr. Gybbon and me.

Jeffreys. There was a writing made, and I was a witness to it, but did not know what it was.

Mr. Justice Page. Mr. Huggins, the questions that you ask, you must first explain to the Court.

Huggins. I desire Mr. Jeffreys may be asked, if he was present at the agreement?

Jeffreys. I was present.

Huggins. Was there any writing signed?

Mr. Justice Page. You must take care to produce the writings if you examine to them.

Huggins. I have sent a man for the receipt of 1,000*l.*
Mr. Justice Page. I cannot comply for the same title made under your grant to be given in evidence for the grantor. It was a title from you, and how you will do to prove this by word of mouth, I cannot see how it can be done; for when a treaty comes into articles and writing, the treaty by word of mouth is at an end without the writing is produced.
Huggins. I was going to explain myself, and was overruled.
Mr. Justice Page. When once articles are come to be a conveyance, except it is to explain that conveyance, and except it is to discover some fraud even in the conveyance when given, it cannot be spoke to.
Mr. Baron Carter being gone out of Court, now returned, and Mr. Justice Page took notice to him of what had passed in his absence.

Mr. Huggins's aim is to show, that Mr. Gybbon was sole, entire, acting Warden; and that no act of Gybbon's should affect him; and had the late Act of Insolvency read, and thought to have read the schedule, but that could not be read. Mr. Huggins asked who brought in that schedule, and asked Mr. Tanner, whether Mr. Gybbon brought in that return as deputy or not; who said that he did not know who was Warden, but that Gybbon was the proper officer. Now Huggins carrying this matter further, would have Gybbon appear to be his deputy, and has now called Jeffreys to prove that deputation. Jeffreys says, that it was in writing, and I could not allow Jeffreys to give in evidence what was in writing. Huggins said in answer, that there was no counterpart, and that Gybbon's widow had such appointment. I submit it (if it was not his act and deed,) if Mr. Gybbon allowed of it.
Huggins. My lord, it is only a receipt.
Jeffreys. My lord, it was a receipt for 1,000*l.* and no agreement.
Huggins. Mr. Gybbon agreed with me for 500*l.* per annum; and liking the bargain made a deposit of 1,000*l.* and this was all the writing between us, and in it declared that he was to pay 900*l.* per annum, on condition of having the rents of the house and shops in Westminster Hall, and required a deposit of 1,000*l.* and a parole of three years may amount to a lease or demise.
Mr. Baron Carter. At six months' end Gybbon desired to have it renewed, and came to the subsequent agreement for 900*l.* per

annum for three years. If the Court could see that agreement, whether it do not amount to a lease, there may be a demise in it, but how far the Court will lay their commands to produce it, we shall not now determine; it would be very hard to have it out of his power, and not to admit him to give evidence.

Attorney-General. The law requires the best evidence that is to be given; supposing that the writing was lost, he might be admitted to give evidence that it was lost. If it was in the hands of any officer of the Crown, and they wanted to be admitted to give evidence as to the contents, whether upon giving evidence, that the thing was in being, and in the hands of a third person, they should give parole evidence [*sworn verbal testimony*] as to that.

Mr. Justice Page. Suppose a man receive money by false tokens, but by some accident it is got into other hands, and he uses all the care and art he can to get it, and proves that he cannot come at it, it would be hard to convict a man, if he cannot come at the writing. It is the same in the cases of life and death, by forgery and false deeds.

Mr. Baron Carter. I agree your notion is right in cases of civil actions, for if he can't give such evidence as the law gives against it, he has a remedy at equity; but in this case, where a man stands indicted for murder, where can he have his remedy? I am sure we should be guilty of murder, if we insisted on it. Huggins ought to give an account that he can't come at such agreement.

Huggins. Mr. Jeffreys says, that he applied to Mrs. Gybbon, and Mrs. Gybbon told him, that it was in the hands of one Wilson, her clerk in court, and he could not tell whose hands it was in.

Jeffreys. I have a copy of that writing, which has been in my hands long before any contest happened to Mr. Huggins, for it was written at the same time the receipt was given.

Mr. Justice Page. Is it a true copy?

Jeffreys. I believe it to be a true copy, and that there has been no alteration made in it.

The Copy of the Writing read —— And it appeared to be witnessed by Mr. Jeffreys, the 26th of June, 1723.

Huggins. Have you had any conversation with Mrs. Gybbon lately?

Jeffreys. Mrs. Gybbon came to me about fourteen days ago.
Huggins. Was there any talk of any such thing as a lease or articles of agreement?
Jeffreys. There was no such word mentioned as a lease or articles of agreement.
Huggins. Do you know of any articles of agreement?
Jeffreys. I don't believe there were any, for I was very conversant with Mr. Gybbon, but never heard him ask after them.
Huggins. How long did Gybbon continue in that office?—
Jeffreys. Three years.
Attorney-General. What do you mean by that office? Did he continue to act for those three years?
Jeffreys. He did, and one year longer, which I applied to Mr. Huggins for him to do.
Mr. Justice Page. You were present at the settling of the account between Mr. Huggins and Mr. Gybbon. At the bottom of the account there are some items that have no sums to them. Pray how did that happen?
Jeffreys. My lord, it was not settled.
Mr. Justice Page. Was anything mentioned, who was to be at the charge of repairs during the four years?
Jeffreys. Mr. Huggins made a memorandum at the bottom of the paper.
Huggins. It was settled at the end of four years.
Mr. Justice Page. The repairs of the prison were left a blank.
Huggins. I answer to that, my lord, that it was settled at the end of four years. Mr. Jeffreys was then present. Your lordship seems to take it for a lease of three years.
Mr. Justice Page. It is neither the one nor the other, either lease or agreement.
Huggins. My lord, Jeffreys said there was no other agreement.
George Welland sworn.
Huggins. When did Gybbon enter upon his office?
Welland. Mr. Gybbon entered at Christmas, 1722, and I was concerned for Mr. Gybbon before, and by his direction acted, and he always paid me my fees, and I never received anything from Mr. Huggins.
Huggins. Who bore all expenses relating to the gaol?—*Welland.* Mr. Gybbon.
Huggins. How long did he act?

The Trial of John Huggins

Welland. Mr. Gybbon was in four years and a half.
Huggins. What do you know about Arne?
Welland. I was there then, and Arne was committed about the middle of May, and at the latter end of September, Hopkins was sent into the country to Shropshire, and I acted till October, and I was requested by Mr. Gybbon to go to the Company of Upholders[15] relating to Mr. Arne. He was brought in May, and put at the Vine, and made his escape, and then grew disordered in his senses. Some of the prisoners came and brought a bed of Mr. Howard's, and I saw him stark naked; and it being desired, he was put in the strong room at the request of the prisoners.
Huggins. What was done upon your application to the Company of Upholders?
Welland. They took care of him.
The witness had a book in his hand, which he called a check-book.
Huggins. Pray give an account, whether I gave any direction relating to the prisoners?
Welland. I never saw Mr. Huggins there but twice, and that was when the protonotaries were there.
Huggins. When had you that book delivered to you?
Welland. Two days before Mr. Fitch died; the book was brought into my hands, which I continued to act in till Mr. Bigrave came in.
Huggins. By the writing in that book, I can prove Hopkins out of town. When was Hopkins out of town?
Mr. Justice Page. I will call Fulthorpe to clear up this matter.
Fulthorpe was called again.
Mr. Justice Page. When was it you saw Mr. Huggins at the Fleet prison?
Fulthorpe. It was some time before I was discharged. It was about a month before Mr. Arne died, and I likewise saw Mr. Farrington at the same time. Mr. Hopkins was there, and then came in with Huggins.
Mr. Justice Page. How often did you see Mr. Huggins there?
Fulthorpe. I saw him twice at the prison, but once at the strong room.
Mr. Justice Page. What time of the day was it you saw Mr. Huggins there?
Fulthorpe. It was between eleven and twelve, and there were there

Mr. Huggins, Mr. Hopkins, and Barnes; and I saw Mr. Huggins walking upon the Bare, when Levinz the Quaker was there, and I believe Mr. Gybbon with them.

Thomas Farrington was again called.

Mr. Justice Page. Who was at the strong room when you saw Huggins there?

Farrington. There were Mr. Huggins, Hopkins, and Barnes there.

Huggins. I beg leave to observe, that Fulthorpe was discharged on the 7th of September, and whether I may not be allowed to examine Welland again, to know if Mr. Gybbon did not give all orders, and to prove that the constant usage was not to have the coroner sit upon bodies in mesne process?

Mr. Justice Page. You may ask what questions you think proper, for I will stay here till to-morrow morning, to give you an opportunity of going on with your defence in your own way.

Huggins. I desire then, my lord, he may be asked, whether Gybbon did not give all orders relating to the prisoners?—*Welland.* He did.

Huggins. Whether the coroner was called in to sit upon any bodies, but in execution?

Welland. We never had the coroner, but upon execution.

Huggins. Whose servant was Barnes?

Welland. Mr. Gybbon's servant, I saw Gybbon pay him money.

Huggins. Did you ever see me and Barnes together?

Welland. I don't believe I ever did.

Huggins. At whose request was Arne put in the strong room?

Welland. At the request of the prisoners.

Mr. Justice Page. Name at whose request he was put in.—*Welland.* I can't tell.

Mr. Justice Page. How came you to know it?

Welland. I was in the Lodge.

Mr. Justice Page. Were you then present?

Welland. I was.

Mr. Justice Page. Can't you name one of them?

Welland. No, none of them are now in gaol.

Mr. Justice Page. Was not Farrington then a prisoner?—*Welland.* He was.

Mr. Justice Page. How long is it since you were concerned in the prison?

Welland. In Michaelmas 1722, and I know nothing of it before.

Mr. Justice Page. Was there not a benefit to the Warden for day-rules?—*Welland.* Yes.
Mr. Justice Page. To whom was the money accounted for?
Welland. It was accounted for to Bishop. The Clerk of the Papers always received the money, and I have been there several times at the payment of money.
Mr. Lee. Was it not usual to give money for the liberty of the rules?
Welland. Mr. Gybbon made it a custom to take two guineas for every 100*l.* for the liberty.
Mr. Lee. Do you know of any money paid to Mr. Huggins?
Welland. I don't know any was.
Mr. Lee. Were you there when the strong room was built?
Welland. I was, and Arne was the first person that was put in.
Mr. Lee. I ask you, whether it was all finished?—*Welland.* I believe it was floored.
Mr. Lee. Was it not an arched vault?
Welland. It was a kind of a vault, and there was a bench in it.
Mr. Lee. Where was it situated?
Welland. It was about three yards from the dunghill.
Mr. Lee. Had Arne a bed there?
Welland. He had a bed in it.
Mr. Lee. Was he not in a naked condition?
Welland. He was in a naked condition, which proceeded from his madness.
Mr. Lee. Was that a place fit for a man in his condition to be kept in?—*Welland.* It was.
Mr. Lee. Is there any place so bad in the prison?
Welland. There was a worse place where I lay, called Julius Caesar's ward.
Mr. Lee. How could it be worse?
Welland. Because many people lay in it.
Mr. Lee. Whether writs were not directed *Deputato*, or *Locum Tenenti* [*to deputy or locum tenens*]?
Welland. They were.
Mr. Lee. Whom were the writs returned by?
Welland. By Mr. Huggins.
John Browning sworn.
Huggins. How long have you known the Fleet prison?
Browning. I have been a prisoner there above twenty years.

The Trial of John Huggins

Huggins. When anybody died in the Fleet, except in execution, was there any coroner's inquest?

Browning. Never, but when in execution, Mr. Dickson, who was Clerk of the Papers before Huggins came, told me so.

Huggins. My lord, the prison being very full, it being against the time of an insolvency, the prisoners grew very riotous, and Mr. Gybbon could not come in, so that there was no place but the strong room to put Arne in.

Mr. Samuel Green sworn.

Huggins. What was the state of the prison, and the condition of it in 1725?

Green. I was had in, in February 1724, and came out the latter end of June 1725, and I applied to Mr. Gybbon in February 1724 for a room. Mr. Gybbon said he could not help me to one; then I applied to the prisoners, and gave a guinea and a half to them for one.

Huggins. Was there a court of inspectors?

Green. Yes, and I was one of them, and every prisoner that came in paid 5*s.* in order to apply to the Court of Common Pleas to regulate the fees.

Huggins. You did place people in rooms. Did you punish any prisoners?

Green. I can't say we did.

Huggins. Did the Warden dare to come in?

Green. He did not.

Mr. Justice Page. Could the prisoners set open the gates?

Green. They could not set open the gates, because there was a turnkey.

Huggins. Did Mr. Gybbon offer to come in?

Green. He did.

Mr. William Howard sworn.

Huggins. Did you know Edward Arne?

Howard. Mr. Arne came in about three weeks before I went out, and he was in the same room where I was, and wanting some goods, Arne offered me much more than I thought they were worth; for which reason I did not apprehend him to be in his right understanding.

Huggins. Did you desire him to bring some friend?

Howard. I think I might desire him to bring some friend.

Huggins. How much might he offer?

The Trial of John Huggins

Howard. He offered me nine guineas, but I took three, when I sold them to his friends.

Mr. Daniel Woodcock sworn.

Huggins. What do you know of Edward Arne?

Woodcock. He came into the Fleet prison in 1725, and I was a prisoner a year and a half before that, in July 1723, and continued there till September 1725: and I remember Arne's being there some time before I was discharged.

Huggins. Were you there when he was carried into the strong room?

Woodcock. I was.

Huggins. Were you in the cellar when he was taken from thence?

Woodcock. I were upon the stairs when he was carried into the strong room. He lay up and down in the gaol in the common hall and cellar, till he was carried into the strong room, and he was in it till I came away.

Huggins. Were you ever in the strong room?

Woodcock. I was.

Huggins. Do you remember the building of it?—*Woodcock.* I do.

Huggins. How near to the laystall and dunghill is it?

Woodcock. Within eight or ten yards.

Huggins. Are there any lights?

Woodcock. There is a place to put in drink at, on the side of the door.

Huggins. What is the wall made of?

Woodcock. Lime and brick, as other walls are.

Huggins. How long was it finished before Arne was carried in?

Woodcock. I can't be certain.

Huggins. Did you see Arne let out at any time?

Woodcock. I saw him let out, and he ran about stark naked.

Huggins. Did you ever see him naked before he was put in there?—*Woodcock.* No.

Huggins. Did you ever see me at the prison?

Woodcock. Yes, when the protonotaries were there.

Huggins. Did you think you should have known, when I came there?

Woodcock. It was as well known, as if the King had made a public entry.

Huggins. Was it not for the prisoners' security to have Arne put there?

Woodcock. I think it was.

The Trial of John Huggins

Huggins. Who sold Arne his goods?
Woodcock. Captain Howard sold Arne his goods.
Huggins. My lord, I must observe that the court of inspectors punished prisoners. Did not the inspectors punish their own prisoners?
Woodcock. Yes, they put them in the stocks.
Huggins. Could Mr. Gybbon come into the prison?—*Woodcock.* He could not.
Mr. Justice Page. Why then did you not all go out of prison?
Huggins. Did not the court of inspectors dispose of rooms?
Woodcock. I can't say.
Huggins. Did you see Barnes carry Arne to the strong room?
Woodcock. I saw Arne as he was going to the strong room with Barnes; and there was a complaint made to the court of inspectors; but not about this man, but about others.
Huggins. Was he a quiet man?
Woodcock. I saw no other, than his running about like a madman.
Huggins. How many days was Arne in the strong room before you were let out of prison?
Woodcock. I was let out about the 4th or 5th of September, there was an application made to the Court of Common Pleas, and I made an affidavit against Barnes.
Mr. Samuel Humphrys sworn.
Huggins. Were not you steward of the court of inspectors?
Humphrys. I was steward for some considerable time.
Huggins. When was the court first erected, and upon what occasion?
Mr. Baron Carter. Mr. Huggins, how you can apply this, I can't apprehend. Mr. Humphrys, what do you know of Arne or the strong room?
Humphrys. Mr. Arne was a prisoner there, when I was there first.
Mr. Baron Carter. Where was he when he came first?
Humphrys. A person of his name came there, whom I knew, and I went with him to see Mr. Arne, and he lived intemperately. This gentleman, after he had been there, had supplied him with money, which he spent in liquors; and after some time he was much altered in his way, and I saw him one day walking with his hat and wig off in the rain, and took notice of it; and after that he proceeded to further extremities, and took up a brick-bat, and throwed it upon the Bare.

The Trial of John Huggins

Mr. Justice Page. Do you believe he had any design against anybody?

Humphrys. I believe he had not.

Mr. Justice Page. Did he ever hit anybody?

Humphrys. I do not know that he did, but we had apprehensions, that he might, after being in that condition; he was an object of great compassion.

Huggins. What was his behaviour?

Humphrys. His behaviour was such, that he was not fit for a bed-fellow.

Huggins. Do you know anything of his being put into the strong room?

Humphrys. Before he was put into that place I was discharged.

Huggins. Do you remember that you saw me there?

Humphrys. I don't remember I saw you there, except when the protonotaries were there.

Huggins. Was that room built when you were there?

Humphrys. According to the best of my memory, that room was built while I was there.

Huggins. Was it not a stable before?

Humphrys. There was a stable, but I don't apprehend it was built on that spot.

Huggins. Were you present at any time, when the prisoners desired to have Arne put into the strong room?

Humphrys. I do not know it; it was after that I came away.

Huggins. Did Gybbon dare to come into the prison without leave of the inspectors?

Humphrys. Mr. Gybbon was very unwilling to come in, and I believe the reason was, he could not come in with any safety. Mr. Gybbon sent one day to some gentlemen of the master side to know, if he might venture with safety to the Fleet prison, for that he had a mind to see the repairs; upon which answer was returned, that he might come in; and Mr. Gybbon came in, and I went about with him.

Huggins. I desire he may be asked, whether if any man was injured, would they not have complained of it?

Humphrys. I was there when Arne came in, and discharged before he was put in the strong room.

Mr. Thomas Dean sworn.

Huggins. Did you see me in the prison during the time Mr. Arne was there?

Dean. During the time I was there, which was till the 12th or 14th of September, you were not there. I was discharged on the 7th but stayed a week after.

Huggins. Was it the opinion of the prisoners that Mr. Arne should be confined?

Dean. It was.

Huggins. Who provided him victuals?

Dean. One Mr. Louden found him in meat and drink, and he was allowed for it. I have seen Mr. Louden in the room.

Huggins. Who kept the key of the strong room?

Dean. I don't know who kept the key.

Huggins. Did you see Arne there?

Dean. I have seen Arne in the strong room.

Huggins. When was he carried there?

Dean. He was committed to the strong room in July, or the beginning of August.

Huggins. Did you see me with Gybbon?

Dean. I went round the Bare when Mr. Gybbon was in the prison, and was upon the Bare with him.

Attorney-General. Did not Gybbon's servants come in?

Dean. They did, and Gybbon came to chapel.

Attorney-General. Whereabouts is the chapel?

Dean. The chapel is within the walls of the prison.

Attorney-General. If Mr. Gybbon dared to venture to come to chapel; how came he not to come at other times?

Huggins. Please to ask, whether, if between the hours of ten and twelve I had been there, I must not have been seen?

Dean. Captain Pattison and others went round the prison with Mr. Gybbon.

Huggins. The question is, if I had been there, whether you would not have seen me?

Dean. I should.

Huggins. Had not Arne a broken constitution?

Mr. Baron Carter. Mr. Huggins, I cannot admit you to go into that evidence, I don't know what advantage it will be to you, you are going to prejudice yourself; for if he had a broken constitution, there was less reason to put him into the strong room.

Mr. John Louden sworn.

Huggins. My lord, be pleased to ask Mr. Louden, whether he had the care and custody of Mr. Arne?

The Trial of John Huggins

Mr. Justice Page. Answer that question.

Louden. I knew Mr. Arne before he came to prison, I had some acquaintance with him. He came into prison about the latter end of June, and some gentlemen spoke to me to have Mr. Arne table with me, and he allowed me 5*s.* per week; but the gentlemen grew uneasy at his dining with them, because that he was something out of order, and some time after growing worse, the gentleman with whom he lay quarrelled with him, and I could not afford to board him any longer, he not being able to pay me; and after he was turned from my table, some of the Upholders' Company came and desired me to dine him as usual; and every morning I carried him a breakfast, and a plate of hot victuals and drink, and I had the key of the room in two or three days after he was put in.

Mr. Justice Page. How came you by the key?

Louden. Sometimes it was half an hour, sometimes an hour before I could find the officer, and I said, if they would not let me have the key, I would not furnish him with victuals.

Mr. Justice Page. You had the liberty of going in, could you let him out?

Louden. Though I had the key, and had the liberty of going in, I had no power to let him out. He was never out, from the time he was put in, but once, and that was when some servants of the Upholders' Company came to see him, and then Barnes locked him up again; and when he was out he was stark naked, and ran into the chapel with the feathers all about him, and I went to take him to carry him in again, but he was very sturdy, and would not let me.

Huggins. In all the time you had the key, and the custody of him, which was from the third day after his going into the room, till three days of his coming out, did you see me in the prison?—*Louden.* I did not.

Huggins. Do you think you should, if I had come?—*Louden.* Yes.

Huggins. If I had been in the house, should you have seen, or heard of it?

Louden. I should.

Huggins. Did anybody sit up with Mr. Arne?

Louden. There was somebody sat up with him a few nights before he died.

The Trial of John Huggins

Huggins. I submit it to you, my lord, whether I shall produce the people of the Upholders' Company that sat up with him.

Mr. Justice Page. That will be of no great use to you.

Huggins. Was there a court of inspectors, who governed the prisoners?

Louden. Yes, there was.

Huggins. Do you remember you saw Mr. Gybbon there then?—

Louden. No.

Huggins. Did the prisoners dispose of their rooms?—*Louden.* Yes.

Mr. Baron Carter. I don't understand very well what way you propose to make your defence. If Mr. Gybbon had the sole power, then the court of inspectors could not. First Mr. Huggins is not concerned, because Gybbon was: and then he could not be concerned, because the court of inspectors was. Mr. Huggins I take to be Warden, and Gybbon, Deputy-Warden.

Attorney-General. What kind of a place is the strong room?

Louden. It is a brick-wall, and arched over with bricks, and the floor is boarded, and at that time a bench went across the room. There is a hole over the door, with four or five iron bars, and a hole big enough to put a quart-pot in by the side; it was a new built room, about six or eight weeks before Arne was put in, there was no chimney, fireplace, nor any convenience to ease nature.

Attorney-General. Was it not the occasion of his death?

Louden. It was possible it might, I believe it might do him prejudice as to his health.

Attorney-General. Did it hasten his death?

Louden. I do not know but it might; I believe it did hasten his death.

Attorney-General. Who gave you the key?

Louden. The turnkey; and I restored it to him again.

Attorney-General. As you came to take charge of it, did you always keep the key?

Louden. Sometimes, I had it, and sometimes they had it.

Mr. Justice Page. Do you believe you could have lived there six weeks, if you had been put in that room?

Louden. I don't believe I could.

Morgan Gwyn sworn.

Huggins. Were you a prisoner all the while Mr. Arne was there? —*Gwyn.* Yes.

Huggins. Did you see me in the house during that time?
Gwyn. I did not hear that you had been in the house all the time he was a prisoner there, nor did I see you.
Huggins. Do you think if I had come, you should have seen me?
Gwyn. I do think I should.
Huggins. My lord, I have witnesses to prove that I was in Hampshire from the beginning of September till the middle of September; that one part of the time that Hopkins and myself are said to be at the strong room I was out of town, and another part that Hopkins was out of town.
William Huggins sworn.
Mr. Justice Page. You are son to the prisoner?
William Huggins. I am, my lord. I have a house in Hampshire, and I remember by several circumstances, that my father came there the 1st of September, and continued till the 14th or 15th.
Huggins. Was I from your house during that time?
William Huggins. Neither my father nor myself were; that being the long vacation, my father was absent from his business, and was out of town at Sir George Oxenden's.
Richard Smith sworn.
Huggins. I desire he may be asked, my lord, whether he saw me in Hampshire, in 1725, at my son's?
Smith. My lord, I saw Mr. Huggins in Hampshire about the 14th or 15th of September in that year; and he was likewise there some time in August.
Mr. Justice Page. Was Mr. Huggins twice there in that summer?
Smith. He was there for a great many days at one time.
Mr. Justice Page. Did he go up to London, and come down again?
Smith. I cannot say whether he did or not.
Mr. Justice Page. Did he come up and down several times?
Smith. He was constantly there for some days.
Mr. Justice Page. What are you?
Smith. I am tenant to the estate which Mr. Huggins purchased.
Robert Knight sworn.
Huggins. Do you know of my being at my son's house in Hampshire, in 1725?
Knight. You were there between the 4th and 11th of September, and stayed fifteen days.
Huggins. When did I return?
Knight. The 15th.

Huggins. Was I there in August too?

Knight. You were there between the 9th and 14th, and stayed seven days.

Charles Bird sworn.

Huggins. Do you know of my being at my son's house, in Hampshire, in 1725?

Bird. You were there in August, 1725, about the 7th, but I cannot say how long you stayed there; then you came down on the 1st of September, and returned the 15th of the same month.

Huggins. My lord, I went from thence into Berkshire.

James Green sworn.

Huggins. Did you see me in Hampshire at my son's in 1725?

Green. I was a servant then, and lived in Hampshire at the same time; and you came there on the 1st of September, and continued till the 11th; and in the same year you were there in August.

John Tucker sworn.

Huggins. Whom are you servant to?

Tucker. To Sir George Oxenden.

Huggins. Was I any time in Berkshire in 1725?

Tucker. You were there in September, 1725; and on the 17th I carried you from Wittenham, in Berkshire, to Henley-upon-Thames.

Huggins. Did you carry me any farther?

Tucker. No.

Mr. Justice Page. When did Mr. Huggins come there?

Tucker. I did not mind that; I know the time when I carried him from thence, but cannot tell when he came there.

Sir George Oxenden sworn.

Sir G. Oxenden. My lord, Mr. Huggins said he came from his son's about the 15th of September, and came to Henley about the 17th. I remember very well that Mr. Huggins was at my house in Berkshire, because Sir Cecil Bishop being there, it was the day before or after Watlington fair, which was the 18th, Mr. Huggins offered to purchase a little farm of him, which Mr. Huggins said he would make a present of to his son, which, I thought, was a kind, goodnatured act. He went away on the 17th or 18th, and I rather believe it was the 18th, because on that day I went to Watlington fair.

Mr. Justice Page. How long did Mr. Huggins stay at your house?

The Trial of John Huggins

Sir G. Oxenden. Mr. Huggins was not there above two days, and said that he came out of Hampshire.
Daniel Hopkins sworn.
Huggins. I must observe, my lord, the witnesses said, that Mr. Hopkins was with me, that he was present at the strong room.
Mr. Justice Page. Mr. Hopkins, pray when did you go out of town?
Hopkins. I went in the Oxford coach on Monday, the 27th of September, 1725, and got to Oxford that night; and on Tuesday took the Worcester coach to Moreton-in-the-Marsh, and went from thence to a place called Barton, to one Mr. Oakley's, a relation's.
Huggins. When did you return?
Hopkins. I came back on the 14th of October in the same year.
Huggins. I desire, my lord, he may be asked, if ever he saw me in the prison in the month of September.
Hopkins. No, nor in October; for you were not come back on the 19th.
Huggins. Were you at the door of the strong room with me?
Hopkins. No, I was there by myself.
Serjeant Cheshire. Do you know Mr. Farrington?
Hopkins. Yes.
Serjeant Cheshire. Don't you remember that he was there with you?
Hopkins. I don't remember any company was there then.
Serjeant Cheshire. Was Barnes there?
Hopkins. No.
Serjeant Cheshire. Who opened the door?
Hopkins. I cannot tell.
Serjeant Cheshire. Did you see Mr. Arne?
Hopkins. I saw him there; he was naked; he had something about him white, but I cannot say what.
Serjeant Cheshire. Had you no discourse about this man?—
Hopkins. no.
Serjeant Cheshire. Did not Mr. Gybbon send you to Mr. Huggins about Arne?
Hopkins. No.
Serjeant Cheshire. When you were at the door, did you not whisper to anyone?
Hopkins. No.
Serjeant Cheshire. Whose servant was Barnes?
Hopkins. He was servant to Gybbon.

The Trial of John Huggins

Serjeant Cheshire. Who named him a watchman?
Hopkins. He was a watchman when I came there; and I saw Gybbon pay him several times.
Serjeant Cheshire. Whom were you appointed by?
Hopkins. I was recommended to Mr. Gybbon by Mr. Huggins.
Serjeant Cheshire. Did you do any business for the prisoner?
Hopkins. Yes, and attended him constantly at his house every morning; but I never had anything for that trouble.
Serjeant Cheshire. Did you buy your place?
Hopkins. No.
Serjeant Cheshire. Did you take all those journeys to Mr. Huggins for nothing?
Hopkins. He had seldom anything for me to do; I was in the morning generally with him about seven o'clock, and left him by nine.
Serjeant Cheshire. Do you know Mrs. Le Pointz?
Hopkins. Yes.
Serjeant Cheshire. Had you no discourse with her about Arne as to his condition?
Hopkins. I do not remember I had.
Serjeant Cheshire. Mr. Hopkins, pray consider with yourself, and answer directly, whether or no Mrs. Le Pointz did not desire you to speak to Mr. Huggins about Arne, and you said you would, and that you came to her after, and told her, that you had spoken to Mr. Huggins, and that he said it was no business of his? Pray consider, and recollect yourself.
Hopkins. I cannot recollect it.
Serjeant Cheshire. How did Arne come into the strong room?—
Hopkins. I do not know.
Serjeant Cheshire. How long was he there?
Hopkins. Six weeks.
Serjeant Cheshire. How long was it in that time before you heard he was there?
Hopkins. It could not be long.
Serjeant Cheshire. How long after the beginning of the six weeks was it that you saw him there?
Hopkins. I cannot tell how long; it could not be long.
Serjeant Cheshire. Was there any matter in the gaol that you did not acquaint Mr. Huggins with?
Hopkins. I seldom acquainted him with any of the transactions.

Serjeant Cheshire. Do you remember you acquainted him with this man's being in the strong room?

Hopkins. I do not know I did.

Serjeant Cheshire. Did you hear any complaint of his being in that place?

Hopkins. I cannot say that I heard any complaint of his being there.

Serjeant Cheshire. I have in my hand, Mr. Hopkins, an examination of yours, and I would have you consider with yourself, and I will ask you one question or two. Do you think the keeping the man in that place was the cause of his death?

Hopkins. I had been very credibly informed of the indisposition of Arne before.

Serjeant Cheshire. Upon the oath you have taken, was not Arne's being confined in that place the occasion of his death?

Hopkins. I cannot say, upon the oath that I have taken, that it was, as he was mad and sick before he was put in the strong room. I believe the madness was the occasion of his death.

Attorney-General. How long after Mr. Arne was confined was it that you saw him?

Hopkins. I cannot say how long; I believe it was in the month of September.

Attorney-General. Did not you see him more than once?—*Hopkins.* I do not remember.

Attorney-General. I ask you again, did not you see him more than once?

Hopkins. I do remember I saw him a second time lying on the floor, and the upper part of his body was then naked.

Attorney-General. Was any prisoner in the Fleet confined in such a strong room before?

Hopkins. None was put in there before, nor in any such.

Attorney-General. What kind of room was it?

Hopkins. The roof was arched; it was built even with the ground, and built not long before Arne was put in there.

Attorney-General. Did you observe the condition of the wall?— *Hopkins.* The room was damp.

Attorney-General. What officer were you belonging to the Fleet?

Hopkins. I was Clerk of the Inquiries.

Attorney-General. Did not you go to Mr. Huggins frequently?

The Trial of John Huggins

Hopkins. I went to Mr. Huggins three or four times a week.
Attorney-General. What did you go to Mr. Huggins upon?
Hopkins. I went to him about his own business.
Attorney-General. Did you never attend him on mornings about the business of the prison?
Hopkins. I have acquainted him with some things.
Attorney-General. Did not you acquaint him with matters of consequence in the prison?
Hopkins. I did, if they were matters of any consequence, or extraordinary.
Attorney-General. Did not you acquaint Mr. Huggins with Mr. Arne's being there?
Hopkins. The reason is why I did not, that I went out of town on the 27th of September, and did not return till the 14th of October.
Attorney-General. I ask you, whether you believe in your conscience you did acquaint Mr. Huggins or not?
Hopkins. It is very likely I did, if I was desired.
Attorney-General. Do you believe in your conscience you did, if you were desired?
Hopkins. Why, I verily believe in my conscience I did, if I was desired.
Attorney-General. How do you know Arne was mad?
Hopkins. I heard that he was.
Attorney-General. Would not his own room have been a sufficient confinement?
Hopkins. I believe it would.
Attorney-General. Did you receive any order from Mr. Huggins for the relief of this man?
Hopkins. I do not know that I did.
Upon which his Examination, which was taken before Edward Hughes, Esq. upon oath, was read, to show his prevarication.
Mr. Justice Page. I ask you, whether in the month of September, there were not a great many people discharged out of custody, and whether there was not any one room that became empty?
Hopkins. I believe there was, for fifty or sixty persons were then discharged; but I had nothing to do with the affair of rent.
Mr. Justice Page. Was there any room better than the strong room empty?
Hopkins. Any room was better than the strong room.

The Trial of John Huggins

Mr. Justice Page. How long was Arne continued there after the 7th of September?
Hopkins. He was continued there till he died.
Mr. Justice Page. Was there any room in the house so bad as that?
Hopkins. I do not know of any.
Mr. Justice Page. When so many were discharged, might there not be a room that Arne might be put in?
Hopkins. I do not remember any disposition of rooms.
Mr. Justice Page. Were there no places empty where the fifty or sixty lay?
Hopkins. Yes.
Mr. Justice Page. Was there not a room then for one man to lie in?
Hopkins. Yes.
Attorney-General. Had you any discourse with Bishop about Arne?
Hopkins. I do not remember he ever spoke to me about him.
Attorney-General. Did Mr. Gybbon never speak to you in the presence of Bishop, to speak to Mr. Huggins, that some care might be taken of Arne?
Hopkins. He did not.
Attorney-General. Did Mr. Gybbon order you to speak to Mr. Huggins to get him into Bethlehem, and to speak to Mr. Taylor to get him in?
Mr. Justice Page. I must observe that Mr. Huggins owned that he only did it (speaking of Arne's being got into Bethlehem) as a friend, and not *quatenus* Warden.
Mr. Lee. Mr. Hopkins. I ask you whether you at any time spoke to Gybbon, or anyone else, to give Mr. Huggins notice of Arne's being in the strong room?
Hopkins. I do not know that I did.
Thomas Smith sworn.
Huggins. What resolution did the Upholders' Company come to, as to the discharging Arne out of the Fleet?
Smith. He was servant to the Company of Undertakers at Exeter Change.
Mr. Justice Page. Do you know if Arne was to be discharged, or how?
Smith. Martin and others, members of the said Company, first arrested him, and he was carried to a bailiff's in Hare Court, and lay there a considerable time, and then was carried to the Fleet; and upon an application to the Company of Upholders, they agreed to discharge him, and get him into Bethlehem.

The Trial of John Huggins

Huggins. My lord, he was a very sickly man before he came there; and I desire the witness may tell you what condition he was in.

Smith. In the month of April, 1725, he was in a weakly condition.

Mr. Justice Page. Mr. Huggins, I cannot admit you into that evidence.

Huggins. I desire to call people to his character.

Mr. Thomas Arne sworn.

Huggins. He was chief mourner to Arne. I desire he may acquaint you what relation he was to him.

Arne. Edward Arne was my uncle's son. I know that he was in prison; he lay some time at an officer's house, and from thence was removed to the Fleet.

Huggins. When did you go to him?

Arne. A week or ten days before he died I saw him there. I inquired for him, and they said he was locked up, and directed me to go to Mr. Louden, Mr. Jerningham's man.

Huggins. Was the door shut?

Arne. It was padlocked; he lay down at the side of the room near the door, and I found some rags about him. He knew me, and took me by the hand; he was then very ill, and could hardly speak. I asked him, what was become of his ring, seal, gold-headed cane, and other things of value? He spoke very faint; I with much difficulty understood by a word now and then, that one Searls, a mercer, had got some of them; and afterwards upon inquiry found, that he had his gold watch, which he had lent him fourteen guineas upon.

Huggins. Did he make any complaint to you?

Arne. He was not capable of complaining, being so very weak.

Huggins. What state of health was he in before he came there?

Arne. I believe he was in a wasting condition before he was arrested.

Attorney-General. Did you hear any complaint as to his being in the strong room?

Arne. By him I did not.

Attorney-General. At the time when you came to visit him, was the room in a condition for a sick or a well man?

Arne. I believe it was not fit for a sick or a well man to be in it.

Attorney-General. How long do you think you could have lived if you had been confined in that room.

The Trial of John Huggins

Arne. I could not have lived six or seven days, and could not believe any man alive could be there six or seven weeks.

Attorney-General. How often were you there?

Arne. I never saw it but once.

Attorney-General. Do you think you could have lived there six weeks?

Arne. I think I could not live six weeks in the damp without fire or candle.

Huggins. My lord, I desire to call some gentlemen to my character.

Mr. Justice Page. That you may do if you think fit.

Sir George Oxenden, Bart. sworn.

Sir G. Oxenden. My lord, I have known Mr. Huggins about nine years, but have been more particularly acquainted with him these four or five years last past. I never took him to be an ill-natured or barbarous man, and do not believe, willingly, he would do an inhumane thing to any one.

Sir John Hinde Cotton, Bart. sworn.

Huggins. Pray give an account how long you have known me.

Sir J. Cotton. My lord, I have known Mr. Huggins about four or five years, and have had occasion to be a good deal with him. I believe him to be a good-natured, humane man; and believe in my conscience, he would not have been guilty of the cruelty laid to his charge.

Robert Viner, Esq. sworn.

Viner. My lord, I have known Mr. Huggins ever since I can remember anything at all. He has been concerned for our family these forty or fifty years, and I lived with him two years together; and I take him to be a good-natured and humane man; and, in my conscience, believe he would not be guilty of a cruel thing to any man.

John Hedges, Esq. sworn.

Hedges. My lord, I have known Mr. Huggins about six years, and always took him for a good-natured and humane man; and have since had an opportunity of knowing several instances of his generosity and good-nature without fee or reward. I have known him six or seven years as a general acquaintance, and he was very good-natured and humane; and some time since I have known some instances of great generosity and good-nature, merely for the pleasure of doing good, without fee or reward.

The Trial of John Huggins

John Knight, Esq. sworn.
Knight. My lord, I have known Mr. Huggins these eight or nine years past, and frequently had opportunities of being in conversation with him, and I always took him to be, as far as any man living from doing anything that was cruel; and always acted agreeable to the character of a humane man; and I am very sorry any such thing should be laid to his charge.

Christopher Tillson, Esq. sworn.
Tillson. My lord, I have known Mr. Huggins these five-and-thirty years, not superficially, but in particular friendship, and have found him in all instances a man unblamable; and I never saw anything tending to cruelty or ill usage; and have always found him so for these thirty-five years.

Major Churchill sworn.
Major Churchill. My lord, I have known him these forty-five years, and have had frequent communication with him, and always found him a friend and a man of humanity, despising of money. There was one thing, in a most particular manner, I will acquaint your lordship of.

Mr. Justice Page. I can't admit you into a particular character, but you may go on with a general one.

Major Churchill. I never thought him capable in thought, word, or deed, of doing a cruel thing.

Thomas Gibson, Esq. sworn.
Gibson. My lord, I have known Mr. Huggins for these seven or eight years past, and found him to act with good-nature, integrity, honour, and humanity.

The Rev. Dr. Pearce (Rector of St. Martin's in the Fields, afterwards Bishop of Rochester,) sworn.
Dr. Pearce. My lord, Mr. Huggins is a vestry man;[16] and I have had more particular reason to converse with him frequently on that account, and I never found anything in him, that was any way consistent with what is laid to his charge, and have constantly found him at church.

Edward Thompson, Esq. sworn.
Thompson. My lord, I have known Mr. Huggins these seven years, and have had frequent experience of acts of his friendship and good-nature, and never discovered anything in his behaviour, but the utmost good-nature.

Thomas Woodford, Esq. sworn.

The Trial of John Huggins

Woodford. My lord, I have known Mr. Huggins many years. I have been with him both sober and mellow, and never have discovered anything barbarous or cruel in him; and I verily believe he could not be guilty of any such act if he knew it at all.

Joseph Taylor, Esq. sworn.

Taylor. My lord, I have transacted a great deal of business with Mr. Huggins, and found him act with candour. Sometimes I have been concerned against him, and sometimes with him; and, if ever I had suspected anything in him tending to cruelty, I assure you, my lord, I would have shunned his company instead of seeking it, as I have done.

Martin Bladen, Esq. sworn.

Bladen. My lord, I have known Mr. Huggins many years, and have lived by him in the country these eight or nine years; and the character that he has had is, that he is a good-natured, humane man. It has been his whole business of life to leave a good character; and therefore, I can't believe he would do an ill-natured act.

John Lade, Esq. (afterwards Sir John Lade, Bart.) sworn.

Lade. My lord, I have known Mr. Huggins these forty years, and have seen a great many kind, compassionate things of him.

Sir Charles Cox, Knight, sworn.

Sir Charles Cox. My lord, I have known Mr. Huggins these forty years, and have had frequent dealings with him, and always observed him to be a man of charity and humanity; and I have courted his company from the good opinion I have had of him, and don't believe that he would be guilty of any inhumanity.

Edward Halsey, Esq. sworn.

Halsey. My lord, I have known Mr. Huggins near thirty years, and have been conversant with him, and the observation I have made of him is, that I have found him zealous to do good offices, where he had no fee or reward and never found him covetous or cruel.

Sir James Thornhill, Knight, sworn.

Sir James Thornhill. My lord I have known Mr. Huggins for these twenty-five years and I was proud of the honour of his acquaintance. I have never seen or heard of the least cruel act that he has done by any one; and if I was to repeat the instances of good-natured acts—

The Trial of John Huggins

Mr. Justice Page. Sir, you can't be admitted to do that.
Thomas Martin, Esq. sworn.
Martin. My lord, I have known Mr. Huggins these thirty years and that he has done a great many kind and good-natured things. I never knew him a vain man but that he did it through good-nature.
Colonel Negus sworn.
Colonel Negus. My lord I have known Mr. Huggins, a great many years and always looked upon him to be a good-natured man; and that it was impossible to think he could do so ill-natured an act, as laid to his charge.
—— *Campbell Esq. sworn.*
Campbell. My lord, I have known Mr. Huggins from fifteen to twenty years, and always found him behave himself with integrity in his profession as a good-natured man, and always thought his genius far superior to do an ill-natured thing. I always had, and still have a good opinion of him.
Huggins. My lord it appeared to your lordship, that Mr. Gybbon was the acting-Warden, and that Barnes was his servant, not mine. No argument can be drawn from the coroner's not sitting, the custom of the place is otherwise, but as to any application to get him into Bethlehem that, my lord, can't be applied to me *quatenus* Warden, for it would be only in me a good-natured act. If Barnes put him in, he is not my servant; if so, then the indictment must fail.

That as to the witnesses they were prisoners, and they are natural haters of their keepers.

I never went to the prison, but had a hundred people about me, and I must have been seen by many. There was no pretence of using any barbarity to any man, no money to be extorted: and when I could no way be benefited by it, no one can think, my lord, I could be guilty of murder, where no benefit or advantage by it could arrive.

Mr. Louden, my lord, who had the custody of the man, and had the key till three days before his death, had never seen me there; and if he that had the key did not know of my being there, who should? I showed, my lord, that I was out of town in September, and Hopkins was out of town till the 14th of October, so that it was impossible that we two could be there together. All the other witnesses that have been called against

The Trial of John Huggins

me, would not have lain from that day to this in prison, had they not lost their honour, nor lost their designs.

I never saw the man, nor heard there was such a prisoner, and to murder a man for nothing, God Almighty knows there never stood a man at this bar with more innocency than myself.

Serjeant Cheshire. It is plain on the King's side, that a subject has been murdered; and what Mr. Huggins has endeavoured to show is, that he never acted, but had a deputy, and that deputy was accountable, if anybody, for he had no acquaintance of this thing. Your lordship has heard the witnesses, and I don't doubt but will relate the evidence fully.

The counsel for the prisoner objected to Mr. Serjeant Cheshire's replying.

Mr. Justice Page. I am of opinion, brother, you can't reply.

Serjeant Cheshire. But I may say something to what has not been given already in evidence.

Attorney-General. Mr. Huggins endeavours to show that Gybbon was the acting-Warden. No, my lord, neither by a lease or deputation Gybbon could not be appointed Warden.

Mr. Justice Page. Mr. Attorney, I cannot admit you to enter into any reply, but if you have any evidence you may call them.

Elijah Beavis sworn.

Attorney-General. Were you a prisoner in the Fleet, in the year 1722?

Beavis. Yes, and I had the liberty of the rules, in the year 1723; and in the year 1724, I was entitled to be cleared by the Act of Insolvency, but because I could not give the Warden money enough, was continued till the year 1725, and I used to see Mr. Hopkins at Pindar's, where Gybbon kept his office, and it was generally accepted by everybody, that Hopkins brought directions from Huggins to Gybbon every day.

Attorney-General. Have you heard Hopkins say, that he had directions from Mr. Huggins to Gybbon, and that he came from Huggins?

Beavis. I did not hear any particular directions.

Richard Bishop sworn.

Attorney-General. Who gave directions, as to the management of the gaol?

Bishop. The particular things were done by Huggins's directions; but the common things without.

Joseph Johnson sworn.

The Trial of John Huggins

Attorney-General. Do you know of any directions brought from Mr. Huggins by Mr. Hopkins, to Mr. Gybbon?

Johnson. I have heard Mr. Hopkins say, that he came from Mr. Huggins, and that he bid him come every morning to him; and that one time Mr. Huggins sent word back by Hopkins, that I should be locked up.

Edward Hughes, Esq. (a Member of the House of Commons) sworn.

Attorney-General. Sir, what have you heard Mr. Huggins declare, as to the acts he did during the time Gybbon was his deputy?

Hughes. My lord, it appeared to me—

Mr. Baron Carter. Sir, you are not to tell us of what appeared to you, but what you know of your own knowledge.

Hughes. My lord, I can't tell how knowledge should come to me, until it appeared to me.

After some pause Mr. Hughes went on.

My lord, Mr. Huggins was ordered to attend the Committee, and while Mr. Huggins was there, he was asked, what escapes had happened during the time he was Warden? He said, he could not give an account of them, there had happened so many. But said, that Oliver Read had escaped, and when he was taken, that he Mr. Huggins had ordered Corbett the tipstaff to put him in irons, which were sent for from Newgate by his, Huggins's directions, and owned that he did it by virtue of his authority for an escape. This confession Huggins made himself, and owned, that he had paid 500*l.* for such escape that Read had made.

Mr. Baron Carter. Was it Mr. Huggins or Mr. Gybbon ordered him to be put in irons?

Hughes. I did not say it was Mr. Gybbon bid him be put in irons, but it was Mr. Huggins, and that he ordered him to be put in irons as Warden, and in all escapes he acted as principal, for he paid 500*l.* for that escape.

Mr. Baron Carter. About what time was this?

Hughes. It was upon the first escape that Read made. It was in the year 1726, that Read got off those irons, and made his second escape, and was re-taken; and then he was put in the dungeon.

Mr. Baron Carter. Was there any particular time mentioned?

Hughes. I have recollected, and it was in the year 1726; what points out the time, is Read's escape.

The Trial of John Huggins

Serjeant Darnell. That paper produced by Jeffreys amounts to a lease.

Mr. Justice Page and Mr. Baron Carter. Whenever an agreement is made to make a lease, that can never be esteemed a lease.

Proclamation was made to keep silence.

Mr. Justice Page. Gentlemen of the jury, this is an indictment against Mr. Huggins the prisoner at the bar, and one Barnes, for the murder of Edward Arne. The indictment is indeed particular. The indictment takes notice, that Huggins was Warden of the Fleet the 1st of October, in the late King's reign; that he being Warden, had the government of the prisoners in the gaol; that Barnes was an agent of his, who is fled from justice. It sets forth, gentlemen, that Barnes seized upon the said Arne, and carried him to a place, called the strong room; and that Huggins was aiding, abetting, and assisting in carrying him to that place, and he was continued there the space of six weeks; that this is a place of cold restraint, and a room newly built, made of brick and mortar, very wet and unfit to live in; that this Barnes did continue him in this place for six weeks in a most barbarous and vile manner, and not allowed him any necessaries, insomuch that he had no chamber-pot, he was without fire or fireplace, and had only a little bed. This is the nature of the dungeon. It is a vault arched over, and in the wall a little hole big enough to put a quart-pot in at. It is built over a common sewer adjoining to a laystall, where all the dirt and filth of the prison lies, which made it not only so noisome, but very unwholesome, that the continuing this person so long in this place was the occasion of his death. That Mr. Huggins was acquainted with it, but showed him no favour. He was not let out, and died in the middle of October. He died, gentlemen, by this duress of the prisoner. I will say but little to what the law is in this case. A prisoner for debt is only taken like a distress, and kept there till he or his friends can pay the debt for him. Imprisonment is no punishment, it is not taken as part of the debt; for let a man lie ever so long, his heirs-at-law cannot be exempt from the debt, but if they have effects, are answerable for it. He is kept only in such manner as he may be forthcoming and safe; this being the case, he is to be kept in here in a becoming way, as the Warden may be safe, and the prisoner forthcoming, but in no other degree that the prisoner should be punished, by any unreasonable restraint. If this Arne was kept in no other way than became the subject of the King, in that reasonable manner, so that you may take it, there was no torture, ill usage, or any act, but such as was fit and decent for confinement, no duress; then and in that case, though he died there, it will not be murder.

But if by the evidence that has been called, it appears that this room was an unfit place to lay this man in, that it must be the means of his destruction, that, being in such imprisonment as the gaoler cannot justify, will be duress. If they carry that point, it is part of the common law, the ancient law, and very rightly observed by the counsel, that it will be murder. It would be very hard to take away this law, though in his own defence; as he was entrusted with the life of the King's subject, he was answerable for him, and the coroner's inquest ought to have sat upon his body. The law is so much afraid of the loss of the life of a subject, that the King will have an inquiry to see what is become of the life of the prisoner. It was opened by the counsel for the King, that it was wilfully omitted; on the other hand it was urged that this custom seemed to be asleep, and that it was hard to lay a great weight, where it had not been so long practised. Gentlemen, there have been great numbers of witnesses called, and therefore I cannot give it word for word, but will repeat as far as is necessary.

Mr. Longborn was called to prove the first part of the indictment, that Huggins was Warden; and he proved the copy of the letters patent granted to Mr. Huggins, who might act by himself or deputy.

Bigrave gave an account, that Huggins's patent bore date on the 25th of July, in the 12th year of the late Queen; that Mr. Huggins, though Warden, did not act himself, but appointed Gybbon as deputy; and that securities were taken by Huggins not by Gybbon, that is to be considered in point of law, that the act must be brought against him as Warden, and the making of a deputy does not discharge him of his duty; in several cases he does not continue answerable, for in civil cases the deputy is answerable, therefore the security is lodged with him. It is a very strong evidence that the Warden still continues Warden, that he ought to see to the escape of prisoners, for that is not only trusted to the honesty of the Warden, but he is to take the best care he can of escapes. He says, that Gybbon did buy his place, that he did oversee and look after the affairs of the Fleet, and filled up several warrants, but always in Huggins's name; that he did apprehend that Barnes was only a servant to Gybbon, and that Gybbon, no doubt, had the immediate trust of the gaol; and that Barnes was a runner to Gybbon, and not Huggins's servant. He agreed what this place was; that it was arched over; that it was eight feet wide, eleven feet long, and nine feet high; that it was built very little time before Arne was committed there. He could not describe the whole situation, but gave an account that it was very nigh the dunghill and filth, had no chimney nor chimney-place, and had only two little holes to let the air in. He gave an account of Hopkins; that he looked upon Hopkins to be Gybbon's servant, besides that he was clerk to Mr. Huggins at his house in St. Martin's Lane, and generally went backward and forward most days to Mr. Huggins, and was able to give him an account of what happened in the gaol.

[*Mr. Justice Page then summarised the evidence of the witnesses. Finally, he returned to the subject of the strong room.*]

The observation that my brother Carter made is very just: that if a strong man, being put into that filthy, vile place it would kill him, to put into such a place him that wanted health, death was more sure. If he was a weak man, there was no danger of his escaping, no danger of going out.

As to his being in that room being the occasion of his death, there need not much be said.

And what is said by Mr. Huggins, except one thing, carries little or no weight; and there is only that can deserve your consideration, whether he did die by the cruelty of Gybbon or Huggins? That he did die by duress, it is not to be supposed to the contrary.

That in point of law, wherever there is a deputy appointed, the superior must answer; for had a prisoner of 20,000*l.* escaped, Mr. Huggins must have paid the money.

In criminal cases I do not think, that the Warden or any

other officer should answer for murder, unless he was privy and consenting. If this sole act was Gybbon's, and Huggins no ways consenting, I think the murder lies upon Gybbon, not Huggins. Though this was the act of Gybbon and Barnes, whoever has a hand in it, and the authority and power as he had, if it is true that he saw him, and he would not give a helping hand to assist him, the excepted rule of Scripture would be true, that 'he that is not for me must be against me': and if he was any way privy to the carrying him and confining him there, he must answer for the murder both in this and the next world.

If this is the act of Gybbon solely, Huggins is not to answer for it; but if Huggins was privy, and he was Warden, he could and ought to have relieved him.

One thing more, in the latter part of the defence Mr. Huggins made for himself, was, to call vast numbers of gentlemen of the first quality; Sir George Oxenden, Sir John Hinde Cotton, in all about twenty he called to his character and credit; and if these gentlemen are not sufficient, I do not know what will be. His character has been fully established. But I must observe to you, whatever the character a man bears, if he is guilty of that act which destroys his character, his character goes for nothing. If there was difficulty, or great doubt happened upon circumstances, whether Mr. Huggins was guilty or not, then it was the constant practice to be governed by a character. I think nobody can have a better; he has had a very great character given him.

Not long since a person produced twenty-seven people, that gave him a character, with no comparison to this, only the greatness of numbers.

Notwithstanding which, it there was not doubted he had committed the fact; and the jury very justly brought in their verdict, guilty.

Verdicts, in convicting of people, are to be founded upon the evidence that the jury has had before them: and I hope I do not express myself so for them to found themselves upon anything I have said; for they will determine according to the evidence that has been before them.

Mr. Attorney-General produced three witnesses, that came to nothing.

The Trial of John Huggins

I must take notice of one piece of evidence given by Mr. Hughes, a gentleman of probity and distinction, one of the Committee appointed by the House of Commons. He tells you, that when Mr. Huggins was under examination before the committee relating to escapes during the time he was Warden, Huggins confessed so many had escaped, he could not remember them all. He owned one Oliver Read had escaped, and was retaken; and that he himself sent to Newgate for irons, and ordered Read to be stapled down and ironed; and that he owned he paid 500*l.* to Read's creditors for the escape of Read: This was whilst Gybbon acted as deputy.

Mr. Huggins does give this answer to that; that Hopkins proved that Gybbon acted, and so he was Warden in law. I cannot tell what condition Gybbon was in, and what security he had given; Huggins was liable for all escapes.

I have taken pains to state the evidence to you as fully as I can; and I hope you will consider it; and that God will direct you to do for the best.

Then one was sworn to keep the jury, and they withdrew, and Mr. Justice Page and Mr. Baron Carter left the bench; and Mr. Serjeant Raby with the Lord Mayor remained there; and in about two hours and an half the jury returned.

Clerk of Arraigns. Are you all agreed in your verdict?—*Omnes.* Yes.

Clerk. Who shall say for you?

Omnes. Foreman.

Clerk. John Huggins hold up thy hand. (*Which he did.*) Look upon the prisoner. Is he guilty of the felony and murder whereof he stands indicted, or not guilty?

Foreman. We are agreed to bring in our verdict special to the Court.

Attorney-General. What is their doubt in point of law?

Serjeant Raby. What that doubt is must be referred to the Court.

Foreman. Was there any medium between bringing him in guilty or not guilty?

Serjeant Raby. You may find the fact specially, and refer the special matter to the Court. If any matter of law arises upon that doubt, it will be explained. You may give a general verdict in order to refer that to the judgment of the Court. You must agree upon the fact; you must state the special matter. It is usual to state the point of law that you doubt in. If you have

The Trial of John Huggins

any doubt as to the law, that you must refer to the Court; but as to the fact, you must determine yourselves.

Attorney-General. What is it makes the question doubtful?

Serjeant Raby. The jury do believe the prisoner in some measure guilty, but not of the whole indictment.

Foreman. We cannot find any of the evidence come up to show he was aiding, abetting, and assisting Barnes in putting him into the room.

Serjeant Raby. Call over the jury.

Clerk of Arraigns. Answer to your names. (*Which they did.*) Are you all agreed in your verdict? Is John Huggins guilty of the murder and felony whereof he stands indicted, or not guilty?

After considering some time among themselves, the Foreman spoke as follows:

Foreman. We agree the prisoner was accessory to the murder committed upon Edward Arne, but that it was not premeditated in him; that he has been privy to the cause of this man's death, and might have prevented it. Two witnesses swore, that Mr. Huggins was at the door of the dungeon, and saw Arne there; and, as he did not discharge him at that time, he was accessory to that.

Serjeant Raby. If he was privy, he was guilty of that. If he was privy and consenting, if he did concur in that act, he is guilty; for it will imply malice.

If he died by duress, and he was concurring and consenting to it, then he was guilty of this act, in that he had power to redress it, and did not. If he was privy, you must consider if he was concurring.

Attorney-General. If he was privy and consenting, it does imply it.

In all special verdicts the jury never find malice.

In no special verdict they find malice.

Foreman. Several of us don't think him guilty of the malice.

Attorney-General. The law will imply the malice.

Serjeant Raby. You are to consider and find the fact.

Foreman. We all agree that Arne died by duress; there are two witnesses to prove that; but that the prisoner had no forethought.

The jury again considered among themselves; but not immediately agreeing, withdrew, and stayed out some considerable time, and then returned.

The Trial of John Huggins

Clerk of Arraigns. Are you all agreed?
Foreman. We are agreed, that there is sufficient evidence to prove, that they saw Mr. Huggins at the strong room.

We agree that he was Warden of the Fleet prison; and that he was Head-Warden at the time the fact happened, as mentioned in the indictment; and that Gybbon was deputy, and acted as such.

That James Barnes appeared to us to be servant to Gybbon, and was employed and acted under him in taking care of the prisoners, and had the custody of them; and particularly of Edward Arne.

Attorney-General. Mr. Tanner, you must write down the verdict of the jury.
Serjeant Raby. Get pen, ink and paper ready. Gentlemen, you must tell him what he is to write:
Which is as follows viz.

That James Barnes, at the time mentioned in the indictment, made an assault upon Edward Arne, being then a prisoner in the Fleet prison; did take and imprison him without his consent, *prout* [*as*] in the indictment.

Attorney-General. They will find the description and situation of the room as in the indictment; they can have no reason to doubt of that.

That James Barnes and John Huggins, at the time of the imprisonment of the said Arne, knew that the room was newly built; and that the walls were moist and damp, as in the indictment.

Mr. Strange. Mr. Huggins did not know it at first, at the time he was there, when the door was open.
Attorney-General. Are the jury satisfied that Mr. Huggins knew the state and condition of the room during the time Arne was there?
Foreman. We agree he saw the building, and that he must know it an unwholesome room, as described in the indictment.
Attorney-General. Let me see the indictment. (*Which he did, and read the words as to the description of the strong room.*) He must know it when he was at the strong room door.
Serjeant Darnell. It is necessary that the jury should know what the Attorney reads.
Attorney-General. Mr. Tanner has twice taken it. How long

(speaking to the jury) before the death of Arne do you find the prisoner knew the condition of the room?

Foreman. I believe it to be fifteen days at least before the death of Arne.

Attorney-General. That during this imprisonment and detention in this room, the said Arne, by reason of the duress of such imprisonment, became sick and languished there, and died, *prout* [*as*] in the indictment.

Huggins. The jury are upon their oaths, will they find him dead by my means?

Mr. Strange. I desire the fact may be found as it is.

Attorney-General. Mr. Tanner, mind, that on the 7th of September he was aiding, abetting, and assisting James Barnes.

Foreman. We apprehend the man continued from the 7th September, and we apprehend he died about the 23rd of October.

Attorney-General. That John Huggins being principal Warden during the imprisonment and detention of the said Arne, was present at the said room, and saw Arne in that room under the duress of that imprisonment; and that he being present, the room was locked up with the said Arne in it.

That fifteen days before the death of Arne, John Huggins being then Warden of the Fleet, and Mr. Gybbon Deputy-Warden, he saw Arne under the duress of that imprisonment; and the said Arne was confined in the said room, and the said Huggins being then present, he was locked up by James Barnes, and continued in the said confinement.

Mr. Strange. That is not according to the evidence. It should be found thus:

That during the imprisonment of the said Arne, and fifteen days at the least before his death, John Huggins being then Warden of the Fleet, and the said Thomas Gybbon, deputy and acting Warden, was once present, and saw the said James Barnes lock up the door of the said room, the said Arne being therein imprisoned.

And at the time Huggins turned away, James Barnes locked to the door; and Arne continued under the said imprisonment therein, until the time of his death; and the jury don't find, that Huggins knew the said Arne was in the strong room when he was first put in there.

The Trial of John Huggins

Attorney-General. I insist upon adding the words, 'aiding, abetting, and assisting'. And 'that Huggins knew of the badness of the room'.

Mr. Strange. They don't find, that during the whole time that Arne was there, Huggins knew of the badness of the room.

Attorney-General. The jury cannot find what they don't know.

Foreman. We find the letters patent constituting John Huggins, Esq. Warden of the Fleet, *prout* in the indictment.

That during the time that Gybbon was Deputy-Warden, Huggins acted as Warden.

Mr. Strange. That does not appear.

Attorney-General. Who sent for irons from Newgate?

Ask whether or no they do find, that at the time Gybbon was Deputy-Warden, Huggins acted as Warden.—Beavis said in 1725, Hopkins came from Huggins about business; that at the same time, during the time that Gybbon acted as Deputy-Warden, John Huggins acted as Warden.

[*At the request of the Attorney-General, the case was argued before the King's Bench judges, to decide the legal implications of the verdict. The final decision was given in June 1730.*

'*Upon the whole, there is no authority against the Court's giving judgment of acquittal upon a verdict that is not sufficient to convict. And therefore, this verdict not finding facts sufficient to make the prisoner guilty of murder, he must be adjudged not guilty. And he was discharged.*']

Chapter Three

The Trial of Thomas Picton (1806)

The trials of General Thomas Picton became one of the great *causes célèbres* of the early nineteenth century. That Picton was a man of great physical courage, with a considerable reputation as a soldier and administrator was beyond question. Yet the facts produced against him in the case of Luisa Calderon seemed an affront to the public conscience of England as a whole, not merely to its newly developed humanitarian element.

Picton was born in 1758 and had become a Lieutenant in the 12th Regiment of Foot in 1777, transferring to the Prince of Wales's Regiment of Foot as Captain in the following year and taking part in the defence of Gibraltar. In 1783 he was placed on half-pay and retired to the life of a country gentleman in Pembrokeshire, the county of his birth. He remained there until the war with France had begun in 1793. In the following year he went to the West Indies as a private citizen and, once there, joined the 17th Regiment of Foot, becoming aide-de-camp to Sir John Vaughan, the Commander-in-Chief, and then to Vaughan's successor, Sir Ralph Abercromby.

Picton distinguished himself in the capture of St Lucia and St Vincent in 1796 and was promoted to Lieutenant-Colonel of the 56th Regiment of Foot. In 1797, with the entry of Spain into the war on the side of France, Picton took part in the attack on Trinidad and was present at the surrender of the island on 17 February 1797. Abercromby appointed him military governor and in the five years of his rule Picton devised a police system for the island and built new roads, as well as assisting the war against other Spanish possessions. When the governors of the remaining Spanish territories offered a reward totalling some £20,000 for his head, Picton replied by personal letters to each, regretting that his head hardly justified such munificence.

The Trial of Thomas Picton

With the conclusion of the war in 1801, the inhabitants of Trinidad requested to remain under British rule and seemed content with the administration of Picton, who was now promoted to Brigadier-General. Yet in England, Colonel William Fullarton and his associates had already begun to circulate gruesome stories of what they claimed was the truth about Trinidad under Picton's government. It was alleged that in eight cases Picton had inflicted summary punishment on accused men or women without even the process of court martial. Celestino, a Spaniard, was hanged after his arrest for disorderly behaviour; Gallaghan, a British soldier, was hanged for raping and robbing a Negress; Pierre Warren, a slave, was condemned to have his ear cut off and died of the wound; Jean-Baptiste Alarcon was hanged for mutiny; Goliath, a slave, was summarily flogged and died in consequence; an Indian sea-trader was shot; an escaped female slave was hanged before her master could intervene, and, lastly, a girl of thirteen, Luisa Calderon, had been interrogated by torture. According to the accusations, justice had been summary. Gallaghan, for instance, was said to have been brought before Picton, who asked him if he had seen the sun rise. Gallaghan said that he had, whereupon Picton promised him he should not see it set, and ordered him to be hanged. The truth of the allegations was difficult to establish, if only because the victims, in seven of the eight cases, were dead. But the eighth victim, Luisa Calderon, was still alive and it was her case which Picton's enemies chose to take up.

When investigations began in 1803, Picton claimed that Fullarton was motivated by personal hatred and vengeance and described Fullarton's witnesses as 'wretches raked out of the most despicable classes of the colony, without property or character, a mixed and spotted breed, to whose evidence little or no attention would be paid by the magistrate of the colony from which they came'. Moreover, he alleged that the witnesses had been 'tutored' by Juan Montes and Pedro Vargas, 'two despicable fellows', who were to appear as witnesses for the prosecution at Picton's trial. Picton defended his own actions in all the cases as being in keeping with the law of the island as he found it and he introduced evidence which made the crimes of those involved seem graver than Fullarton had suggested and his own actions less arbitrary. As a general principle, he pointed out that at its surrender Trinidad was almost in a state of anarchy and had he not dealt severely with his own men, as well as the population, the situation would have been beyond control.

At the other extreme, Fullarton was describing Luisa Calderon, whose capacity for theft or duplicity had never been in much doubt, as 'this blessed innocent'. Attempts were made by the prosecution to suggest that she had been only ten years old at the time of her ordeal, whereas the truth was that she was thirteen or fourteen. While living with Pedro Ruiz as his mistress, she had robbed him in partnership with her lover Carlos Gonzalez. When arrested, she refused to give information and, with Picton's sanction, she was picketed, a common military punishment which consisted of hoisting the victim up on a rope and obliging him to support himself on one foot on a sharp piece of wood. By comparison with other military punishments it was not severe but the infliction of it to force a confession from Luisa Calderon was bound to rouse widespread repugnance. Picton's counsel, Robert Dallas, argued that the practice was nonetheless legal under Spanish law, which had not been replaced in Trinidad by English law at the time in question. Indeed, he pointed out that it was as well for Luisa Calderon that she had not been subject to the criminal law of England, which punished such crimes as hers with the gallows rather than the picket. Dallas was an ingenious advocate of considerable experience. In 1787 he and Picton's trial judge, Lord Ellenborough, who was then Edward Law, had been two of the three counsel for the defence of Warren Hastings. In the following year, Dallas had appeared for Lord George Gordon who was prosecuted for libelling the Queen of France, the French Ambassador, and the administration of justice in England.

In 1802, Picton had been replaced as Governor of Trinidad by three commissioners, of whom he himself was to be one, Fullarton a second, and Sir Samuel Hood, who was on the whole sympathetic to Picton, a third. When the other commissioners arrived in Trinidad, Picton resigned and returned to England, though the inhabitants of the island petitioned the king to refuse his resignation. With the arrival of Fullarton, the collecting of evidence against Picton went ahead. Sir Samuel

The Trial of Thomas Picton

Hood, who shared no part of Fullarton's enthusiasm for this, soon became a target for Picton's enemies as well. When Hood chose to be a candidate in the Westminster election, he was greeted by a long political lampoon, *The Picton Veil; or, The Hood of Westminster*, which accused him of covering up the crimes of Picton and other public figures. The following verse, which couples Picton and Castlereagh, is typical of the poem as a whole.[1]

> See Castlereagh, with dauntless front,
> Who in Hibernia bore the brunt
> Of flogging, torturing without end,
> In soul allied as Picton's friend:
> No wonder he his voice should raise
> To sound aloud a murd'rer's praise.
> It bodes our country little good,
> When crimes are cover'd by a Hood.

Picton's first trial, held in 1806, is reprinted here. The prosecution was led by William Garrow, who as Attorney-General was to defend John Hatchard in 1817 and, on that occasion too, argued the humanitarian case. Picton himself did not appear as a witness but, according to the *New Newgate Calendar*, 'Governor Picton walked the hall of the courts during the whole of the trial. He was a tall man of a very sallow complexion, and was dressed in black. He was accompanied by several of the civil officers of the island.'[2] Among other offers of financial assistance, which Picton refused, the population of Trinidad collected £4,000 towards the costs of his defence. After the first trial, the Privy Council decided that no further proceedings against Picton were justified, though he was granted a new trial, as a matter of law. The second trial, in 1808, ended with a special verdict. Unlike the first jury, the jury at this trial found that torture was sanctioned by the Spanish law applicable in Trinidad and that though Picton had committed the acts alleged, he had therefore done so without malice or criminality. Further legal argument was abandoned in 1810, William Fullarton having died in the meantime.

Picton joined the Walcheren expedition and then, in 1810, commanded the Third Division in the Peninsula, winning a minor battle at San Antonio and then taking part in the defence of the lines of Torres Vedras during the winter of 1810–11. After fighting at Ciudad Rodrigo in 1812 he commanded the attack on Badajoz and fell, wounded, while leading his men. The wound was serious enough for him to return, temporarily, to England, where he took his seat in the Commons as Member for Carmarthen, and received the unanimous thanks of the House for his services in the war. On 27 April 1812, Lord Liverpool had said of him in the House of Lords,

> The conduct of General Picton has inspired a confidence in the army and exhibited an example of science and bravery which have been surpassed by no other officer. His exertions in the attack [on Badajoz] cannot fail to excite the most lively feelings of admiration.

After a spell at Cheltenham, to which he had gone as a matter of habit for recuperation, Picton returned to the Peninsula in December 1813 and fought throughout the rest of the campaign. His initiative won the battle of Vitoria for Wellington, and Picton himself rode through the thick of the fighting, wearing a top hat and clutching an umbrella. After the French army under Soult had been driven from Spain, Picton and his men entered Toulouse on Easter Day 1814.

Picton returned to England as one of the heroes of victory and was knighted early in 1815. After Napoleon's escape from Elba, he was given command of the Fifth Division and made his way to Brussels. Throughout the journey from Wales, he referred to his premonitions of death. At Quatre Bras on 16 June he was hit by a musket ball. Two ribs were broken and his body was badly bruised. He ordered his servant to strap him up and tell no one. Two days later, Picton, top-hatted as ever, held part of the ridge close to the centre of the allied line at Waterloo. In the early afternoon, Napoleon launched D'Erlon's infantry in a massive attack, which swept all before it. As 8,000 French troops swarmed towards them, Picton led his men in a desperate counter-attack. Sword in hand, at the head of the troops, he shouted, 'Charge! Hurrah! Hurrah!' At that moment he was hit in the head by a French bullet and fell dead from his horse. Yet the rally which he had begun was to break the French attack.

The Trial of Thomas Picton

Picton was soon the subject of impressive obsequies, including a monument in St Paul's Cathedral; a remarkable obelisk at Carmarthen, for which the king contributed by proxy; a poem by Thomas Moore, 'Oh, give to the hero the death of the brave', and a reputation, particularly in Wales, which gave his name to streets and public houses. Whatever the reactions of the twentieth century to his conduct in the case of Luisa Calderon, for his contemporaries it was to be an insignificant matter by comparison with the splendour of their later acclaim.

> Criminal Cause relative to the Theft of Two Thousand hard Dollars from PEDRO RUIZ, before His Honour Don Hilario de Begorrat, common or ordinary judge, in the Port of Spain in the Windward Island of Trinidad, on 22 and 23 December 42 GEORGE III. A.D. 1801. [*Extracts*]

[*Act of Process.*]
On the seventh day of the present month, between six and seven o'clock in the evening, Pedro Ruiz appeared in the court of the government, complaining of having that instant been robbed of two thousand hard dollars in specie, the lock of one of his trunks having been broke open, which trunk was deposited in the middle room of three apartments, held or possessed by him, near the marine and government parade or square, and having, to effect the same forced away one of the planks of the side of the house towards the sea. In consequence of which, His Excellency [*Governor Picton*] gave orders to secure the persons of Luisa Calderon and her mother Maria Calderon, domestics of the said Ruiz, and also Carlos Gonzalez, and Pedro Josef Perez, partner of the said Ruiz. Which cause His Excellency has transmitted to His Honour the judge for the adjudication and termination of the same. Accordingly, he pronounced that he ought to give orders, and did give orders, to proceed to the summary examination of the witnesses that may be obtained; also of such persons who may know anything relative to the cause in question, and especially the nearest neighbours to the said house.

[*Deposition of Theresa Alen, a free mulatta, residing in this port, and next-door neighbour to the house of Pedro Ruiz.*]

On the seventh day of the present month, it being about half-past six o'clock in the evening, she saw Carlos Gonzalez, a free mulatto, pass by; that he wished the deponent a good evening; that she then saw him enter the house-door of Pedro Ruiz, and having conversed with or spoke to Luisa Calderon, he immediately went away, and retired the back way of the said house of Pedro, being towards the beach and to the eastward.

[*Deposition of Josef Rodriguez, 'who by trade keeps a liquor and chandler's shop near the house of Pedro Ruiz'.*]

On the seventh day of the present month, he being in his shop, there came the mulatta Luisa Calderon, housekeeper of Pedro Ruiz, after the firing the evening gun at sunset. That she entered into conversation with deponent's wife, and Luisa invited her to take a walk as far as the bridge, beyond the church, and that his said wife refused. That at this moment Carlos Gonzalez approached them, and the deponent asked him to sit down, which the said Carlos declined, saying that he was in haste. That he notwithstanding stopped some time, for Cuno Puentas inquired of Gonzalez the state of the vessel newly bought by him, and he replied that said vessel prospered, and that he was then fitting her out. And at this time Luisa Calderon went away home to the house of Pedro Ruiz, and immediately afterwards Carlos disappeared, without his observing which way he went. That he has heard it reported that Pedro Ruiz had been robbed, but does not know by whom.

[*Deposition of Honore Birot, 'bedridden with the palsy'.*]

On the seventh day of the present month, being about the time of evening prayer, the deponent heard the passage door of the house of Pedro Ruiz being opened, and at about a quarter of an hour afterwards he heard blows, as of the breaking open a trunk, and that a short time after, in like manner, he heard the iron bolt drawn. That on the following day he was acquainted by Hilario Arnaud that Carlos Gonzalez was in custody for the said robbery.

[*Deposition of Nely, the female slave of Theresa Alen.*]

On the seventh day of the present month, it being about half-past six o'clock in the evening, after the evening gun being fired, she saw Carlos Gonzalez, who went into and stood on one side of the house passage of Pedro Ruiz, and made water there. And at this time or moment the deponent asked him why he should make water there, being the place where kitchen articles were usually put. That thereupon the said Carlos, without speaking a word, went away from that place, and went further up the passage, and stood on some timber or planks, and seemed as if he was making water there, when she, the deponent, retired.

[*Deposition of Pedro, 'a native negro, the slave of Pedro Ruiz'.*]

On the seventh day of the present month, at about noon-day before dinner, he, the deponent, went with his master's cart to the city of St. Joseph, to carry sundry provisions for the troops there. That at half-past seven o'clock at night of the same day he arrived back again, and at the house of Luisa, the housekeeper of Pedro Ruiz, who lives near the church, and having met her at the door of the said house, she inquired of him, the deponent, where his master Pedro was. To which he replied that she who was at the house-door ought to know better than him where his master was, for he, the deponent, was but just arrived from the city of St. Joseph. That after this he went to take a walk and to get some drink at the shop of Beltri, a black woman near the Green Market, and on going out of the house of the said Beltri, he went towards his master's house. And a little before getting there he heard a negro cry out (whom he did not know) that a robbery had been committed. And on his arrival at his said master's house, he found a great many persons therein, and the said Pedro told him, the deponent, that someone had robbed him. That being within the said house, together with his master, he and his master searched the same, and they found no partition or wall whatever broke open, and only the lock of the trunks.

[*Deposition of Pedro Josef Perez.*]

One afternoon, about the time of the siesta (afternoon's sleep) subsequent to the robbery, Carlos Gonzalez came to the dwelling-house of the deponent, and sitting down, Carlos said to him, 'What do you think has happened?' He then related that the judge now present with the officers of justice had been that morning to his house, and had searched the same in consequence of the robbery of Pedro. And at this instant Pedro came in, when he, the deponent, said to Carlos, 'Why should you be uneasy, as you are clear and innocent? God keep you so.' And Carlos repeated to him the same words. And then the deponent said to him in a free manner, 'Never mind me. In case they should call on me, I will acquaint them what I saw on the night of the robbery.' Then Carlos said, 'What, are you against me?' And the deponent answered, 'No.' Then Carlos went away. The deponent remaining alone with Pedro, they conversed on the same subject.

[*Deposition of Luisa Calderon.*]

Being questioned respecting the contents of the aforegoing act, and the other circumstances that had occurred, with the intent to ascertain the truth relative to the cause in question, she fully denied knowing who were the perpetrators of the robbery.

[*Act.*]

In consequence of the strong suspicions His Honour entertains of the mulatta, Luisa Calderon, a domestic of Pedro Ruiz, concealing the truth relative to the aforesaid robbery, expressed in these proceedings; and His Honour being persuaded that he will discover the truth of the matter by means of a slight torment being inflicted on the said Calderon: and whereas His Honour is not invested with power to execute the same, His Excellency the Governor and Captain-General of this island must be made acquainted hereof, with the summary of this process by virtue of this document, to the intent that His Excellency may determine, as may appear to him justice, the usual and requisite forms for that purpose to be adopted and observed by the notary in this cause.

[*Order.*]

Apply the torture to Luisa Calderon.

(Signed) Thomas Picton.

[*Act of Torment.*]

His Honour, for the *first time*, admonished her to tell the truth relative to the persons who had been parties in the said robbery, and in what manner the same was committed. For that otherwise the torment would be inflicted on her to which she had been condemned, and that in case she should sustain any hurt or injury, or that should she die, the same must be on her own head, and not to be attributed to His Honour, who only endeavoured to investigate the truth. And she said and deposed as before. And His Honour again admonished her, for the *second and third* times, when she answered that she did not know who were the delinquents that committed the robbery. Whereupon His Honour, the said judge, ordered the said Luisa to be conveyed to the place appropriated for the said torment, where were present the officers of justice, Josef Flores and Rafael Chando, and there being a picket with a rope hanging from the ceiling, being the instrument for executing the torture. On sight thereof, the said judge admonished her, *for the last time*, to relate the truth. For that should she not comply, the said torture would be inflicted on her, and would be on her own head, and could not be attributed to His Honour. And on the aforesaid being made known to her, she replied that she could not depose anything else than what she had done before. Then His Honour ordered the said officers of justice to uphold and bind her, as till then she was in no way bound or fettered. And it being about half-past eleven o'clock, as by the dial of a watch or clock, His Honour, the judge, questioned the culprit what she knew of the robbery committed on Pedro Ruiz, in what manner it was perpetrated, and bidding her speak the truth. To which she replied that she knew nothing more than she had said before. Then the said judge ordered the aforesaid officers to tie the said Luisa up by one hand perpendicularly, with one of her feet resting on a picket of wood; and to tie the other foot and hand together. In which posture the said Luisa cried, 'Ay, ay,' repeating the same several times, calling on God and the Holy Virgin, saying, 'I do not know anything, my lord judge. If I did, I would have told it.' The said judge again bid her tell the truth, and she replied, 'I do not know anything. Most Holy Virgin, assist me.' Then the said judge ordered her to be suspended in such a manner that her great toe touched or rested on the said picket, and in this situation she remained, repeating her former expressions. Then the said judge ordered the rope to be drawn in such a manner that she should be suspended without her toe touching the said picket, at which time she desired them to loosen her and that she would relate the truth. And accordingly she confessed that Carlos Gonzalez, with whom she once only had had a carnal connection, notwithstanding the intimacy with Pedro Ruiz, that it was him that had stole the money from the said Ruiz; and this she knows from having been an eye-witness thereof. When she came a second time to the house of the said Pedro, she opened the door with the key that she had,—she lighted a candle, and having heard blows, as of breaking open a trunk, she retired further back, put out the light, locked the door, and concealed herself in the passage, close to where Carlos had moved the said trunk, whom she also saw while he was taking out the sundry bags in which the money was contained, and which he carried off. And at the time that Carlos went away, she concealed herself the more that he might not see her. That she does not know where the said Carlos has deposited the said money. That he has not given any portion thereof to her, neither did Carlos ever propose to her the committing the said robbery. And on being reminded and questioned from what motive, when she saw Carlos committing the robbery, she did not cry out, nor lodge an information to a magistrate; she answered that she did not know what she was to do. In like manner she was questioned whether Carlos ever had communication and entrance into the house of Pedro. She replied that she remembers that one day, about four or five months ago, that the said Carlos, towards night, came and entered the second room in the house of Pedro, and stood at the door of the same room wherein the robbery was committed. And said Carlos requested Pedro to change him some gold coin for Pistreens [*small silver*]; and Pedro, opening the trunk which has been since broke open and wherein he kept his money, he took out a bag and changed him the gold coin.

And in the procuring this said confession the said Luisa was about one hour on the picket. The rope was then loosened and she was released therefrom.

> [*On the following day, 24 December 1801, Luisa Calderon was again placed on the picket with the aim of making her confess that she was an accomplice in the robbery and that she knew where Gonzalez had hidden the money. After twenty minutes the attempt was given up, 'His Honour perceiving that she was about to faint, notwithstanding her pulse was still regular'. Gonzalez maintained his innocence but in 1802 he was sentenced to pay Ruiz 1,800 dollars, to pay the costs of his trial, and to be banished from the island. Luisa Calderon was released from prison.*]

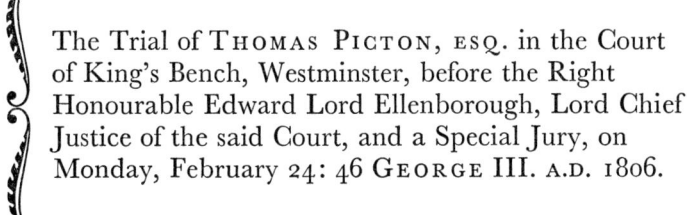

The Trial of THOMAS PICTON, ESQ. in the Court of King's Bench, Westminster, before the Right Honourable Edward Lord Ellenborough, Lord Chief Justice of the said Court, and a Special Jury, on Monday, February 24: 46 GEORGE III. A.D. 1806.

Counsel for the Prosecution
Mr. *Garrow* (afterwards a Baron of the Exchequer):
Mr. *Adam* (afterwards Lord Chief Commissioner of the Jury Court of Scotland):
Mr. *Harrison*.

Counsel for the Defendant
Mr. *Dallas* (afterwards Lord Chief Justice of the Common Pleas):
Mr. *Lawes*:
Mr. *Abercrombie*.

The Indictment was opened by Mr. Harrison.

Mr. *Garrow*. Gentlemen of the jury; the task of stating the particulars of this most extraordinary and horrid transaction, was originally confided to much greater abilities than those upon which it has now unfortunately devolved. I feel, however, some consolation in reflecting that the present is a case which, addressed to a British jury in a British Court of Justice, requires no embellishment of eloquence, nor any factitious aid, to impress it upon the minds of those who are to hear and to decide upon it. Unless the facts, clearly and fully substantiated by proof, force from you a reluctant verdict of guilty, I have no hesitation in declaring that the defendant ought not to be convicted:—I say 'a *reluctant* verdict of guilty', because there is no individual present, not excepting even myself, whose duty it is to conduct the prosecution, who would not rejoice if you could justify yourselves to your consciences and your God, in doubting the truth of this accusation.

The indictment, which has been stated to you by my learned friend Mr. Harrison, alleges, that a representative of our Sovereign, and Governor of one of our colonial dependencies, who was therefore bound to protect his fellow-subjects, has abused the station to which he was raised, and has disgraced the country to which he belongs, by—what no one in England has heard of, without horror and detestation—inflicting torture upon one of His Majesty's subjects, without the least pretence of law, without the least moral justification, but solely to gratify his tyrannical disposition, by the oppression of the unfortunate and defenceless victim of his cruelty.

Gentlemen, in the year 1797, the island of Trinidad surrendered to His Majesty's forces under the command of the illustrious Sir Ralph Abercromby, whose name must ever be mentioned by Britons with gratitude and admiration. That great man entered into stipulations by which he conceded to the inhabitants of this Spanish settlement, the continuance of their laws and institutions; and he appointed a new governor until His Majesty's pleasure should be known, or, in other words, until the Sovereign of Great Britain should have, in his paternal kindness towards this new dependence of his empire, extended to it all the privileges and advantages of English laws.

This colony, prior to its surrender to the British arms, had been governed by a code of laws, abating very much of the severity of that of Old Spain; and I have the authority of the defendant himself for stating, that, previous to his appointment to the government, the juridical regulations of Trinidad were extremely mild and benignant, and well adapted to the protection of the subject in this remote insular establishment.

The person, whose sufferings form the subject of this day's inquiry, is a young woman of the name of Luisa Calderon. About the age of ten or eleven years, this young person was seduced by a man of the name of Pedro Ruiz, to live with him as his mistress; and although it may to us in this country appear singular, that she should be in such a situation at that tender period of life, yet in that hot climate where the puberty of females is much accelerated, it is common for them to become mothers at the age of twelve; at that early period they either marry, or enter into a state of concubinage if they cannot form a more honourable connection. Having been seduced by Ruiz, and living with him as his mistress, it appears most clearly (for I have no desire to keep any part of the case secret), that she was engaged in an intrigue with Carlos Gonzalez, who in the month of December 1801, availing him of the access to the house of Pedro Ruiz, which his connection with Luisa Calderon afforded, robbed Ruiz of a quantity of dollars which were there deposited. Gonzalez was apprehended, and a suspicion arising that she was acquainted with the circumstances of the robbery, if not an accessory to the crime, she also was taken into custody, and examined before an officer of the laws, equivalent to our magistrate or justice of the peace. In the first instance she denied any knowledge of the transaction. The magistrate felt, that according to the laws of Spain, his functions were nearly at an end. She persisted in her denial, and whether her object in so doing was to protect herself or her friend from injurious consequences it is not at all material to inquire. The magistrate felt that he had no authority to adopt any coercive means in order to procure any confession of her own guilt, or any accusation of Gonzalez; and therefore he resorted to the defendant, who was invested with the supreme authority of the island, to supply the deficiency; and, gentlemen, I shall produce in the handwriting of General Picton himself, and subscribed with his signature this bloody sentence: 'Inflict the torture upon Luisa Calderon.' You will readily believe that there was no great delay in proceeding to obey this order. The unhappy girl when taken to the gaol was told by the judge, that, if she would confess all, her life should be saved; but unless she did so, she should be put to the torture; that if she suffered the loss of a limb, or should be deprived of life itself, the consequences would be upon her own head, and that he should be absolved from all blame. In order to impress this admonition upon her mind, two or three young negresses were brought before her in the room where torture was usually applied, who were to undergo the same severities, on a charge of sorcery and witchcraft. Here then, we behold a British Governor for the first time introducing torture into a British settlement as a punishment for sorcery and witchcraft, and as the means of extorting confession from a person under accusation.

  Notwithstanding all this, the young woman persisted in declaring her innocence, and the punishment was applied which has been improperly called *picketing*. I say improperly, because picketing is a known military punishment, but this is properly distinguished by the name of *the torture*. Indeed it is a libel upon picketing to call the torture inflicted upon Luisa Calderon by the same name. True it is that there is some resemblance between the one practice and the other; in both cases the foot is placed upon a sharp wooden point, but in the former that mercy which always attends the infliction of punishments in this country has assigned for the sufferer a means of reposing or raising himself by the interior of his arms, a rope being placed round the body, and passing under the arm, so that when fatigued, he can rest upon it, by which the agony to the foot is diminished. Not only for the sake of correctness, but for the sake of humanity, I hope this practice will not receive the appellation of *picketing*, but that of *Pictoning*, that it may be described by the most horrid name by which it can be known, and be shunned as a disgrace to human nature.

I will briefly state to you the particulars of the situation of this unhappy creature during the time she was thus exposed to this exercise of cruelty. While her body was supported by the great toe projected on a sharp piece of wood, the wrist of the hand on the opposite side was drawn up by a pulley, so that her whole weight was sustained by the pulley and the spike; and lest she should afford herself any momentary relief by struggling in such a situation, the other hand and foot which were not concerned in the dreadful operation were tied together behind her. She complained bitterly and requested to be lowered. She was then told that if she would confess she should be let down, and then she said Gonzalez had certainly stolen Ruiz's dollars. Nothing but the incontestible evidence which I have to produce, could make you believe, that this unhappy creature continued for fifty-three or fifty-four minutes in that dreadful state. The time was ascertained by a watch which the magistrate had before him, not from any fear that she might suffer too much, but because there was some notion of a supposed law, that the torture could not be inflicted for more than an hour; and had it not been for the watch, the pleasure of inflicting the punishment might have induced the magistrates and the spectators to have continued it for a longer period than the time supposed to be allowed. She was then lowered, but her confession not being deemed satisfactory in less than twenty-four hours the torture was again applied.

The Trial of Thomas Picton

This, gentlemen, is a faithful representation of it (*producing a drawing in colours*), and may give you some notion of the suffering which a human being in such a situation must have undergone.

It appears to me, that the case which I shall lay before you in support of the prosecution is complete. Our charge is, that Governor Picton, abusing his station, has, without reasonable cause or legal justification, inflicted the torture upon this young female. But I understand I am to be told that, although the highest authority in this country could not inflict such a punishment on the meanest individual, yet, that Governor Picton was justified by the laws of Spain as they applied to the island of Trinidad. Subject to my lord's correction, however, I state with confidence that if it were written in characters which no man could misunderstand, and which he who runs may read, that the laws of Spain as applicable to Trinidad, permitted, in any given circumstances, the infliction of torture, this would afford no justification to a British Governor. Nothing could justify him but the law of imperious necessity, to which we must all submit: he must show that he had no alternative. What was the duty of a man placed in his honourable and important station? It was his duty in the first moment of his government to have impressed on the minds of the people of this new colony a conviction of the perfect security they would acquire, of the abundant advantages they would derive, from the mild, benign, and equitable spirit of British jurisprudence; and, above all, that the moment they were received within the pale of the British government, the torture would be for ever banished from the island.

But I moreover assert, that the defendant cannot make out any pretence of a justification, for there is nothing even in the law of Spain as applicable to Trinidad, by which such a pretence can be supported; and I also have no hesitation in declaring, that even if he could establish a right in some cases to inflict the torture, it would not avail him here. He must make out a case of absolute and irresistible necessity, and show that it was his *bounden duty* to inflict it. He ought to have remembered, that in England torture is unknown, not because the subject has never been discussed, but because it is so abhorrent to all our feelings, to our regard for personal liberty and the fair administration of justice, that it never has been and never can be tolerated here. What is the language of our legal institutions, as they are explained by a learned and elegant writer adverting to this subject?

'The trial by rack is utterly unknown to the law of England; though once when the Dukes of Exeter and Suffolk, and other ministers of Henry VI had laid a design to introduce the civil law into this kingdom as the rule of government, for a beginning thereof they erected a rack for torture; which was called in derision the Duke of Exeter's Daughter, and still remains in the Tower of London, where it was occasionally used as an engine of state, not of law, more than once in the reign of Queen Elizabeth. But when, upon the assassination of Villiers, Duke of Buckingham, by Felton, it was proposed in the Privy Council to put the assassin to the rack, in order to discover his accomplices; the judges, being consulted, declared unanimously, to their own honour and the honour of the English law, that no such proceeding was allowable by the laws of England.'[3]

General Picton should have carried this with him to Trinidad, he should have borne in mind the folly of supposing that an instrument of torture is an instrument to extract truth. The subject has been reduced by a foreign writer (Beccaria, chapter 16);[4] quoted by Mr. Justice Blackstone into the form of a mathematical problem: 'The force of the muscles and the sensibility of the nerves of an innocent person being given, it is required to find the degree of pain necessary to make him confess himself guilty of a given crime.' Nothing indeed can be so absurd and preposterous as the application of this process in the administration of justice. But what are we to say of this man who comes here to defend himself, saying, that he has found a law under which he can obtain shelter, when I tell you that it appears by all the volumes sent from Trinidad, that so far from Governor Picton having found torture in daily use under former governors, so far from his being bound by any circumstances of necessity to inflict it, he has all the merit of the invention. Like the Duke of Exeter's Daughter, it never had existence until the defendant cursed the island with its introduction.

The Trial of Thomas Picton

Gentlemen, that I shall prove this case to you I am most confident, for I have read the depositions, which have been most laboriously collected, and laid before the Court; and if I show that for the first time General Picton, a British governor, erected this instrument of torture, and that with his own hand he wrote the bloody order for its infliction, I set before you a man without the least shadow of defence.

The date of this transaction is removed at some distance. In the opinion of those who were to advise His Majesty as to the manner in which the government of this remote island should be managed, it was deemed expedient that commissioners should be sent over, and among the persons appointed to this important situation was Colonel Fullarton. Upon the arrival of those commissioners, this affair was disclosed to Colonel Fullarton, who felt it to be his duty to put it in a train of inquiry. The result of which is that he has found it necessary to bring this defendant before you, and also to bring before you the unfortunate victim of his tyranny, whom I have this day accidentally seen, in consequence of my being by mistake conducted to a consultation into a room where she was. She will be presented before you, and you will find that she at this moment bears about her the marks of the barbarity of the defendant.

Gentlemen, I shall hear with patience and attention and with as much pleasure as any man what my excellent and learned friend has to offer in behalf of his client. I state the case at present with full confidence in your verdict. I ask nothing from your passions; nothing but justice do I require, and I doubt not, that, at the conclusion of this trial, you will be found to have faithfully discharged your duty.

EVIDENCE FOR THE PROSECUTION

Luisa Calderon sworn.
Mr. Garrow.—Can you speak English?—A very little, sir, indeed; I can understand it but very little.
Mr. Sergeant was then sworn as an interpreter.
Luisa Calderon examined by Mr. Adam.
Were you at Trinidad in the year 1798?—Yes.
Were you acquainted with a person of the name of Pedro Ruiz?— Yes.

Did you live in his house?—Yes, I did.
In what year did you first live in his house?—I do not know in what year.
Were you there in 1799 and 1800?—I cannot say positively that I was.
Were you there at the time Mr. Picton was Governor?—Yes.
Do you remember any robbery having been committed in the house of Pedro Ruiz?—Yes.
Who was the person suspected of that robbery?—A person called by the name of Carlos Gonzalez.
Do you remember his having been taken up, and committed for that robbery?—Carlos was taken up for the same thing.
Were you and your mother likewise taken up for that robbery?—Yes, the same night.
Before whom were you carried in the first instance? Were you carried before Governor Picton?—Yes, before the same Governor.
Did he order you to be committed to prison?—Yes, I was sent by his order.
Under what guard were you sent to prison?—Under the guard of three soldiers.
Were you committed to close confinement in prison?—I was sent to the woman's side of the prison, to that part which belongs to the women.
Before you were sent to prison by Governor Picton did he say anything to you?—Governor Picton told me if I did not confess who had taken the money, the hangman Ludovigo was to put his hand upon me.
Mr. Garrow. That she was to be turned over to the hangman, is that what she means?—*Interpreter.* Yes, it is.
Mr. Adam. Did he say anything more to you?—No more, but he sent me to prison.
Do you know a person of the name of Begorrat?—Yes.
Is he an *alcalde*, a judge?—He is like a lord mayor there.
Did Mr. Begorrat come to you in prison?—He was with me in prison.
Did he examine you upon the subject of the robbery by Gonzalez? —Yes.
Did he examine you frequently upon it?—Yes, at various times.
On different days?—Yes.

Did you make any declaration to Mr. Begorrat respecting the robbery?—Yes, I did.

Was there a person present of the name of Francisco de Castro, an *escrivano*?—Yes.

Present with Mr. Begorrat?—Yes, de Castro was a clerk.

Interpreter. Escrivano means a scrivener.

Mr. Garrow. From the depositions it appears he is a mere writer, something like a clerk at Bow Street.

Mr. Adam. Were those examinations carried on while you were confined on the woman's side of the prison?—At the first examination I was in a separate room.

Were you afterwards carried to a room where there was a picket erected in the gaol?—Yes.

What was the nature of that instrument of torture, can you give an account of it in English, and the manner in which it was applied?—This hand (*the left hand, raising herself*) was tied up, and then this hand (*the right hand*) was tied to the left foot.

Was it your left foot that was tied to your right hand?—Both; they put me first of all on one side, and then they took me down, and tied me up on the other side.

The first time they tied you up, did they tie you by the left hand? —Yes.

Which foot was tied to the right hand?—This foot (*the left foot*).

Then your left hand was tied by a rope?—Yes.

Was it fixed to the ceiling, or did it pass through a pulley?— Yes, through a pulley.

What was your right foot placed upon?—Upon the picket.

Mr. Garrow. The toe resting upon a sharp point of wood?—Yes.

Is that a faithful description of it? (*Showing the witness a coloured drawing.*)—Yes, very good indeed.

Mr. Garrow. I wish your lordship could have seen the involuntary expression of the sensations of the witness upon looking at the drawing.

Lord Ellenborough. I do not approve of exhibiting drawings of this nature before a jury, and I shall not permit it till the counsel for the defendant has seen it. I have no objection to your showing a description to the jury, but the colouring may produce an improper effect.

Mr. Dallas. I have no objection whatever on the part of my client that the jury should see it, but it certainly is not the usual course of proceeding in a case of this sort.

Lord Ellenborough. The jury will consider it merely as a description of the situation in which she was placed. Whether she was justifiably so placed is the question between you.

Mr. Garrow. I have one to which there can be no objection. It is a mere pen and ink sketch.

Is that a correct representation? (*Showing it to the witness.*)—Yes, this is correct.

The last-mentioned drawing handed to the jury.

Lord Ellenborough. Gentlemen, you will consider that as a description of the position, which we can easily understand from the words of the witness. Nobody wishes that any improper impression should be made by that drawing, it is only to show the nature of the process. You see the suspension by one arm, and the resting upon the opposite foot.

Mr. Adam. At what time of the day were you first tied up in this way?—In the afternoon.

Of the first day?—Yes.

Can you tell how long you remained upon it?—Three quarters of an hour, they said.

Was your foot allowed to rest upon the spike of wood all that time?—Yes.

Were you at any time drawn up by the rope?—Yes.

So as to suspend you?—Yes.

Had you seen any persons placed in the same situation before you yourself were?—Yes, I had.

How many?—Two of them.

Mr. Dallas. Is that evidence?

Lord Ellenborough. I do not think that should have been asked.

Mr. Adam. I will not insist upon it. What effect had this torture upon your body the first time you were put upon the picket?—A great deal of pain.

What effect had it upon your wrist?—The wrist swelled very much.

And what upon your foot?—My foot was very much swelled also.

Were you asked to make any declarations respecting the robbery while you were tied up?—Yes, I was.

Were you sworn before you were tied up?—Mr. Begorrat asked me if I would declare who took the money.

Was any oath administered to you?—No more than the Holy Cross being held up to me.

Did you make any declaration? What did you say respecting the robbery at this time?—I declared to the Lord Mayor that Carlos Gonzalez had taken the money; that was while I was suspended.

Do you recollect whether this first time that you were tied up was on the 23rd of December 1801?—I do not recollect the day.

Lord Ellenborough. Do you recollect whether it was in the month of December?—Eleven days after I was sent to prison.

Mr. Adam. Was it about Christmas time?—Yes, it was about Christmas time.

When you were taken down what was next done to you this first time?—They took me into a lower room called by the name of Mr. Vallot's room.

Who was Mr. Vallot?—The gaoler.

Were you kept in the room all night?—No, I was taken there to own to Mr. Vallot who had taken the money.

When you were taken down to the gaoler's room did you see Carlos there?—Carlos was there.

How long were you kept in the gaoler's room?—Not long. I cannot recollect how long.

You were not detained there all night?—No.

Where did you go after you left the gaoler's room?—Into the same room where I had been suspended.

Were you kept there all night?—Yes, all night in that room.

Were you put in irons?—Yes, in the *grillos*.

Describe the *grillos*.—

Mr. Adam. That, my lord, is the name of the fetters.

Witness. There is a piece of wood, and a hole just below, and an iron bar runs through it, with two iron rings for the legs.

Were you fixed to that iron bar?—All that same night.

How were you fixed to it? By the legs, or how?—The iron went down to my ankle.

Mr. Garrow. This is a representation of the iron. (*Showing the witness a drawing of it.*) Is that like it?—Yes, it is.

Mr. Garrow. It is a long iron bar, to which the leg is fastened by a ring.

Mr. Adam. Did you remain fastened to this iron all night?—Yes, all night.

Were you put upon the picket again the next day?—Yes, the following day.

Were you put upon the same instrument of torture, and in the same manner as you had been the day before?—Yes, the very same.

At what hour in the day?—In the beginning of the morning.

Was this the day before Christmas?—The day before Christmas day.

How long were you kept upon this instrument of torture on that day?—Twenty-two minutes.

Was there a watch placed in order to tell the time, upon a barrel or anything?—Yes, there was a watch.

Who was present this second day, when you were put upon the instrument?—Mr. Begorrat and Francisco de Castro.

Mr. Garrow. These are the same persons, the justice and his clerk.

Mr. Adam. Was any other person present?—Mr. Rafael.

Lord Ellenborough. Who was he?—An *alguazil* [*officer of justice*].

Mr. Adam. By which arm were you tied up on the second day?—By both arms.

One at a time?—Yes, first one, and then they changed it to the other.

Were you drawn up by the rope the second day so as to remove your foot from resting upon the spike of wood?—I could just touch it with the end of my toe.

Were your shoes taken off both days?—Yes.

Your feet were naked?—Yes, I had no shoes on.

What effect did this produce upon you; did it make you sick?—I fainted away.

Lord Ellenborough. Did you faint away on both days, or only on one of those days?—No more than one day.

Was that the latter day, or the former?—The last day.

Mr. Adam. Do you know whether you were taken down upon your fainting away?—I do not recollect whether I was or was not.

Was that owing to your insensibility, or have you forgot it?—I do not recollect anything of the kind.

Did they take you down before you fainted away or after you fainted away?—I do not recollect whether they took me down first or after, but I did faint away.

Did they administer any relief to you, or give you anything?—Mr. Vallot, the gaoler sent some vinegar to rub my nose with.

The Trial of Thomas Picton

To what place were you taken after you were put upon this instrument the second time?—In the same place where I was upon the picket.

Were you again put in fetters?—Yes, I was put in irons.

How soon were you put in irons after you were taken down?—The same night; the day that I was taken down, the same evening they put me into irons.

How long did they keep you in irons?—All the time that I was in prison.

How long were you in prison?—Eight months.

Were you at any time taken from the prison to the house of Pedro Ruiz?—Yes.

How long was that after the last time the torture was inflicted?—This Mr. Begorrat the Lord Mayor took me to the house of Ruiz one time.

Do you recollect how long that was after the torture?—I cannot recollect the time.

Was it a month?—I cannot say.

Were you able to walk there without assistance?—I was so very bad that I went all the way quite lame.

To what was that lameness attributable?—The irons that I was put into.

What age were you at the time you were confined eight months in gaol?—Thirteen years, and going for fourteen.

How came you to be released from the prison at the end of eight months?—I do not know what the reason was that I was liberated; I cannot tell the reason.

Had Colonel Fullarton arrived in the island of Trinidad before you were liberated?—After I was liberated Colonel Fullarton arrived in the island of Trinidad.

Were you liberated after he arrived, or before?—Before.

How soon after did he arrive in the island?—I cannot recollect the time.

Are there any marks of the injury you received from the torture or irons now remaining?—On my hands I have some, but none on my feet.

On which hand?—Upon both hands, upon my wrists (*showing them.*)

Are those the seams of the cord that was tied round your arm?—Yes, the marks the cord made.

Luisa Calderon cross-examined by Mr. Dallas.
What space of time elapsed between your release from prison and your coming to England?—I do not recollect.
Was it many months?—I cannot say how long a time.
Did you come with Colonel Fullarton?—Yes, I came with him here.
By whom have you been supported since you have been in this country?—By one Mr. White.
Who is Mr. White?—A gentleman in London.
Lord Ellenborough. I suppose she means Mr. White, Solicitor to the Treasury.
Mr. Dallas. That is all I want, my lord.
Rafael Chando sworn. Examined by Mr. Garrow.
Perhaps you speak English enough to answer a few questions?—I understand you.
Were you one of the *alguazils* of the Port of Spain in the island of Trinidad in December 1801?—Yes.
Mr. Dallas. I do not know whether this is the usual way in which witnesses are sworn in that country; for the sake of regularity, I wish to have that explained.
Mr. Garrow. You are a Christian, I apprehend?—Yes.
When you call God to witness, you consider yourself bound to tell the truth?—Yes.
Is there any other mode of swearing more binding upon your conscience than the oath you have now taken?—No.
You feel yourself bound to speak the *whole* truth when you call God to witness it?—Yes.
You were sworn in the same way before the Privy Council?—Yes.
You said you were one of the *alguazils* of Trinidad in December 1801?—Yes.
Do you remember returning from the country where you had been engaged in some business on the day but one before Christmas day in that year? On the 23rd of December?—Yes.
Do you know a young woman of the name of Luisa Calderon?—Yes, very well.
When you arrived at the gaol on the 23rd of December, did you see Luisa Calderon?—Yes, I saw Luisa.
Under what circumstances did you see her?—I saw her with the gaoler-man, Mr. Begorrat, Mr. de Castro, and Josef Flores.
He was one of the judges?—He was one of the *alguazils*.

What were they doing with Luisa Calderon when you came in?—
They were giving her a glass of wine and water.
On what account were they giving her a glass of wine and water?
—They had just been bringing her down from the torture.
Was she at that time in a state of suffering and pain which
required some relief?—Yes, I think very much so; she was
very much swelled in the hands and feet at the time they gave
her the wine and water.
What position was she in?—She stood close by a table to support
herself with her hand, and seemed suffering very much.
You said something about her feet and hands. It had been done
before you came, and she appeared to be suffering from that?
—Yes.
What time in the evening of the 23rd was it?—About seven or
eight o'clock at night, I do not know exactly.
Did she recover after she had had this wine and water?—No, Mr.
Begorrat asked questions of Luisa.
Was Carlos there?—No, Mr. Begorrat said 'Luisa, you will tell
before Carlos the same that you have told me.' Luisa said,
'Yes, sir.'
What passed then?—Mr. Begorrat then desired me to fetch Carlos
up.
You brought Carlos into Luisa's presence?—Yes.
What passed then?—In about two or three minutes he sat down.
After he came into Mr. Begorrat's and de Castro's presence, did
anything pass?—No, he never spoke, only I was to bring him
before Mr. Begorrat.
What became of Luisa that night?—She was put into the *grillos*
directly.
Is this a true description of the iron? (*showing him the drawing*)—
Yes, just the same.
Two rings for the foot, and then a long iron?—Yes.
In what room was she confined that night?—In the same room
where they gave her the torture.
What was the form of that room as to its ceiling?—Like a garret,
the middle high and the sides very low.
Was there room enough for her to sit upright?—No, she could not
sit upright.
Not in the middle of the room?—No, she was obliged to crouch
down.

The Trial of Thomas Picton

Where the iron was placed, she was obliged to stoop?—Yes, so as to sit down.

Did she remain in that room all night?—Yes, all the while she was in custody, all night and all day long about eight months.

You have been now describing to us what passed upon the 23rd? —Yes.

Was she again put to the torture the next day?—Mr. Begorrat told me to go to de Castro to know whether he was ready to go to the gaol, and he told me yes.

When was this?—On Thursday, the day after the first torture, they gave her the second torture.

Do you know whether that was the day before Christmas day?—I know it was the day after the first torture.

In what part of the day was the second torture applied?— Between eleven and twelve in the forenoon.

The first torture had ended about seven at night?—Yes.

Describe to my lord and to these gentlemen what was done to Luisa upon the second day?—He gave her the torture again.

Describe what they did to her?—They hung her up in the torture.

In what way?—This hand and this foot tied in this way (*the left foot passed behind the right leg, and received by the right hand*).

Lord Ellenborough. The girl described it the other way.

Witness. The left hand fastened up, and the left foot passed behind her right leg, and tied in the hand, and then a very little bit of the toe just touching the spike.

Is that a true description of it? (*showing him the drawing*)—Yes, just the same.

How long did she remain in the situation you have been describing the second time?—By my own watch twenty-two minutes.

Did she appear to you to suffer very much by this torture?—She fainted twice into my own arms.

Did she while she was suffering make any application to be in any manner relieved by altering the mode of the torture?—Never, no further than speaking for a little drop of vinegar.

You do not understand the question. Did Luisa ask to be let down at all?—No, at the time that she fainted and fell into my arms Mr. Begorrat got some vinegar, and put it to her nose.

Was that while she was tied up?—Yes.

Then somebody applied vinegar to her nose?—Yes, Mr. Begorrat gave it to me.

After she had fainted twice, and been tied up twenty-two minutes, was she taken down?—Yes.

Did it appear to you that she could have endured it any longer?—No, I cannot tell you any more than that in twenty-two minutes they took her down from the torture.

Did it appear to you that, without danger to her life, she could have endured it any longer?—I think at the time she fainted away twice into my own arms she could not.

Was there any defender appointed for her, or anybody to take care of her interests?—I saw no one.

Was there any one there besides this thing called a judge, the *escrivano* and the gaoler?—There was nobody else there when she fainted away at the time they brought up the vinegar.

Was there any surgeon to take care of her in case of any accident happening?—No, the negro of Mr. Vallot, the gaoler-man, pulled the rope.

What became of this poor creature after she was taken down?—They put her in irons directly.

In the state in which she had been before?—Yes.

You told us she continued in this state for eight months?—Quite eight months.

Was she during any part of that time permitted to go at large or to leave those irons, and this miserable and wretched confinement?—No, they carried her once or twice to the house of the man that had been robbed.

She was in the custody of the gaoler at the time?—Yes, I went there with a constable.

Except that, she was closely confined for the eight months?—Yes.

Was she deprived of the assistance and society of her friends?—I did not see anybody. I have seen the sister bring her some victuals, but never go to see her; she gave it to the gaoler.

They never permitted her to go to the dungeon?—I do not know whether they permitted her or not, I did not see it.

How long had you lived in the Port of Spain?—About eight years.

Did you live there before the island surrendered to Sir Ralph Abercromby?—Yes, about four or five months before.

Had you been an *alguazil* all the time you were there?—No.

How long had you been an *alguazil*?—About four or five years.

Did you ever hear or know of torture being inflicted upon a person in custody till after Governor Picton arrived there?—Never.

You know the place in which this instrument of torture was erected?—Yes.

You told me you never knew or heard of anybody being tortured. Was there any instrument to inflict the torture before General Picton arrived?—The first place of torment that I ever saw in the island was among the soldiers in the barracks.

Was even that erected before Governor Picton arrived?—No. Governor Picton, for the first time, ordered me and the gaoler to make that which was called the picket in the barrack yard after he became Governor.

Did you ever see anything of that kind there before?—Never.

How long was it after the instrument of torture was used in the barrack yard before any instrument of torture was used in the gaol?—That was the first torment I ever saw in my life.

How long after that was it before any instrument of torment was erected in the gaol?—I cannot tell how long it was erected before Luisa was tormented.

Was it a short time before?—Five or six months.

Are you quite sure it was after Colonel Picton became Governor? —Yes; I was the person he ordered to go to the gaoler-man to desire him to inflict the torture upon a black man of the picket guard.

Colonel Picton said to the gaoler, 'Go you and fetch the black man of the picket guard to be put upon the torture;' that was the first instance of torture that you ever heard of in Trinidad?—Yes.

And you are quite certain that was the first instrument of torture you ever saw or heard of in Trinidad?—Quite sure, I never saw or heard of any in this place before.

And none in the gaol?—No, I went there frequently.

You were an officer of justice?—Yes.

And according to your belief it was erected about five or six months before Luisa was tortured?—Yes, about five or six months.

You have told us she remained about eight months. Was she ever brought to trial?—Yes. She was brought to what you call here

the Parliament—(*after some hesitation*) the justices, and they said, 'Luisa, what did you do with the money?'
Carlos and Luisa were both discharged afterwards?—Yes.
Rafael Chando cross-examined by Mr. Lawes.
When was Carlos discharged?—At the time that the judge ordered him to be discharged, upon payment of the money.
What became of him afterwards?—He went to a place called Margarita.
He was sent out of the island, was not he?—Yes.
Mr. Garrow. By Begorrat?—I cannot tell you whether by Mr. Begorrat or Colonel Picton.
Juan Montes sworn. Examined by Mr. Harrison.
Can you understand what I say in English?—Very little.
Are you acquainted with the handwriting of Colonel Picton?—Yes.
Look, at that (*showing him a book*), is that his handwriting?—It is.
Is the signature only his handwriting, or the writing before it?—It is all his handwriting.
(*It was read*) Appliquez la question à Louisa Calderon. Thomas Picton.
Mr. Garrow. That is, apply the torture to Louisa Calderon. Thomas Picton.
Mr. Dallas. My lord, it appearing clearly, whether it be written in Spanish or in French, that it is an answer to something, I submit to your lordship, that we are entitled to have that read to which this is an answer.
Mr. Garrow. I do not take this to be an answer, I take it to be an order; the words purport to be an order, not that I am at all anxious about it.
Lord Ellenborough. It is certainly written in consequence of some application to the defendant, which I suppose that paper contains, for liberty to inflict the torture; if it does, we should have the whole before us.
Mr. Dallas. All I either wish or desire is, to have that representation laid before the Court which was made to Colonel Picton, and to which what has been already read is an answer.
Mr. Garrow. The only question here is, whether my learned friend can, in the course of my case, read that to which this is supposed to be either an answer or an order. It is a matter of

very little importance to me; but when I find a paper, the whole of which is written by Colonel Picton, I think I am entitled to read it: but I have no difficulty in stating, that there is a representation of Mr. Begorrat, in which he says he has no power to inflict torture, without the consent of the Governor. He asks leave to inflict a slight torture, and then comes the order for the torture. I have no objection to Mr. Begorrat's representation being read, if your lordship thinks it proper.

Lord Ellenborough. It is impossible to understand it without.

Mr. Garrow. Does not your lordship think it must be received as their evidence, and not mine?

Lord Ellenborough. No.

Mr. Lawes. Be so good as read the preceding act of Mr. Begorrat.

Mr. Garrow. It is, perhaps, unnecessary to caution such a jury as this, that the representation of Mr. Begorrat proves no fact; it is only his *representation*.

Mr. Lowten reads it.

Mr. Garrow. I will thank you to read a little further, and his lordship will see Mr. Begorrat's account of the manner in which he executed this order.

Mr. Lowten reads it.

Lord Ellenborough. Does it appear, that this subsequent matter was known to Colonel Picton?

Mr. Dallas. No, my lord, not at all.

Lord Ellenborough. All that is attested as notified to him is evidence against him.

Mr. Harrison resumed the examination of Juan Montes.

How long have you known the island of Trinidad?—Since 1793.

In what capacity?—In a military capacity, as an assistant to the engineers.

Were you in any legal situation there?—Before the conquest, my capacity was military.

Did you ever know torture applied in that island?—Never.

When was it first introduced? When did you first see or hear of it?—After the conquest, by order of Governor Picton.

How long after?—The first instance of torment was in 1799.

When was it first introduced into the gaol?—Luisa Calderon's was the first that was in the gaol.

The Trial of Thomas Picton

Where was the other instrument of torture that you alluded to before?—In the picket guard-room.

Was it first introduced into the gaol or the guard-room?—The picket guard-room.

By the picket guard-room, you mean the room where the soldiers were upon picket?—It is a guard of soldiers.

How long after that was it introduced into the gaol?—I cannot say positively, I know very well it was in the year 1801.

About two years afterwards?—Pretty near two years.

Mr. Garrow. In order to save time I will state, for my learned friend's consideration, that I have many witnesses to prove, that the instrument of torture was not introduced till after Colonel Picton arrived, and became Governor. If that is not disputed, there will be no occasion to call them; but I have persons of the first respectability to prove it.

Lord Ellenborough. I dare say it is not disputed; if it is, Mr. Dallas will tell you so.

Mr. Dallas. I do not mean to dispute it.

Mr. Garrow. We have alleged that the defendant, was in a civil and military capacity in the island. This order is made by him in that character, and I shall consider the allegation as proved. For your lordship will observe in the proceedings he recognises himself to be Governor, and is addressed as 'His Excellency.' He has taken the character upon himself, as appears upon the face of the proceedings.

This is my case, my lord, on the part of the Crown.

Defence

Mr. Dallas. Gentlemen of the jury; the case on the part of the prosecution has certainly not been, either in statement or in proof, a very long one; and it now becomes my duty to address you in behalf of the defendant General Picton. I can with perfect truth and sincerity assure you, that the situation in which I am placed this day has been by no means a matter of choice;—having ceased to be in the habit of attending this court, it will hardly be supposed that I could have had so much confidence in myself, or so little sensibility for the dearest interests of others, as to have undertaken the defence of my honourable and gallant client upon the present occasion, if the determination had in any degree depended upon *me*. But unfortunately, I have failed to convince General Picton of what every other man would at once have admitted—that my feeble abilities were ill adapted for his defence, and that upon my being withdrawn, the task would have devolved upon a gentleman better qualified in every respect (except in anxiety to serve the defendant to the utmost possible extent) to fulfil it. Such are the circumstances of my present situation: but in declaring them, I hope I shall not be misunderstood. Let it not be supposed, that I mean to insinuate that there are any difficulties *peculiar to the case* which would have deterred me from undertaking the defence of the honourable person whom I represent. Neither let it be imagined, that I feel at all discouraged by any degree of unpopularity which may be supposed to attach to the cause I shall maintain. These are disadvantages which I hope in common with every gentleman at the bar, I can boldly and manfully encounter. What I mean to say is, that when I consider how much General Picton has at stake upon this occasion, I would, if possible, have spared myself the anxiety which the conduct of his defence must necessarily engender in the mind of any man—even of such of my learned friends as are most accustomed to address juries in this place—and which anxiety is increased by the consciousness of my not having those qualifications which constant practice and experience in this court must necessarily bestow.

I agree with my learned friend, that the case now before you is novel and extraordinary: nor do I mean to deny, that in whatever light it is considered, whether as affecting the public or the individual under accusation, it is of the greatest magnitude. On the one hand, nothing can be of more importance to the public than that extensive powers, entrusted to a representative of our Sovereign for the purposes of justice, should not be converted into engines of malice and oppression. On the other, it is of the deepest concern to the gentleman whose conduct is arraigned, that, if it should appear upon the evidence that he has done no more than what a faithful discharge of his duty required, he should not be consigned to ruin, and—what to a mind like his is infinitely worse than ruin—dishonour, by the verdict which you shall deliver—a verdict which, (to repeat the concession made by my learned friend in his opening speech) nothing ought to induce you to pronounce, unless the facts proved in evidence should reluctantly force it from you.

It is impossible for me, gentlemen, rising to address you upon a subject so momentous, not to feel myself, even at the outset, surrounded and pressed upon by difficulties which, for the sake of impartial justice, I would fain if possible remove. I cannot but have felt that a case of this nature, stated as it has been, and supported as it has been by the exhibition of prints and drawings, exposed to the view of every person in court, and assisted by a species of acting which I at least have for the first time witnessed in a criminal prosecution—I say I cannot but have felt that such a case, founded upon a charge of torture, and so stated and supported, must in its progress have created powerful sensations, even in men determined to keep their minds as indifferent and impartial as possible— sensations very unfavourable to the party for whom I appear.

Lord Ellenborough. I would not permit the drawings to be shown to the jury, until I had your consent.

Mr. Dallas. My lord, I acknowledge it; and perhaps therefore I am not correct in now adverting to any advantage that may have been taken of such a concession.

Gentlemen, I was proceeding to state, that living as we do in a country where that law which has been truly called the perfection of reason is, as far as human circumstances will admit, most perfectly administered, and the chief characteristics of which are mildness and humanity, it is impossible not to feel how difficult it must be to win the mind, if I may so express myself, to the contemplation of a different state of things, and to a conviction that a system diametrically opposite to that pursued in this country may be absolutely necessary in a distant clime and in different circumstances, and may consequently be strictly defensible in this court. Difficult, however, as the task must unquestionably be, I am fully persuaded, gentlemen, that with whatever feelings you may have been impressed from the manner in which this cause has been conducted, and from the exhibitions which you have beheld, you will endeavour to divest yourselves of their influence; and that, with impartial and unprejudiced minds, attending only to the facts that shall have been proved, and applying to those facts the legal principles which I shall lay down, and which will be confirmed by the sanction of his lordship, you will ultimately pronounce a calm and dispassionate verdict.

Before I proceed to consider the charge in this particular case, and which, with great deference to my learned friend, I must say will require a more correct examination than he has thought fit to bestow upon it, I will shortly state what I conceive to be in point of fact the sum and substance of the case even as it has been disclosed to you by the evidence adduced in support of the prosecution.

It appears, that some time previous to the year 1801 General Picton had been appointed Governor of the island of Trinidad, and that as such he was invested not only with the supreme military but also with the supreme civil authority of that settlement. It is now admitted, that in the month of December in that year, a robbery had been committed in the dwelling-house of a man named Pedro Ruiz; that at the time when the robbery was committed, the person who has this day appeared as a witness before you was living as a domestic in the house of Ruiz, and in a state of prostitution with him; that the robbery was to a very considerable extent; and that it was committed by Carlos Gonzalez, a man with whom the witness Luisa Calderon was indulging herself in a criminal intercourse during the time she was living with Pedro Ruiz as his mistress. This robbery would have been, by the laws of England, a capital felony; and if Luisa Calderon was privy to and an accomplice in the offence committed by Carlos Gonzalez, even according to the mild and merciful law of this country, they both would have forfeited their lives. For it is hardly necessary to remind you, that if a domestic servant becomes a party to a robbery of this description, it is a case the most painful to an English judge, for it is one in which he can never interpose in behalf of the offender, the law is invariably suffered to take its course, and the crime is expiated by an ignominious death. Such are the facts which have been disclosed to you by the statement of my learned friend; they are in part substantiated by the evidence which he himself has brought forward, and will be fully developed by that which it will be my duty to adduce.

The Trial of Thomas Picton

Under these peculiar circumstances, information was laid before General Picton at the Government House, in consequence of which this young woman was brought before him, and the conversation took place to which she has this day deposed. You will observe then, gentlemen, that all that General Picton did in the first instance, on receiving this information of a capital offence having been committed—and committed under circumstances which, to adopt an expression of Mr. Garrow's, involved my learned friend's own witness in a considerable degree of suspicion of being an accessory to the crime—was to dismiss from himself all consideration of the subject, and to refer the investigation to the ordinary and competent tribunal of the colony. It appears, that the defendant ordered all the parties accused—not only this young woman whom it is now alleged that he had a *particular* desire to oppress, but also her mother, Carlos Gonzalez, and another person—to be committed to prison for the purpose of being examined by Mr. Begorrat, whom my learned friend chooses to represent as a justice of the peace, but whose powers and authority were of a very different description. Admitting however, for argument's sake, that his office corresponded with that of our justice of the peace, the evidence adduced by the present prosecutrix merely proves, that strong suspicions having arisen that she had been guilty of a capital felony, she was committed to prison by General Picton, to undergo an examination before a justice of the peace, in order to ascertain if possible, how far she was implicated in the transaction.

Such is the history of these proceedings, according to the evidence which my learned friend has laid before you; and you will permit me to pause here for a moment, that I may call your attention to a distinction which strikes my mind at least as being very material, and which I think will hereafter be found to have most important bearings upon all parts of the case. This charge is not instituted against General Picton and Mr. Begorrat for a conspiracy to accuse a person of a capital felony whom they knew to be innocent, in order to subject that person to the imprisonment and torture which afterwards took place; but instead of thus attacking the source of the affair it breaks in, if I may so express myself, upon the full tide and current of it, and imputes to the defendant as an act of great criminality that which took place during the progress of an inquiry into a highly penal charge, *the first step not having been taken by himself*.

Under the circumstances which I have described, reference was made to Mr. Begorrat, who then held the situation of *alcalde* or criminal judge; and it appears even in this stage of the case, and from the evidence given on the part of the prosecution, that the torture, such as it was, was not applied until every means had been in vain resorted to by Mr. Begorrat to avoid it—this torture which it is now the object of my learned friend to represent to you that General Picton was, from the mere love of oppression, so desirous of inflicting upon the young female who has appeared before you. Witness after witness had been called, day after day had been consumed in the examination of them, and it was only after repeated prevarications on the part of Luisa Calderon, and after the suspicions of the judge had been confirmed, that Mr. Begorrat in the last instance made that representation and application to the Governor, which you have this day heard; and you will there find, that it was after eleven days investigation, in the course of which a great number of witnesses were examined, that this memorial was laid before the proper tribunal.

Here, gentlemen, in this second stage of the proceedings, it is important to remark that the application of torture appears most clearly not to have originated with General Picton. He merely received the representation of the ordinary criminal judge, before whom the inquiry had been conducted, and who was sworn to perform the duties of his office according to the laws of Spain, as established in Trinidad; that representation stating, that it would be proper to inflict a slight torture, he acquiesced in the suggestion and suffered the law to take its course. It is most material that you should bear this in mind; because when we are considering a criminal charge the essence of which is (as it was avowed by my learned friend in his opening speech) the allegation of malice —of a desire on the part of General Picton to oppress the particular individual, it is highly necessary to investigate every part of the case that we may discover the commencement of this malice, from which all the subsequent proceedings are stated to have sprung, and to which consequently they must be traced. It is most extraordinary to impute malice to General Picton, when it appears that instead of the torture having originated with him, or any order having been given by him in the first instance, he never entertained a thought of the kind, he never issued any order or took any step until it was suggested to him in the regular and ordinary course by the judge, as fit and expedient. Whether it was fit and expedient is a different consideration, but when you are to decide upon the motives of the defendant, it is important to bear in mind that all he did in the first instance, was, upon a reasonable suspicion of guilt, to commit for examination; and in the next instance, merely to confirm a suggestion made to him as Governor by the ordinary criminal judge, before whom the affair had been investigated in the court below.

* * *

Let it not be taken for granted, that the defendant must be found guilty of the offence imputed to him by the indictment, because he would have been deemed criminal if the law of England had been the rule by which he was to be guided. You, gentlemen, well know, that no two systems of jurisprudence can be more opposite, than the law of our West Indian colonies and that of the mother country. Many instances might be adduced but I will only call your attention to one in illustration of my position. I will suppose, that a gentleman, after having passed many years of his life in the island of St. Vincent's, and having there held certain magisterial situations should, upon his arrival in England, be taken into custody, on a charge of maiming and disfiguring a particular individual during his residence in St. Vincent's. This, according to our law, would amount to felony. I will further suppose, that in support of such a prosecution, a witness should appear in this court, not in the circumstances in which Luisa Calderon has presented herself before you, for she has sustained no permanent injury, but horribly maimed and disfigured, with his nose slit and his right hand amputated, and should tell you on his oath, that this was inflicted by order of the defendant, for no other reason, than that he had obstructed and resisted a constable, who was taking him to be flogged for having lifted his hand against some cruel taskmaster. Nay, I will go further, and suppose, that instead of being thus maimed and disfigured, the person had actually suffered an ignominious death at the place of public execution; and, that the indictment had charged the foul crime of murder—would not every Briton, possessing feelings and principles founded upon the law of his country, on hearing, that the punishment of death had been inflicted upon a man for raising his hand against a constable, instantly and emphatically exclaim, 'The man who hath done this thing shall surely die!' But, when the defence should be heard, it would be found fully adequate to the occasion. The magistrate's justification would instantly be admitted, and his lordship would direct an aquittal as soon as the law of the island, which I will now read, had been referred to. It is this:

Here Mr. Dallas read the law of the island of St. Vincent's, which he had cited and which imposed the punishments mentioned by him, at the discretion of two magistrates, upon any slave who should be guilty of the offence described by the learned counsel.

What is this? Not the law of Spain, but the law of an English colony, and which was passed in that colony, upon a petition to His Majesty at home. By the English law therefore, as applicable to one of our own settlements in the West Indies, any two justices of the peace, to whose office my learned friend has thought fit to assimilate that of Mr. Begorrat, may, at their own discretion, and without the intervention of a jury, for such an offence as I have described, cause a fellow-creature to be disfigured and maimed, or even consign him instantly to the scaffold.

Can the two cases be compared? Luisa Calderon, the present prosecutrix, has undergone a punishment which is not uncommon in this country; but, were this otherwise, would any man, acting upon the feelings of natural justice, tell me that in point of enormity any comparison can be instituted between the case of that young woman who is in as full possession of health as she was at any time before the infliction of the torture—and that of a person, who with his face so disfigured as to have lost the character of humanity, and with his body deprived of its most valuable member, should prosecute an English magistrate of the English island of St. Vincent's, for

The Trial of Thomas Picton

proceeding according to the colonial law of England? And yet, however it might shock our feelings, however repulsive it might be to our sense of natural justice, however we might regret for the honour of human nature, that such a law would exist in any country of the earth, still the law being in force, it would be your bounden duty in such a case, not to be misled by your feelings, or to follow the law of England; but to apply the law of the particular place to the facts under your consideration, and to return a verdict of not guilty. It is, therefore, most important to consider the place where the transaction, which is the foundation of these proceedings, occurred; you have been already apprised, that the island of Trinidad was the scene of action, and I shall for the present assume, that a different system of jurisprudence exists there from that which is established in Great Britain.

* * *

First, I shall contend, that General Picton is entitled to your verdict, because by the Spanish code which he was bound to administer, the infliction of torture in this particular instance was lawful. If I substantiate this, my case is made out; the unlawfulness of the torture is charged in every count of the indictment.

Secondly (for impregnable as I know my first position to be, I shall not confine my line of defence to that alone), I shall submit to you that, as by this indictment the infliction of the torture is charged not only to have been unlawful, but also to have been malicious and without any reasonable or probable cause, even supposing, for the sake of argument, that the act was unlawful, it was not malicious, and that you must, therefore, acquit the defendant.

Lord Ellenborough. Everything against law is presumed to be malicious.

Mr. Dallas. Whether the existence of malice and the want of reasonable or probable cause be a question of fact, or a legal inference, General Picton is entitled to his acquittal.

Thirdly, gentlemen, under my lord's correction, I assert, that although you should be of opinion (for I have considered this subject in every possible point of view), that the infliction of torture was inconsistent with the law of Spain, still if it should appear to you, that General Picton had been misinformed as to this, and had been led to believe that the proceeding was strictly legal, this case resolves itself into one of mere error of judgment, for which no criminal responsibility attaches upon my client; and that, therefore, the indictment cannot be sustained.

Upon all of these grounds, whether considered separately or collectively, you must pronounce a verdict of not guilty.

* * *

You, gentlemen of the jury, have listened to the eloquent appeal of my friend Mr. Garrow—always animated, always ardent, always impressive—delivered in the most emphatic language that this great master of declamation could employ. You have moreover, beheld drawings and engravings—

Lord Ellenborough. That you must attribute to me, or perhaps to yourself, for I distinctly asked you whether you would consent to their exhibition, and on your concurring, I cautioned the jury not to suffer their minds to be inflamed, but simply to look at the representation of the position of the prosecutrix, in order to understand the testimony of the witness. I should be very sorry to permit the case to go to them under any improper impression.

Mr. Dallas. If your lordship had heard the conclusion of my sentence, you would have seen that I did not mean to cast any imputation upon the manner in which the prosecution has been conducted.

Gentlemen, we have heard the statement of my learned friend, and we have seen drawings, the display of which I hope for the honour of justice has been confined to this court; I hope that they have not been exhibited elsewhere to influence the judgment and inflame the passions of the public, and, as a part of that public, of you who sit in judgment on the defendant. I do not mean for a moment to insinuate, that my learned friend would lend himself to such a base contrivance; he is the last man in the world to pursue conduct so dishonourable. In addition to the evidence of the witnesses, a sort of acting has been introduced by the gentleman upon the floor (*Rafael Chando*); but I do not complain of this. I consented to it at the time; I wished the case to be presented to you in any manner which to my learned friend might seem advisable, and it would be most unreasonable that, having given my consent, I should now make it a subject of complaint. My only object was that you might have every opportunity of forming a correct notion of the sort of punishment inflicted upon this young woman. And what was it? My learned friend has said there is a process (namely picketing) in this country very similar to it in many respects, but different from it in one, and he treats you with a sort of pun, telling you, that the punishment inflicted in this case should be called *pictoning* and not *picketing*. We have had no drawing of the picket, and have not seen any theatrical exhibition of that process by the gentleman upon the floor, and therefore I do not understand in what my learned friend's distinction consists. But I have no hesitation in declaring, that if you look into any dictionary of Arts and Sciences, or any book in which the term is defined, you will find the description of the picket to correspond exactly with the punishment inflicted upon Luisa Calderon.

['The picket was another corporal punishment, chiefly used by the cavalry and artillery, and in the former often inflicted by the order of the commanding officer, without the sentence of a court martial. The mode of inflicting it was thus: a long post being driven into the ground, the delinquent was ordered to mount a stool near it, when his right hand was fastened to a hook in the post by a noose round his wrist, drawn up as high as it could be stretched; a stump, the height of the stool, with its end cut to a round and blunt point, was then driven into the ground near the post before-mentioned, and the stool being taken away the bare heel of the sufferer was made to rest on this stump, which, though it did not break the skin, put him to great torture; the only means of mitigation was, by resting his weight on his wrist, the pain of which soon became intolerable. Soldiers were frequently sentenced to stand on the picket for a quarter of an hour. This, like the riding of the wooden horse, has been for some time left off, it having lamed and ruptured many soldiers.'—Grose's *Military Antiquities*, 1812, vol. 2, p. 104.][5]

We see then that in this land of liberty, in this land which is proverbial for the humanity of its laws, the punishment of the picket prevails. And upon whom is it inflicted? Upon those brave men who shed their best blood, and risk their lives in the service and for the defence of their country. In the case of Luisa Calderon, who, if she had been convicted, would by the law of England have been doomed to suffer death, all that General Picton did was to order the infliction of this English punishment that the truth might be discovered; and this he did at the suggestion of the magistrate, who was bound to inquire into the nature and circumstances of the offence in the first instance. Now, was this proceeding consonant or not to the law of Spain? My learned friend has stated, and I readily agree with him, that torture is unknown in England; he has referred to a book with which we are all acquainted, and (notwithstanding some few defects) an abler treatise never proceeded from the pen of man.

[*Dallas then produced evidence for the legality of torture under Spanish law.*][6]

In the *Curia Philippica*, fol. 229, No. 2, it is laid down that 'The *question*, or torment, is to be applied for confirmation or proof, there not being sufficient.' In fol. 229, No. 4, it is stated, that 'In the same crimes for which the *question* is applicable to the delinquent, in the same it is applicable to the witness who varies and prevaricates in his evidence, or who denies the truth, or who refuses to declare it, there being a presumption that he knows it; not being of those persons to whom the torment cannot be applied, according to the law *de Partida*, and its Gregorian glossary.

[Persons exempted: A minor under fourteen, an old decrepit person, a pregnant woman, a woman forty days after parturition, and who suckles, a priest, soldier, knight, king's councillor, or magistrate.]

And for the same crimes in which the torment is applicable to the delinquent, in case an evidence of vile character and bad morals is admitted, he is to testify under torment, otherwise his evidence is of no validity.' Citing *Law de Partida*.

And in fol. 230, No. 12, 'the torment that may be ordered

to the delinquent for the crime, may also be ordered to force
a declaration from his accomplice (if there be appearance or
presumption that he had any) in crimes of religion, treason,
that against nature, coining, theft, &c. as well as in all others
which cannot be committed without accomplices, in all which
those who are so may be admitted as evidences.'—Citing
Antonio Gomes.

In another book, entitled *Elizondo: Practica Universal Foranse
Juicio Criminal,* fol. 277, No. 12, vol. 1, it is said, that
'Appearances to authorise the application of the *question,* should
be weighty, apparent, urgent, and probable; and not light,
doubtful, and equivocal; *except* in hidden crimes, and difficult
of proof, such as *theft,* sodomy, crimes committed at night,
coining, &c. in which the slightest are sufficient to authorise a
departure from the ordinary forms of law, and the receiving of
such proof as can be met with.' And in the same treatise,
fol. 275, No. 5, slight appearances are held to be sufficient to
authorise the *question* against persons entrusted with the care of
property in cases of theft. And you will remember that Luisa
Calderon was the housekeeper of the person robbed, and had
the charge of his property.

All these authorities derived from Spanish law-books, which
have been long of high reputation, and in general use in the
colonial courts, tend directly to the establishment of General
Picton's defence. And let us for a moment consider the
advantages resulting to my client from such support. This is
not an exposition of the law of Spain by the *viva voce* testimony
of men ignorant of its principles or unacquainted with its
practice, and which might be adapted to any particular
occasion. These venerable authorities are removed from all
possibility of corruption. They declare the ancient established
laws of the land, and cannot give a false representation in
order to serve the turn of any particular person; they
pronounce before you the same unchanged and unchangeable
sentiments which they uttered when they first appeared before
the world.

Thus, whether we advert to the parole evidence of the
witnesses who have been called, or to the documentary proofs
which are contained in the return to the mandamus and in the
volumes now before me, we shall find it unquestionably and

The Trial of Thomas Picton

universally laid down, that in such a case as that of Luisa Calderon, the person invested with the supreme civil and military authority in Trinidad, and sworn to administer the Spanish law, was fully justified in the infliction of the torture.

But not to detain you, gentlemen, by going through these authorities one by one—

Lord Ellenborough. Have you any precedents as to the *degree* of torture, and the mode of inflicting it?

Mr. Dallas. There is a book of forms, which I shall produce; but the species of torture is not fixed by law, but is left to the discretion of the judge.

Lord Ellenborough. Should not the judge have *exercised* that discretion? I am sorry to interrupt you, but I do so in order to draw your attention to what may constitute the most important difficulty.

Mr. Dallas. I am much obliged to your lordship, because I wish to meet fairly every difficulty that can be started. I shall therefore address myself to what your lordship has pointed out.

With respect to the different species of torture, I shall beg your lordship's attention to this passage in the *Curia Philippica, Juicio Criminal*, fol. 230, No. 13, 'The species of torment and the quality is not determined by the law, but left to the arbitrement of the judge, according to the complexion of the delinquent, the crime, and its appearances; though he should not make use of new torments, but the usual ones, such as dropping of water, small cords and pulleys, and of that nature.'

It is laid down in the same book, that 'There are to be present at the torment only the judge, *escrivano*, executioner, and person tormented. And it is to be applied in a secret place, without any other person being present, or in hearing.' *Law de Partida.*

[*Curia Philippica, Juicio Criminal*, fol. 231, No. 6.]

And that is the way in which the punishment appears to have been applied in the case of Luisa Calderon.

Lord Ellenborough. Does not this mean the judge by whose arbitrement the torture was inflicted?

Mr. Dallas. With great deference to your lordship, I apprehend not. But if it were so, that will only make way for a new line of argument, which I shall hereafter pursue.

The Trial of Thomas Picton

Lord Ellenborough. My interposition arises only from an anxious wish that no part of the case may escape you.

Mr. Dallas. As to the persons present, the words of the law of Spain, as laid down in the authorities I have quoted, are satisfied; the judge, the *escrivano*, and the executioner were present. The question is, whether the judge, who must be present at the infliction, ought or ought not to be the judge who has the power of appealing to a superior authority. Now the passage before us relates to the common cases in which there is no power of appeal; in the present case the inferior judge could not carry any punishment into execution without the authority of General Picton. Supposing the torture to be legal, it was only requisite that he should apply to the Governor for permission to inflict it; and having obtained his permission, the criminal judge was the person who should be present at the infliction, and he was present in the case before us. Such is the law of Spain.

* * *

Gentlemen, the case, as I now understand it, is confined to the questions, whether torture was in this instance applicable by the law of Spain; and whether, supposing General Picton to have exceeded his authority and to have acted unlawfully and erroneously, the situation in which he stood will not furnish a complete answer to the charges of this indictment? I contend, with submission to his lordship, that it will, upon these grounds. You will find from the evidence which I shall produce, that General Picton was the supreme criminal judge; and it has already been proved, that what he did upon the particular occasion was done in the regular course of judicial inquiry. An information is laid before the supreme criminal judge, who, by the law of Trinidad, is bound to institute an inquiry, which inquiry is referred to the ordinary and competent tribunal, and upon the report and suggestion of that tribunal (upon which he, as judge, is bound to proceed), he orders the infliction of the torture. The question is not whether he was, technically speaking, a judge; but whether he was clothed with that judicial authority which brings him within the protection of the law. I do not mean to say, that he was formally invested with the robes of office, and seated upon the bench of justice; but I contend, that he possessed all the powers necessary to give him that protection to which by the law of England a judge is entitled, while exercising his judicial functions.

* * *

It is laid down, 'that no one is liable to any prosecution whatsoever, in respect of any verdict given by him in a criminal matter, either upon a grand or petit jury.'

[William Hawkins, *A Treatise of the Pleas of the Crown*, Bk.I, ch. 5, section 5.]

The law of England, therefore, with respect to persons in your situation, gentlemen of the jury, is this; if you were to proceed not merely erroneously, but even maliciously, no indictment could be maintained against any one of you, for it would be a sufficient answer for such person to say, 'I acted maliciously, but when I did so, I was serving as a juryman;' no juryman for anything done by him as such, even although he has acted maliciously, is subject to an indictment.

Now, gentlemen, what says the law of England, with respect to persons in the situation which General Picton held at the time of the transaction in question? In the same book to which I have already referred, you will find it laid down, that 'as the law has exempted jurors from the danger of incurring any punishment in respect of their verdict in criminal causes, it hath also freed the judges of all courts of record from all prosecutions whatsoever, except in the Parliament, for anything done by them openly in such courts as judges.'

[Hawkins, *Pleas of the Crown*, Bk. I, ch. 5, section 6.]

I therefore submit—

Lord Ellenborough. I take the distinction to be this:- If a judge, in the ordinary exercise of his jurisdiction commit an error, he cannot be prosecuted; but if he commit an error while acting out of such jurisdiction, he is not protected.

Mr. Dallas. I am well aware of the necessary and important distinction which his lordship has pointed out. Where a juror or a judge acts maliciously, but within his jurisdiction, he will be protected, and no action or indictment will lie. Such is the difference between those who perform public functions, and private individuals. But even with respect to the question of jurisdiction, I can state some very strong passages from Lord Hale, where the whole doctrine is collected.

Lord Ellenborough. Some of these points are highly important, and make it very proper that this case should be turned into a special verdict.[7]

Mr. Garrow. We have not the smallest objection, my lord.

Lord Ellenborough. I suppose, Mr. Dallas, you will be relieved from the difficulties of *proving* the Spanish law, which might otherwise embarrass you. To prove the written law of any nation, a copy of that law should be produced. If I were sitting at Guildhall, and proof of foreign commercial regulations were necessary I should require an authenticated copy of those regulations.

Mr. Garrow. I should be ashamed if in a public prosecution of such importance, I did not immediately fall in with your lordship's suggestion. I trust that I know what your lordship means, and I will not object to their proving that it is written in some Spanish law book. I should be extremely sorry to obtain a verdict in a case where anything can be supposed to be shut out.

Lord Ellenborough. If a book of this sort is produced, stating the law of Spain in such a manner that Mr. Garrow thinks it reasonably made out to be the law of Spain, there would be no difficulty in having it stated in the special verdict so to be.

Mr. Garrow. Suppose some document should by and by be produced, which your lordship would not in strictness receive, yet if there be reasonable evidence of its containing a correct representation of the law, I shall consent to its being stated in the special verdict that such is the law of Spain. I take that to be what your lordship means.

Lord Ellenborough. I should be disposed to go still farther. The text writers furnish us with their statement of the law, and that would certainly be good evidence upon the same principle which renders histories admissible. There is a case in which the history of the Turkish empire by Cantemir was received by the House of Lords, and received after some discussion. I shall therefore receive any book that purports to be a history of the common law of Spain. Mr. Garrow says he will not take a formal objection; you have the facts upon the evidence already given; I will now take down your evidence, and if there be any question of fact, I will put that fact to the jury, and you may frame the special verdict.

Mr. Garrow. It will still be open to me to contend, that whatever the law of Spain may be, it is no defence to General Picton. I say he was not under the law of Spain at all.

Lord Ellenborough. Then it will be open to you to contend upon that point to such extent as your case will admit.

Mr. Dallas. Gentlemen of the jury, in consequence of the conversation which has taken place within the last five minutes, it will not be necessary for me to trouble you any farther. I understand, that the facts of the case are to be reduced to a special verdict; and whether there is any justification in point of *law* will be the subject of discussion hereafter.

My lord, we shall first put in the instructions from Sir Ralph Abercromby to General Picton.

Lord Ellenborough. You take it up with the capitulation of the island?

Mr Dallas. We will take it up, if your lordship pleases, with the capitulation. We have the *Gazette* in which the capitulation is contained; after which we shall give in evidence, General Abercromby's instructions, General Picton's commission, then His Majesty's instructions, and so on.

Evidence for the Defendant

The articles of capitulation read from the London Gazette *of 27th March 1797, as follows:*

'Articles of Capitulation for the surrender of the island of Trinidad, between His Excellency Sir Ralph Abercromby, K.B. Commander-in-Chief of His Britannic Majesty's land forces; His Excellency Henry Harvey, Esq. Rear Admiral of the Red, and Commander-in-Chief of his Britannic Majesty's ships and vessels of war: and His Excellency Don Josef Maria Chacon, Knight of the Order of Calatrava, Brigadier of the Royal Navy, Governor and Commander-in-Chief of the island of Trinidad and its dependencies, Inspector General of the troops of his garrison, &c. &c.

'Art. 1.—The officers and troops of His Catholic Majesty and his allies, in the island of Trinidad, are to surrender themselves prisoners of war, and are to deliver up the territory, forts, buildings, arms, ammunition, money, effects, plans, and stores, with exact inventories thereof, belonging to His Catholic Majesty; and they are thereby transferred to His Britannic Majesty, in the same manner and possession as has been held heretofore by His said Catholic Majesty.

'2.—The troops of His Catholic Majesty are to march out with the honours of war, and to lay down their arms at the distance of three hundred paces from the forts they occupy, at five o'clock this evening, the eighteenth of February.

'3.—All the officers and troops aforesaid of His Catholic Majesty, are allowed to keep their private effects, and the officers are allowed to wear their swords.

'4.—Rear Admiral Don Sebastian Rieuz di Apodaca, being on shore in the island, after having burnt and abandoned his ships, he with the officers and men of the squadron, under his command, are included in this capitulation, under the same terms, as are granted to His Catholic Majesty's troops.

'5.—As soon as the ships can be conveniently provided for the purpose, the prisoners are to be conveyed to Old Spain; they remaining prisoners of war, until exchanged by a cartel between the two nations, or until the peace; it being clearly understood, that they shall not serve against Great Britain or her allies, until exchanged.

'6.—There being some officers, whose private affairs require their presence at different places of the continent of America; such officers are permitted to go upon their parole, to the said places, for six months, more or less, after which period they are to return to Europe. But as the number receiving this indulgence must be limited, His Excellency Don Chacon, will [give] previously to the British commanders, a list of their names, rank, and places they are going to.

'7.—The officers of the royal administration, upon the delivery of the stores with which they are charged, to such officers as may be appointed by the British commanders, will receive receipts, according to the custom in like cases, from the officers so appointed to receive the stores.

'8.—All the private property of the inhabitants, as well

The Trial of Thomas Picton

Spaniards as such as may have been naturalized, is preserved to them.

'9.—All public records are to be preserved in such courts or offices as they may be now in; and all contracts or purchases between individuals, which have been done according to the laws of Spain, are to be held binding and valid by the British government.

'10.—The Spanish officers of administration, who are possessed of property in Trinidad, are allowed to remain in the island, they taking the oaths of allegiance to His Britannic Majesty, and they are further allowed, should they please, to sell or dispose of their property, and retire elsewhere.

'11.—The free exercise of their religion is allowed to the inhabitants.

'12.—The free coloured people, who have been acknowledged as such by the laws of Spain, shall be protected in their liberty, persons, and property, like other inhabitants, they taking the oath of allegiance, and demeaning themselves as becomes good and peaceable subjects of His Britannic Majesty.

'13.—The sailors and soldiers of His Catholic Majesty are, from the time of laying down their arms, to be fed by the British Government, leaving the expense to be regulated by the cartel between the two nations.

'14.—The sick of the Spaniard troops will be taken care of, but to be attended and to be under the inspection of their own surgeons.

'15.—All the inhabitants of Trinidad shall, within thirty days from the date hereof, take the oath of allegiance to His Britannic Majesty, to demean themselves quietly and faithfully to the government, upon pain, in case of non-compliance, of being sent away from the island.

> Done at Port d'Espagne, in the Island of Trinidad, the 18th February 1797.
> (Signed)   R. Abercromby.
> Henry Harvey.
> Josef Maria Chacon.'

The following document was then put in and read:

'Head Quarters, Trinidad,
1st March, 1797.

'Sir;—Lieutenant-Colonel Maitland having laid before me your letter and paper, containing notes, relative to the office of chief magistrate, which is continued in you, in consequence of the proclamation issued for the maintenance of the former laws of the colony, until His Majesty's pleasure is known:

'I have the honour to return you such answers as the occasion calls for, directing you, at same time, to consider this letter as your sufficient authority for acting according to the directions contained in it.

'As it has been necessary to remove the person *who filled the office of auditor and assessor*, and that no proper person can be at present found to succeed him, you will in all civil causes, previously convene three of the most intelligent and upright men in the colony, or consult any able lawyer, and having received their opinion upon such points as you want, proceed upon their judgment, and give sentence in the case.

'John Nihell, Esq. appointed *alcalde*, and to execute the duty of auditor, for the time being in Trinidad.

'In criminal causes, an appeal lies to the Governor.

'With respect to the chief magistrate's salary, I am sensible of the propriety, and even necessity of making a just provision on this head: although it is my wish, as much as possible, to reduce fees in general, yet certain limited ones will be authorised. Lieutenant-Colonel Picton will be directed to ascertain the amount of what these may be, and such addition shall be made as is proper. At all events, you may rest assured, that a complete allowance shall be paid you for your service to the public.—I have the honour to be, sir, your most obedient humble servant,

(Signed)   R. Abercromby, L.G.
Commander-in-Chief.'

'TRINIDAD.—I certify the above to be an exact and true copy of a letter received from Sir Ralph Abercromby, the original of which is in my possession.'

John Nihell, Chief Justice.

Sir R. Abercromby's instructions to the defendant were then put in and read as follows:

'Instructions to Lieutenant-Colonel Picton 56th regt., appointed commandant of the Island of Trinidad.

'Art. 1st.—The articles of capitulation, the proclamations which have been made by the commanders in chief, and that moderation which has been the leading feature of the measures adopted towards this colony, are as far as is practicable to guide Lieutenant-Colonel Picton's conduct. At the same time, he must have respect to the mixture of inhabitants, and their characters which call for great circumspection and for the quickest intelligence of what is passing in every quarter.

'He will continue to assure the inhabitants that nothing more is expected from them than the preservation of internal tranquillity, that no one will be called upon to bear arms, or act against an open enemy, unless it be a voluntary act of their own.

'2.—It has been determined to be expedient to maintain the former laws of the colony, used under the Spanish government. This, however, is not to prevent the commandant from removing any officer in the courts, or elsewhere, whose conduct may give general offence to the inhabitants or to himself.

'3.—The force left to garrison the island consists of about
British and foreign artillery.........52
         Queen's........500
         Buffs.......... 150
         Hompesch's.....300
         Soters...........40
              1042

'Of these, the Buffs are only here for a time.

'The staff consists of:
Lieutenant-Colonel Picton, commandant, at 30*s*. per diem, being the same as allowed Brigadier-General Moore, at St. Lucia, until His Majesty's pleasure is known.
Captain Clapham, 14th, his secretary at 10*s*. per diem.
Mr. Lacoste, resident commissary.
Mr. Collin, assistant to the deputy paymaster of the forces.

Lieutenant Collins, 53rd regt. assistant in the quarter-master general's department, who is to do all duties in the barrack department, and 2 m.g.s. [*Quarter-master General's staff.*] Captain Boland, 38th, town major at 5*s.*—town serjeant at 1*s.*—a mate of the general hospital.

Mr. Diggins, who came as a guide is to be employed in any way in which he can be most useful; to be allowed 5*s.* per day, a ration for himself, and a forage for a horse.

'4.—The Commander-in-Chief leaves his warrant to Lieutenant-Colonel Picton, for convening general courts martial, including the authority to appoint a deputy judge advocate, *pro tempore.*

'5.—*Defence of the Island.* It is probable, that this colony will remain undisturbed; as there is no reason to apprehend an attack from any quarter, but from Old Spain. In the event of an armament appearing, Lieutenant-Colonel Picton must be active, to make the best observations possible of their strength and intention. Sending off as soon as possible, a swift-sailing vessel, with an account thereof to the Commander-in-Chief; and if he can, a second, lest the first should be captured. He must do all in his power to oppose a landing; and to resist the progress of the enemy when landed. From the nature of the Spanish troops, great expectation may be formed of success, even against very superior numbers by an enterprising conduct; when their progress can be no longer opposed, he must take the best position he can, and endeavour to protract the siege, until the time when he may calculate upon being relieved. Having done all that his own judgment points out to be the duty of an officer upon such an occasion, he must make the best capitulation he can.

'6.—Returns of the garrison are to be transmitted on the 1st of every month, to the Adjutant-General. If no direct opportunity offers, they must be sent *via* Grenada, as the safest and speediest channel.

'7.—Lieutenant-Colonel Picton will avail himself of every safe conveyance to report the position of affairs to the Commander-in-Chief.

'8.—A fast-sailing vessel will be left to be at the orders of Lieutenant-Colonel Picton, to be dispatched, should any important intelligence or event require it.

'9.—Lieutenant-Colonel Picton will make it his study to keep upon good terms with the commanding officer of the Royal Navy upon this station, and with the Royal Navy in general. This is a matter of consequence.

'10.—Constant vigilance must be preserved at all the posts. The order and cleanliness of the troops cannot be too much attended to.

'11.—The custom-house has been established; copies of the Commander-in-Chief's instructions to the superintendent are here given. The commandant is required to know, from time to time, that no fees, in any shape, are taken which are not authorised.

'12.—In commercial maritime cases, the commandant will summon assessors from the most intelligent merchants unconcerned in the matter, to assist him in the award or sentence he may give. The proceedings in all these cases to be preserved in writing.

'13.—Lieutenant-Colonel Picton is authorised to make small disbursements for secret services; to reward people for bringing intelligence, or for any particular instances of service rendered; it is evident that he must be discreet in the use of this power. The reward must be proportioned to the rank of the person, and the service done.

Head Quarters, Trinidad.
1st March, 1797.
R. Abercromby, L.G.'

Lord Ellenborough. You should show that the law of Spain prevailed in the colony prior to the capitulation.

Mr. Garrow. Not the law of Old Spain, but a code applicable to these settlements, relaxing very much the severity of the law of Old Spain.

Lord Ellenborough. You have that code to refer to?

Mr. Garrow. I cannot admit generally, that the law of Old Spain obtained. I may admit that the law of Old Spain obtained under certain qualifications.

Lord Ellenborough. But then it is incumbent upon you to produce those qualifications.

Mr. Garrow. Whenever they show that the law of Spain obtained, it will be shown to have existed under certain qualifications.

The Trial of Thomas Picton

For example, speaking generally, we should say Jamaica is governed by the law of England; but it would not be accurate to assert that the two islands are governed by the *same* laws. In like manner, in order to encourage cultivation, there was a particular code of laws applicable to Trinidad, which were much milder than those of Old Spain.

Lord Ellenborough. You mean that the people were subjects of the King of Spain, and governed by the general law of Spain, except where that law was altered by the particular code applicable to Trinidad.

Mr. Lawes. We know of no particular code framed for the island of Trinidad, or for any of the colonial dependencies of Spain, and therefore must resort to the laws of the mother country.

Lord Ellenborough. There can be no doubt of their liability to the laws of Old Spain, and that they were governed by those laws, unless some other code is shown. It is said, that there is some qualification of the law of Spain, but it is incumbent upon the prosecutor to show that; I dare say there will be parole evidence of it. You will give such evidence as you think proper. Some gentleman's name was mentioned, I think Mr. Gloster.

Mr. Dallas. Unfortunately, my lord, Mr. Gloster went to the island long after the capitulation. The evidence we offer is, that Trinidad was a Spanish colony, and therefore governed by the Spanish law. I do not know of any such law as that to which my learned friend has alluded, nor have I seen anything like it.

Lord Ellenborough. It lies with you in the first instance to give some evidence as to the law.

[*The Crown claimed that Spanish colonial law was milder than that of Spain but Ellenborough ruled that the Crown must prove any difference between them. Sir Ralph Abercromby's letter appointing John Nihell as chief magistrate of Trinidad (1 March 1797) was then read. It referred to 'the Spanish form of law' having been continued on Abercromby's authority. In a second letter to Nihell of the same date, also read at this point, Abercromby refers to 'the proclamation issued for the maintenance of the former law of the colony, until His Majesty's pleasure is known'.*]

Lord Ellenborough. This does not contain anything more than a

The Trial of Thomas Picton

recognition of the *former law*; he says nothing about the criminal law.

Mr. Garrow. Yes, my lord, that in all criminal cases an appeal lies to the Governor.

Lord Ellenborough. That is, after judgment.

The following extracts from His Majesty's instructions to General Picton, dated 1 June 1801, were then read:

'Extracts from the King's Instructions to General Picton.

'5th. It is our will and pleasure, that, for the present, the temporary administration of the island should, as nearly as circumstances will permit, be exercised by you according to the terms of the capitulation hereunto annexed, in conformity to the ancient laws and institutions that subsisted within the same previous to the surrender of the said island to us, subject to such directions as you shall now or hereafter receive from us, under our signet or sign manual, or by our order in our Privy Council, or to such sudden and unforeseen emergencies as may render a departure therefrom absolutely necessary and unavoidable, and which you are immediately to represent to one of our principal Secretaries of State for our information. But it is nevertheless our special command that all the powers of the executive government within the said island, *as well civil as military*, shall be vested solely in you our Governor, or in the person having the government of the said island for the time being, and that such powers as were heretofore exercised by any person or persons separately, or in conjunction with the Governor of the said island, shall belong solely to you our Governor, or to the person having the government of the said island for the time being; and it is our will and pleasure, that all such public acts and judicial proceedings which before the surrender of the said island to us, were in the name of His Catholic Majesty, shall henceforth be done, issued, and performed in our name.'

'7th. It is our will and pleasure, that, for the present, and until our further pleasure shall be signified, the same courts of judicature which subsisted in the said island previous to the surrender thereof to us, shall, for the present, be continued in the exercise of all the judicial powers belonging to them in criminal and civil cases, and that they shall proceed according to the laws by which the said island was then governed;

and that such judicial powers as previous to the surrender of
the said island to us were exercised by the Spanish Governor,
shall be exercised by you our Governor, in like manner
as the same were exercised previous to the surrender of the
said island.'

[*General Picton's commission, dated 1 June 1801 was read and the
evidence for the defence continued with the testimony of Michael
Gourville, an* alcalde.]

*Monsieur Michael Gourville sworn. Examined by Mr. Lawes with the
assistance of an interpreter.*
When did you first go to the island of Trinidad?—In 1774. I was
one of the first foreigners that settled in Trinidad.
How long did you continue there?—Until about two months ago,
when I set out for this country.
Who was Governor of the island when you first went there?—
Don Manuel La Falques.
When did Monsieur Chacon became Governor of the island of
Trinidad?—I do not exactly recollect the time. He was
Governor eleven years.
Did you act in the character of an *alcalde* there, and of what
description?—I was *alcalde* for one year.
Under whose government were you *alcalde*?—Monsieur Chacon's.
Were there different classes of *alcaldes* or only one?—There was a
first and second class, but the jurisdiction was the same.
Had the Governor any jurisdiction at that time concurrently
with the *alcaldes*?—Equal with the *alcaldes*.
Lord Ellenborough. Does he mean acting in the same manner as a
judge, and hearing the same sort of causes?
Mr. Lawes. Did they both act as judges, or was the sentence of the
one appealed from to the other?
Lord Ellenborough. They cannot have been the same; the Governor
had not only an equal jurisdiction with the *alcalde*, but a larger.
Witness. They appealed in criminal cases to the royal audience of
the Caraccas.[8]
Mr. Lawes. My lord, I believe it was not exactly as your lordship
stated, at that time I believe neither at that moment could
execute the sentence. Did they act concurrently over the same
subjects?—No, they did not act jointly.

How were the sentences of either of them executed, and by what authority?—By the authority of the judge himself.

Mr. Dallas. Every matter of police in the island would be executed from day to day upon the spot, but in cases of life or death they were sent to the Caraccas.

Mr. Lawes. I wish to know, whether the *alcalde*, or the Governor, could pronounce any sentence without an assessor?—They do, but they are responsible when they are not attended by a man of the law.

They could not pronounce the sentence without a man of the law?—If they do it, they are responsible.

Under what authority were their sentences at last executed?—(*The witness did not understand the question.*)

Were their sentences at that time referred to the court of Caraccas?—I do not know whether they appeal now; but at the time General Picton was Governor, it was impossible to do it.

I am not talking about this transaction, but whilst Monsieur Chacon was Governor?—The appeal was always made to the audience of Caraccas.

Do you know how sentences were executed or enforced, when the appeal to the Caraccas ceased?—Trifling matters in questions of police were decided on the spot without reference.

Lord Ellenborough. Are we talking of Chacon, under the Spanish law?

Interpreter. He says, 'in the time of Chacon, I have seen the Governor inflict punishments of different natures by his own authority, such as flogging.'

In what cases were those sentences inflicted?—Robbery in the streets, or highway, or violence against a woman.

Lord Ellenborough. You can refer to the law. The Governor would not exercise the ordinary jurisdiction of the judge?

Mr. Garrow. No, my lord, except in this instance.

[*The witness explained that under Spanish law an assessor was present to give his opinion on points of law, during a case, to an alcalde.*]

Mr. Lawes. When do you first remember a lawyer being on the island?—On the arrival of Monsieur Chacon.

Do you know whether Mr. Justice Nihell was removed from

his situation as chief justice, and when?—Five years ago. About a year after the conquest.

Was there any chief justice or officer of that sort in the island till after the conquest, when Sir Ralph Abercromby appointed one?—Never any other than the two *alcaldes*.

Lord Ellenborough. I have it down, 'no judge but *alcaldes* in the time of the Spanish government.'

Mr. Lawes. Has any other person been appointed chief justice since the removal of Mr. Justice Nihell?

Lord Ellenborough. Where is his appointment? Let us see what the description is.

Mr. Garrow. He is described in this way: 'Chief magistrate, chief judge, and auditor, during His Majesty's pleasure, in and over the whole and every part of the said island.'

Mr. Lawes. Has anybody been appointed to the office since the removal of Mr. Nihell?

Mr. Garrow. He has not been removed.

Lord Ellenborough. He says he has.

Mr. Garrow. It is not the fact. He has ceased to act, in consequence of General Picton's orders.

Lord Ellenborough. Then you may cross-examine him as to that.

Mr. Lawes. Has any person been appointed in the place of Mr Justice Nihell?—No.

Has Mr. Justice Nihell since sat in any other court, or in any other place and what?

Mr. Garrow. I must object to your proceeding on the assumption of his having been removed; it is not the fact. It is true he does not act, because General Picton quarrelled with him.

Lord Ellenborough. Whether he was or not, you may ascertain by cross-examination.

Mr. Garrow. He was appointed in writing, and his written appointment is before the Court. I submit that his removal must be proved in the same way.

Mr. Lawes. When did he cease to act as chief magistrate?— I was in England when Nihell was displaced, and therefore know nothing about it.

Who acted as judge of the Court of Consulado for the last five years?—There never has been one for the Consulado, which is an assembly of the commercial inhabitants who decide matters.

Who acted as judge there?—The judge was appointed by the General.
Who was that judge, and when was he appointed?—Mr. Nihell.
Who was appointed judge of the Consulado, and when?—Mr. Nihell.
Lord Ellenborough. Is the Consulado a civil or a criminal court?
Mr. Dallas. A civil court.
Lord Ellenborough. It is really trifling with the Court to be putting questions concerning this civil court, which cannot in any way affect the present case. You are abusing the indulgence which has been granted to you of having a special verdict. I have been most anxious to obtain every possible information respecting the criminal courts of Trinidad, to which alone our inquiries are directed; and much time has been wasted by these interrogatories about the Consulado, which turns out to be a civil court.
Monsieur Michael Gourville cross-examined by Mr. Garrow.
Did not Mr. Nihell continue in the island until you came away?—Yes he did.
Did he not continue to act as chief magistrate until you came away?—He was judge of the Consulado.
Did he not continue in the office of judge in the same manner as when he was first appointed?—No I believe not.
Why so?—Because he was appointed only to the Consulado.
We learn the contrary from the written document which names him the chief magistrate. Before that nomination, did the Governor, in the first instance, interfere with regard to prisoners and witnesses in cases which were before the *alcalde*?—Never; because the party that complained, had always a right to choose his own judge.
Were there at that time two *alcaldes*?—Yes, always.
Then, the party complaining had a right to go to whichever of those two he thought proper?—Yes, he had that right, or to choose the Governor if he pleased.
In case he chose one of the *alcaldes*, did the Governor then at all interfere?—No; the Governor was forbidden to intermeddle.
I am speaking of complaints of a criminal nature?—There was no interference in either case.
Did you ever know, in the time of M. Chacon, any instance of

torture being applied to persons either accused, or suspected of crimes?—Never.

Before the arrival of Governor Picton in Trinidad, was there any instrument for the infliction of torture?—No; I never heard of any.

If there had been any instrument of that sort during the year in which you were yourself *alcalde*, must you not have known it?—Sometimes they tied the thumbs of criminals together.

Did you, during the year of your being in office, attend the gaol?—Yes.

Do you know the room in which the torture was applied to Luisa Calderon?—No, I do not know the room.

Lord Ellenborough. That no torture was inflicted before General Picton became Governor is not contradicted. We have heard distinctly that no torture was applied during the year this witness was in office, and this has not been contradicted; if there is any contradiction, you will go on.

Mr. Garrow. I like to take it from one of their own witnesses.

Lord Ellenborough. There was no *practice* of torture; but if there was any such *law*, it must be shown.

Mr. Garrow. Did you ever know an instance of tying the thumbs of a *witness* together?—No.

In what cases of criminality did they tie the thumbs?—People of colour, who had robbed them of trifling things.

A slight punishment for a small theft?—A slight punishment upon loose people of that sort, for a slight offence.

Do you remember the first introduction of torture by Governor Picton?—I was not in Trinidad, I was in this country.

Do you mean to say you were absent from the island, during the first part of General Picton's government?—I was there at the conquest, and remained there one year.

While you remained there, had the Governor introduced the torture?—No.

As to the circumstance of tying the thumbs, did you ever know an instance of it, except in the case of people of colour who were slaves? Did you ever in your life know it done to a free person?

Lord Ellenborough. We have ascertained the period when the torture was introduced.

Mr. Dallas, if you can show that there was any law of Spain, applicable to the colonies, which authorised torture, you had better do so. Your case now remains just where it was at the beginning, with this difference, they say that the *alcaldes* had concurrent jurisdiction with the Governor, but that if applied to, the case remained with him.

[*The defence called John Nugent to give an account of Spanish legal procedures and then produced one of its most important witnesses, Archibald Gloster, who was the Attorney-General of Trinidad.*]

Archibald Gloster, Esq. sworn. Examined by Mr. Dallas.
How long have you resided in Trinidad?—From the 3rd January 1803.
Do you hold any official situation in the island?—I do.
What is that situation?—His Majesty's Attorney-General.
How long have you held that situation?—From 15th October 1802, when my warrant was signed by the King.
Do you hold any other situation?—Yes, I am a member of His Majesty's Council.
In your situation have you had occasion to consult the books of authority in the Spanish law?—I cannot say I am conversant with the Spanish law. I never made it my study. I have had Spanish books brought before me in the Privy Council, and laid before me as being books of authority.
Has the Council acted upon them?—I conceive they have.
Mr. Garrow. This gentleman does not state himself to be competent to speak upon the subject; he had certain books laid before him, upon which he acted, without knowing whether they were books of authority.
Lord Ellenborough. You may cross-examine him by and by; he adopts these books as containing the law of Trinidad; he received them as containing the law of Trinidad.
Mr. Garrow. If he was asked whether they contained the law of England, he might answer in the affirmative with as much reason.
Mr. Dallas. Did the courts act upon these books?—I so seldom went into the courts of the country, that I cannot say. I have referred myself to one or two books which they consider as authorities, and which are so looked upon in the offices of the *alcaldes*, the judges; I have seen the books upon the table, and seen them turning them over.
What are those books?—The *Bobadilia*, a very old book, but

there is a new edition of it lately published, which is a practical book; *Elizondo* is another, and *Curia Philippica*. *Elizondo* is like Tidd's, Sellon's, or Impey's Practice.
Are they considered as law by Spaniards resident in the island?—Yes, I mentioned a strong circumstance that they were cited before me as a member of His Majesty's Privy Council.
They were cited and referred to for you to act upon?—They were referred to and the members of the council returned them with a report annexed upon the authority of those books.
You believe them to be authentic?—Certainly I do.
Archibald Gloster, Esq. cross-examined by Mr. Garrow.
I should hardly suppose I was correct in understanding you to say you never studied the Spanish law?—Never; I said I was not skilled or versed in it.
You do not pretend to know more of it than we who have passed all our lives here?—I have not perused them as a student, or as a person would who intended to practise by them.
Have you read them as a matter of science or study?—No.
Are they translated into English?—No, I believe not.
I take it for granted you are familiarly acquainted with the Spanish language?—No, not familiarly; I can translate it with the assistance of a dictionary when I wish to look into one of the Spanish law books, or I would get a friend to translate it for me.
Have you been speaking to us now of all the books of authority that have fallen in your way on the subject of the Spanish law, as applicable to the government of the colonies?—No.
Do not you know, on the contrary, that there is another expressly and exclusively applicable to the colonies which you have not named? what think you of the *Royal Schedula*?—What? The *Schedula* published by the Spanish Court?
Yes, which contains the 'Regulations for the Population, and the Commerce of the Island of Trinidad?' I dare say I have translated that pretty near, though I am not a Spaniard; have I made a tolerable hit for the first time as a dipper? This is a code which had not fallen under your experience?—Yes; I was perfectly aware of it, it is the *Royal Schedula*.
But it did not occur to you to mention it, which contains the rules for the population and commerce of the Island of Trinidad;

The Trial of Thomas Picton

there is another book which is called *Recopilacion de Leyes*?—Yes; I know that book perfectly.

It is a collection of laws respecting the Indies?—Yes, royal letters and ordinances of the Indies.

You conducted this cause for General Picton in Trinidad, I believe? You examined his witnesses, and cross-examined those on the other side?—I attended as his friend.

It may have occurred to you to consult these two books, the *Schedula* and the *Recopilacion*?—I do not know that I have particularly.

Is there one single syllable from the beginning to the end, that justifies inflicting torture in any one of the Spanish islands?—I do not know that there is.

Upon your oath, do you not know there is not?—Upon the oath I have taken, I do not know that there is not.

Those are the books used in the island, as the law of the island?—I do not know, except the general law.

When we have an express law for the colony, you must not tell us it is the general law of the state?—I believe from my memory, there is in that very book some reference to the general law of Spain.

Mr. Garrow. No doubt of it—I will tell you what that reference is. Where there is no remedy for a particular case, and a new case shall arise, then they apply to the general law of Castile.

Lord Ellenborough. Is there in that book any law of Trinidad to regulate the treatment of contumacious witnesses, or of witnesses guilty of prevarication? Does it state the treatment of witnesses who are contumacious?—I do not know that there is, or that there is not.

Mr. Garrow. How long have you been in Trinidad?—Only since 1803.

Lord Ellenborough. You do not found yourself on that book, Mr. Dallas?

Mr. Dallas. No, my lord; we found ourselves upon the books we put in as containing the general law of the island. I shall now put in the books in general use in the island, and which Mr. Gloster has mentioned were the books cited as authorities in the island. We will first of all read an extract from *Curia Philippica*, p. 229. We have a translation upon the depositions, that may perhaps save time.

Mr. Garrow. I am told, that instead of this being the text law of Spain, it is the comments of some person upon the law, which comments may be absurd.

Mr. Dallas. It is written by a person who held the office of criminal judge for a considerable length of time.

The Title of the Book read. 'A code of laws in a first and second volume; the first divided into five parts, wherein is briefly and compendiously treated, decisions in the civil criminal ecclesiastical and secular judicatures, with the determinations and opinions of lawyers; useful for judges and advocates:— the second volume divided into two parts, and three books, wherein is treated the affairs of commerce and inland government; useful to merchants and professors of jurisprudence.'

The following extracts were then read.

Curia Philippica, fol. 229, No. 2.—'The *question* or torment is to be applied for confirmation, or proof; there not being sufficient.'

Curia Philippica, fol. 229, No. 4. —'In the same crimes for which the *question* is applicable to the delinquent, in the same it is applicable to the witness who varies and prevaricates in his evidence, or who denies the truth, or who refuses to declare it, there being a presumption that he knows it; not being of those persons to whom the torment cannot be applied, according to a law *de Partida,* and its Gregorian Glossary. And for the same crimes in which the torment is applicable to the delinquent, in case an evidence of vile character and bad morals is admitted, he is to testify under torment; otherwise his evidence is of no validity. (*Law de Partida.*)'

Curia Philippica, fol. 230, No. 12.—'The torment that may be ordered to the delinquent for the crime, may also be ordered to force a declaration from his accomplice (if there be appearance or presumption that he had any) in crimes of high treason, coining, that against nature, theft, &c. as well as in all others which cannot be committed without accomplices, in all which those who are so may be admitted as evidences. (*Antonio Gomes.*)'

Curia Philippica, fol. 231, No. 6.—'There are to be present at the torment only the judge, *escrivano,* executioner, and person tormented; and it is to be applied in a secret place, without any other person being present or in hearing. It is thus expressed in a law *de Partida*.'

Mr. Dallas. These are all the extracts I propose to read from the *Curia Philippica*. We shall next read some extracts from *Bobadilia de la Politica*.

Lord Ellenborough. With reference to the passage last read, I wish to be informed, whether there is any description of the judge who ought to be present. Does it appear whether the judge who tries the cause is intended?

Mr. Dallas. No, my lord.

Lord Ellenborough. It should be understood that these books are to be produced, in order that both parties may have access to them.

The following extracts were then read.

> *Bobadilia de la Politica*, fol. 964, No. 22.—'In high treason, homicide, theft and robbery, and crimes of atrocious nature, suspicions being strong, and the accused hardened, learned lawyers are of opinion that unusual torments may be applied.'

> *Bobadilia de la Politica*, fol. 965, No. 25.—'In applying the question judicially, though the criminal should die, or lose the use of his limbs, the judge cannot nor ought to be answerable for it, according to common opinion and a law *de Partidas*, which says:—"If the judge order a man to be tormented, for any offence he may have committed, in order to discover the truth, he cannot be answerable for any wounds the party may have received. And I well remember, that in the gaol of this court, an assassin died under torment, and another had his arm broken, without consequences."'

> *Bobadilia de la Politica*, fol. 962, No. 16.—'In notorious, concealed, and atrocious offences, charged against wicked persons of evil fame, if the judges order the question or torment upon slight evidence or suspicion, and in the information or summary mode without communication to the accused, as in the common opinion, they shall be held exculpated *in residencia*; though *Paris de Puteo* says, that it is only allowable to superior judges and not to inferior ones. But I know that the contrary is the practice; and in twenty-one years that I was *corregidor* and judge, I always practised it in such cases; and though I was accused *in residencia* I was always acquitted. And in the superior council in the account that I rendered of the

The Trial of Thomas Picton

corregidorship of Soria, they approved of the torment I had ordered to Sarzala and other robbers whom I had caused to be apprehended in Navarre and Aragon in the year 1773.'

Lord Ellenborough. I believe I must strike that out; for it is by far too questionable.

Mr. Lawes. The next is folio 959, No. 10.

This extract was read as follows:

Bobadilia de la Politica, fol. 959, No. 10.—'If the action is for having committed any one unjustly to prison, I say, if the crime is of a serious nature, although the accused shall not have confessed it, he may not only be put in irons, but into the stocks and chains.'

Lord Ellenborough. That is only by way of restraint. It is too remote from the subject before us; it is quite wide of the mark.

Mr. Garrow. These books themselves are only received upon the evidence of a man who cannot read them, or make them out without a dictionary.

Mr. Dallas. The next authority I shall read is the *Colom.*

The following extract was then read:

Colom, vol. 1, folio 231.—'It is the part of the professional or graduated lawyers, to determine the appearances which are sufficient to authorise the torment, and not mine. But the question cannot be ordered by the ordinary judge or examiner, without consulting the superior tribunal.'

Mr. Garrow. Mr. Gloster said, he never saw that book in the island.

Mr. Dallas. These are all the extracts we shall read.

Archibald Gloster, Esq. re-called.

Mr. Lawes. Look at the first volume of the book called *Colom.* Is that a book of authority in the island of Trinidad?—Upon my word, I cannot say. To the best of my recollection, I think I have seen this book in the offices of the *escrivanos.*

Have you seen it there among other books they have recourse to, in the execution of their duty?—I think I have.

Mr. Garrow. As instructions to a notary.

Mr. Lawes. It is a practical book, certainly.

Lord Ellenborough. There should be somebody to accredit it as a book of some acceptation in the country.

Mr. Dallas. It appears to have been printed at Madrid in 1795 with the royal licence—*Cum Privilegio.*

Mr. Garrow. This author is an *escrivano*; he describes himself as an *escrivano*, with many other pompous titles; and having collected all the cases that had passed through his office, he has written this book for the information of some of his brother *escrivanos*. Suppose Payne the constable had written a book upon the office of constable, would that be considered a book of authority?

Mr. Dallas. This is a book of the same description as Impey's *Practice*, which we all take as our guide.

Lord Ellenborough (to Mr. Gloster). You saw this book in the island? —Yes, I think I did.

Lord Ellenborough. Then it stands on the same footing as the others.

Mr. Garrow. Very much so, my lord.

Mr. Dallas. War having broken out between England and Spain since this transaction took place, the present relative intention of the two countries places us under peculiar difficulties.

Lord Ellenborough. I am ready to take it with all its defects.

Mr. Lawes. I am now going to put in another practical book, something like our *Crown Circuit Companion*. *(to Mr. Gloster)* Is the *Elizondo* a book of authority?—Yes, it is: I mentioned it before.

Mr. Lawes. We only wish to have the form of the petition for the infliction of torture.

Mr. Gloster. I cannot say that I can translate it, because of the number of legal terms.

It was read by the interpreter as follows:

   Elizondo Practica Universal, fol. 273.—'A petition requesting torment on the ground of defective proof. T. in the name of R. In the cause that in my behalf is prosecuted against D. for, &c. I declare that the proofs for evidence being seen by your honour, brought forward in my behalf, that you will be pleased to order an infliction of torture on the said D.; it being but justice, and, by carrying into execution, a favourable result may happen.'

Mr. Dallas. We will now proceed to the evidence under the mandamus. We shall first read the Act of Process in consequence of the information laid before General Picton, his ordering the commitment of Luisa Calderon, and referring the cause to Mr. Begorrat.

The Act of Process was read.[9]

Mr. Dallas. If your lordship pleases, we will now take the depositions in order as they are numbered, and they can be entered as read.

Mr. Garrow. I doubt whether they can be received; it does not appear that these were ever communicated to the defendant, and that he acted upon them.

Mr. Dallas. Yes, they were.

Lord Ellenborough. I understood that they meant to prove such communication; you may as well lay the foundation now, Mr. Dallas.

Mr. Lawes. It does appear from Begorrat's act, that all these proceedings were laid before the Governor, previous to his signing the order.

Lord Ellenborough. That proves that something was laid before him. Whereabouts do you find the signature of General Picton?

Mr. Garrow. To the order for inflicting the torture.

Mr. Dallas. We now, my lord, mean to read the depositions.

Mr. Garrow. As there is to be a special verdict, I may perhaps save a good deal of time. I apprehend that their object in proposing to read these depositions is, to show that there was strong suspicion that Luisa Calderon must have been concerned in the robbery; that is certainly the result to be obtained from the depositions; and I have no objection that my learned friend should so take it, or that any depositions, prior to the signature of General Picton, which he may think will conduce to that end, should be entered as read. If, upon forming the special verdict, they omit any which it may by us be thought material to insert, your lordship will give us leave to insert them?

Lord Ellenborough. Certainly; but you must be very guarded, for there are some which are extremely trivial.

Mr. Garrow. Some there are, which are neither evidence, nor anything like it.

Lord Ellenborough. I press this upon you, because, if it be not attended to, the special verdict will be sent back to be corrected.

Mr. Garrow. If it should become necessary, your lordship will, I dare say, allow us to have the use of your notes?

Mr. Dallas. That being understood, I believe we have nothing more to trouble your lordship with.

Lord Ellenborough. I have made a note that, on the requisition of either party, any deposition or document, *which is legal evidence*, is to be inserted in the special verdict.

Mr. Garrow. My lord, I propose to call a witness to show that the island is governed by the *Recopilacion*; they never resort to the laws of Old Spain, but where the code of the Indies does not apply.

Lord Ellenborough. I understand you, that where the *Recopilacion*, which they referred to in preference to the law of Spain, is silent, they may refer to the law of Spain.

Mr. Garrow. We put it more strongly: we put it, that the law binding upon a Spanish colony is the *Recopilacion*, although there may, perhaps, be an extreme case, which may render it necessary to resort to the law of Old Spain.

Lord Ellenborough. You recollect it has been sworn by this gentleman, that *that* is the rule; but it will be for the jury to say whether they are satisfied that the evidence of Mr. Gloster is conclusive.

Mr. Garrow. It is very important to bear in mind, that the date of Mr. Gloster's knowledge of the laws of Trinidad commences in 1803, long subsequent to this transaction; and that he did not know of these books being in existence at the time this circumstance occurred. I think it stands so at present; but we had better have that ascertained.

Mr. Gloster re-called.

Mr. Garrow. When did you first arrive in Trinidad?—On the 3rd of January, 1803.

Previous to that date you did not even know of the existence of those books?—No, for my visits to the colony previous to that, were only for a week or ten days and not more.

You did not know anything more of them than if they had been books in the Persian language, which had never travelled out of their own country, and you had never travelled into theirs? —I did not; I had no occasion.

Don Pedro de Vargas sworn.—Examined by Mr. Harrison.

How long have you known Trinidad?—I have known it since the year 1803; I arrived, I believe, at the same time as Mr. Gloster.

How long have you known the Spanish West Indies?—Ever since I was born.

The Trial of Thomas Picton

How many years have you been acquainted with them?—I was born in South America, where the 'Regulations' and 'West India Laws' are in force.
What was your situation there?—I have been in four situations; I was brought up to the law.
Lord Ellenborough. You practised in the profession of the law?—Yes, as an advocate.
Mr. Harrison. Where have you practised?—At Santa Fè, the capital of the new kingdom of Grenada.
Have you been in various parts of the Spanish West Indies?—I have been in several parts.
Enumerate those parts of the Spanish West Indies in which you have been?—I have been in the greatest part of the new kingdom of Grenada; in the province of Caraccas; in the island of Porto Rico; in the Havannah; in Cuba, and in New Spain.
Are you able to say, that you are acquainted with the laws of the Spanish West Indies?—I think I am.
You have studied them in fact as your profession?—Yes, I have.
Take that book, and state to his lordship and the jury, whether that is the book you consider as containing the law for the government of the Spanish West Indies?—I conceive this book contains principally the laws of the colonies of South America; this book principally respects the government of the West Indies.
Lord Ellenborough. What is it called?—The *Recopilacion of the laws o, India, relating to South America,* ordered to be printed and published by His Most Catholic Majesty King Charles II.
Mr. Harrison. Are you acquainted with the contents of that book?—Yes; that is to say, more or less: I may have forgot part of them.
Is there any thing that justifies or alludes to tortures?—No, sir; according to my knowledge of it, there is not anything.
Does your knowledge of the Spanish West Indies enable you to say whether torture is there exercised under the Spanish government, and considered as part of the law?—To my knowledge it never was exercised or practised in the province of Caraccas.
You are acquainted with the practice of the Spanish law in the new kingdom of Grenada?—Yes, in the province of Caraccas.
Is that the Caraccas to which the appeal lies?—Yes; Santa Fè

was the capital of the Kingdom of Caraccas, and is newly established within these few years.

Was it in Cuba?—I do not know, because I passed very little time there, only two months in the harbour of Cuba.

Was it in Porto Rico?—I have been more there—I never heard such a thing.

Did you, in any of the islands, or in any part of the Spanish West Indies, hear of the practice of torture upon any person, or by any person?—No, I never heard that it was practised.

Could it have been practised without your knowing it by some means or other?—I think it would have been known; it could not have been in general practice, I am quite certain of that.

Could they have put persons to the torture without it coming to your knowledge some way or other?—No, I do not believe they could.

Lord Ellenborough. It could not have been the general practice without your knowledge?—Certainly not, my lord.

Mr. Garrow. Had they any instruments for inflicting the torture in any of the gaols or places of custody, for the purpose of inflicting it upon offenders?—No, I never saw any.

In your judgment as a lawyer, could torture be legally inflicted in the Spanish West Indies?

Lord Ellenborough. I do not think that the question should be so put. You may ask him whether he knows any law that authorises the practice.

Mr. Harrison. As a lawyer, do you know any law that justifies the infliction of torture in the Spanish West Indies?—I think, if there was any deficiency in the law actually existing in the West Indies, for some particular crimes—

Mr. Garrow. The question which that gentleman has put to you is this. According to the law as you know it, could torture be legally inflicted?

Mr. Harrison. Do you know any law authorising the infliction of torture?—Yes; there is an ancient law of 1260, or 1266, or thereabouts (I am not precise in the date) which authorises the infliction of torture.

Where is that law?—It is the law of *Partidas*; it is a law belonging to Old Spain.

Then in the law of Old Spain there are parts that justify the infliction of torture in certain cases?—Certainly; but if you will give me leave to comment upon it, I will do so. One celebrated author of Old Grenada, in Spain, speaking of torture says, 'the torture in the Spanish settlements was held in general abhorrence; and I do not think anybody will endeavour to inflict it.'

Mr. Dallas. This is not evidence.

Lord Ellenborough. Having been conversant with a great part of the Spanish West Indies, he does not know an instance of the torture having been inflicted. He says he has heard of the old law of 1260, but which has got into such disrepute, that it is held in abhorrence.

Mr. Garrow. Did you ever know the law of 1260 acted upon, or considered as binding on anybody in the Spanish West Indies?—No, I do not consider it as binding.

Lord Ellenborough. Was it ever in your time acted upon, or considered as binding in the Spanish West Indies?—No, I believe not; the laws of *Partidas* are so old, and we have other laws.

Mr. Garrow. You say that you found it in reading a treatise upon the subject; but that in practice it is not followed; though the laws of *Partidas* would justify the supposition of torture having been used?—Yes.

Lord Ellenborough. Mr. Dallas, you should by some means or other, show that it is the *existing* law. It is too much to found your case upon so old a book.

Mr. Dallas. My lord, the observation would be strong if our case rested solely on a law so ancient as 1260.

Lord Ellenborough. The question 'what is the law that prevails?' must go to the jury independently of the other facts of the case. It will be for them to say, whether there was any law in force which authorised the infliction of torture in the island of Trinidad. That must be stated as a fact. I thought it would have been admitted one way or the other without contest; but as there is conflicting evidence, I cannot dispose of it, and it must therefore be left to the jury. We cannot find evidence; we must find facts; it must be disposed of, otherwise the verdict would be imperfect.

Mr. Dallas. Then, if that be the case, we must give further evidence upon this point.

Don Pedro de Vargas cross-examined by Mr. Dallas.

You say you have practised as an advocate?—Yes.

The Trial of Thomas Picton

For what length of time?—Two years.

Two years only. In what court?—In Santa Fè.

You practised for two years only, as an advocate in Santa Fè, and your whole experience is derived from your practice during that period?—I must tell you, that those who study the law, are obliged by the laws of Spain to study for the space of five years; after that they must practise two or three years; and after that they are examined in full audience; and after that, if approved of, they have a licence to practise; after I was approved of, I practised two years.

Then the extent of your experience, as far as practice is concerned, is those two years?—Yes.

You have produced a book, which you tell us contains regulations for the government of the Spanish colonies. Is there any part of that book which directs what the proceedings should be when a person is apprehended for theft? Turn to any part that directs what is to be done in a case of robbery?—I think I can produce some; but there are three volumes; it will be something difficult. You intend I should produce only one instance?

I want to know, whether those books contain any directions to the criminal judge, how to proceed in matters of robbery, or of criminal accusation?—I am not prepared for that: but, notwithstanding, let me see if I can find it.

Will you swear, that there is from the beginning to the end of those three volumes, a single passage that *forbids* the application of torture in the Spanish colonies in any case whatever?—In the Spanish colonies I believe there is nothing: not any law.

You will not swear there are in those three volumes any passages that directly forbid the application of torture in any Spanish colony?—It will be very difficult for me to have all the laws in my head, I think there is none, except for a slave.

When did you arrive in this country?—I arrived in 1799, I believe. I am not quite certain.

That was before the peace was concluded between France and Spain?—Yes, I arrived the first time in England in 1799.

Did you give in your name at the Secretary of State's office, under the Alien Act?—I think I cannot answer that question.

Lord Ellenborough. You must not ask him that question. He may subject himself to penalties; I think it should not be put.

Mr. Dallas. Did you at any time pass in this country by the name of Smith?—Yes, I did.

You passed not by your own name, but by the false name of Smith?—Yes, I was entered in the office of the Secretary of State at that time. I believe Lord Hobart was Secretary for the Colonial Department; and it came to the knowledge of the Secretary of State at that time, before the peace in 1801.

Have you been at any time employed by Colonel Fullarton, in taking examinations against General Picton?—I believe not, I was not employed officially.

I repeat the question to you. Upon your oath, have you not been employed by Colonel Fullarton, to take the examination of different persons against General Picton?—I have been employed as an interpreter by Colonel Fullarton, and gave him the assistance of my legal advice; he appointed me as his assessor.

Have you been employed by Colonel Fullarton to take the examinations of different people against General Picton?—I was employed.

You were employed by Colonel Fullarton as an interpreter, to take these examinations?—Yes.

Mr. Garrow. There were persons who spoke the language with which you are conversant, and you assisted to translate what they said?—Yes.

[*In the initial inquiry into Picton's conduct, held in Trinidad in 1805, both Hilaire Begorrat and Francisco de Farfan, each of whom had been involved as an alcalde in Luisa Calderon's case, had given evidence. The answers which they gave at that time to the questions put by the Attorney-General of Trinidad, far from incriminating Picton, were an attempt to justify his conduct in terms of Spanish law and to praise his administration of the island. The witnesses against Picton were also discredited in the answers given. The penultimate question put to Farfan during the Trinidad inquiry, and his answer to it were as follows:*

'*As an old inhabitant of this colony and a Spaniard, what was the opinion of your countrymen of General Picton?—Amongst the honest part of my countrymen, he was considered as a man of considerable talents, doing honour to his own country.*'

Farfan denied that Picton had ever been guilty of cruelty as

Governor, and insisted that the only punishments ordered were those 'necessary for the tranquillity of the colony'.

At this point in the 1806 trial, the evidence of Begorrat and Farfan from the Trinidad hearing was read out.]

Lord Ellenborough. Do you, Mr. Dallas, call any parole evidence to prove torture to have been practised in any other parts of the Spanish settlement?

Mr. Dallas. No, my lord, I have no other evidence.

Mr. Garrow. Gentlemen of the jury—

Lord Ellenborough. Mr. Dallas was stopped, when a special verdict was agreed upon. I ought therefore now to hear him upon the contradictory evidence as to the law; if I hear you now, I thereby preclude Mr. Dallas from making any observations which he may think necessary upon that point.

Mr. Dallas. I had not concluded my address, when I was stopped by the suggestion of a special verdict.

Lord Ellenborough. It rests with you; but it must always be understood, that I cannot put down contradictory evidence.

Mr. Dallas. I understood it was agreed to be a special verdict.

Lord Ellenborough. Yes; but if there is a contradiction in the evidence it must be left to the jury to determine. Perhaps it will be as well that both parties should comment on the question, whether the law of torture did exist in Trinidad or not. The jury will then dispose of it one way or the other, and the special verdict will be framed accordingly.

Mr. Dallas. Gentlemen of the jury, I can have no objection, under his lordship's direction, to take the course now marked out for me; and indeed I should, at all events, have been entitled to address you again.

Mr. Garrow. As we are in this stage of the business, I think it will be as well if your lordship will add to your notes that Vallot had been gaoler ten years, and that during his time there had been no torture, nor any instrument of torture, in the gaol.

Mr. Dallas. Then the whole of his evidence must be read.

Lord Ellenborough. You gave evidence by Vargas, and you ought to have followed it up then.

Mr. Garrow. My lord, I stated that I had many witnesses to prove that no torture was ever practised; but as it is, I have no wish to have Vallot's evidence read.

Mr. Dallas. Gentlemen of the jury; the case is now confined to a single point, and, as I stated to you before, I have no objection to adopt the course chalked out for me by his lordship. But at all events I should most undoubtedly have been entitled to address you again upon a part of the case, I mean upon the evidence which my learned friend has adduced in answer to mine; for upon evidence of that sort, in any court and in any prosecution, it would have been open to me to animadvert.

Reduced as the case now is to a single point, I will, under his lordship's correction, state what I conceive to be the only question for your decision—a mere question of fact, and involving no legal considerations—namely, whether, upon the evidence before you, you can upon your oaths declare, that by the law of Spain torture was not applicable in the island of Trinidad in any case, the circumstances of which corresponded with those of the case of Luisa Calderon; or whether by the law of Spain, the criminal judge could, in any instance, order the infliction of torture.

I confess, I thought that upon this point I had made out an extremely strong case in behalf of the defendant General Picton: I did not content myself with calling persons who had practised for a longer or shorter period of time in the Spanish colonies; but I produced before you the works of different authors—some being commentaries on the laws of Spain by distinguished practitioners of those laws, others containing decisions which had from time to time taken place; and I also established the important fact, that it was the bounden duty of those who were concerned in the administration of criminal justice, to consult these books as containing the rules by which their conduct should be regulated.

* * *

All these authors, down to 1795, state that there are cases (and according to them the present is one) in which, by the Spanish code, torture may lawfully be inflicted. And such being the fact in respect of Spain itself, let us consider whether the case stands upon any different footing with regard to the colonies. We have proved as well by parole evidence as by the production of those very books which are the sources of knowledge, and to which the judges themselves must apply for information, that by the law of Spain torture may be inflicted upon criminals. Now can my learned friends turn to a single passage in which any distinction is even attempted to be taken between the colonies and the mother country? They have, indeed, endeavoured by examining a witness to the contents of these volumes, to show that the rule which applies to Spain, does not apply to the colonies of Spain; but when I find it laid down as a general proposition, that in Spain the torture is legal, and there being, in regard to the colonies, no exception which breaks in upon the general rule, this is sufficient to convince me that the law is the same in both places. But, strong as it is, my case does not rest even here. How is it affected by the examination of this gentleman, who, according to his own account, is a graduated advocate, and has practised two years, and whose experience is confined to those two years of his practice? He states that the law of Old Spain does not prevail in the colonies; and my learned friend says, that the books I have laid before you are trash; and that they are produced here for the purpose of misleading you. Why? Because he holds in his hand a compilation of laws which contains rules for the regulation of the Spanish colonies, and which lays down maxims for the conduct of those who are to administer the law in those colonies. Mr. Vargas tells us, that nothing with regard to torture is to be found in that book. I might say, be it so; and since nothing about torture is to be found in it, that book may be put out of the question altogether. But I am standing upon a general rule; and if that book which he has produced contains no passage in which an express exception to the general rule is to be found, the production of the book is a direct corroboration of my case.

You cannot, I am sure, have forgotten one question which I put to the witness who now sits before me. I called upon this experienced jurisconsult—this ingenious advocate—to declare whether, in this compilation of the laws of Spain, he could find any passage that prescribes the mode of proceeding in the case of a person charged as a principal or accessory in a robbery? He went from place to place; he turned the volumes over in confusion page by page; and he concluded his evidence without referring us to any text upon the subject!

And I must say that my learned friend has adopted a most singular course for overpowering the testimony I have adduced, and in which I pointed out each page and passage bearing on the particular point; for three volumes have been produced to an advocate, not now practising in any court of any colony belonging to the Spanish empire, who cannot fix upon or point out one single text, not only as to the matter to which he has been called, but even as to any other. But, gentlemen, you will remember that I put this further question to him, 'Will you, upon your oath, undertake to say, that torture being consonant to the general law of Spain, from one end of those books to the other, there is a single passage that prohibits it from being applied in the colonies of Spain?' he would not undertake to say there was. Then, I assert, that there is no evidence whatever delivered by him, that can be put in opposition to the evidence given on the other side; because our evidence is positive as to the prevalence of the system, and they have not cited a single passage from any authority, pointing out an exception to the general rule.

Gentlemen, Vargas, who appears now in the character of a Spanish advocate, has passed under another name—that of Smith; but under the circumstances of his situation, I scorn to detain you by any personal observations upon him. I will only remind you of his having been employed from time to time in going between Colonel Fullarton and the witnesses. In a case so important to the defendant, and after the strong positive evidence of the general law of Spain, I ask, whether, upon the production of a book, out of which not a single passage has been read—upon this negative evidence, in direct opposition to all the positive evidence written and parole which I have produced—you can conscientiously believe that the Spanish law did not sanction the application of torture in the case of Luisa Calderon?

I am sorry to have troubled you at so much length upon this single part of the case; but I trust it will be imputed to my anxiety that no material circumstance should escape you.

REPLY

Mr. Garrow. Gentlemen of the jury; it is with extreme concern, that I feel myself called upon at this time of night, to address to you any observations on the present most important case; but the manner in which, on the part of Governor Picton, it has been thought proper that his defence should be conducted, and especially that speech which has lately been delivered, make it my indispensable duty, with reference not only to the prosecutor, but also to the honour and character of our country, to trouble you with some remarks upon the topics of which my learned friend's speech has consisted.

To me my learned friend has been, as he always is, extremely courteous; and indeed he is the last man to volunteer harsh observations; and therefore nothing but the distress of his case could have urged him to treat the gentleman before me in the manner you have witnessed. I say, 'the distress of his case', because unless his lordship blots out of his notes, and you erase from your memories what this learned *jurisconsult*, as my learned friend denominated him, has stated, General Picton has not even the slightest shadow of defence. We will now, gentlemen, proceed to inquire what degree of credit does belong to this gentleman, and to examine the pretensions of that witness with whom my learned friend has the courage to contrast him.

Mr. Vargas tells us, that he was born in Spanish America, that he was bred to the profession of the law, and that he practised in that profession for two years. These two years, says Mr. Dallas triumphantly, comprise the whole extent of his experience; but I think my learned friend was unlucky in making this attack upon Mr. Vargas, whose qualifications as a witness were to be contrasted with those of Mr. Gloster, the Attorney-General of Trinidad, and counsel of the defendant. Let us compare their respective merits.

The one is a man educated from his infancy in the laborious study of the laws of his country, and speaking the language in which those laws are written. Like all his countrymen of the same profession, he was under the necessity of practising, for a considerable time, in the courts of inferior jurisdiction; he then underwent an examination before a full court, and on obtaining their certificate of his fitness, was authorised to manage the concerns of others, in which occupation he has been employed two years. Having therefore had every means of investigating the authorities on this subject, he has given the account which you have heard,

but which my learned friend has not stated with perfect
fairness. Mr. Vargas did not say, that on consulting the books,
no written law would be found, by which, in particular cases,
torture could be inflicted in Old Spain. He said that the
Spanish settlements in the West Indies were, at the cession of
Trinidad to the British forces, governed by a separate code of
laws, which we have put in, and which I showed to Mr.
Gloster, and not by the laws of Old Spain. I observe it is
printed by authority, in 1783, expressing itself to be a 'Code
for the Regulation of the Population and Commerce of the
Colonies', published by the court of Madrid, as a code of laws
by which their settlements are to regulate themselves. He says,
that on looking into this, he finds no authority for the
application of torture to any person, under any circumstances
whatever, but being asked whether he knows any text that
justifies the infliction of torture, he does not reply like a rash
man, as my learned friend represents him to be, because a
rash man would have said, there is no such text. But he says,
I do recollect to have somewhere seen an edict of 1260, in
which torture is spoken of as legal; but I state to you, as far
as concerns the West Indies, that during the whole of my
connexion with them, I have never seen or heard of the
infliction of torture. He went on to say, that although this was
formerly the law of Old Spain, yet even there the good sense
of modern times, if it has not entirely abolished it, has nearly
done so, and has made the principle of torture a subject of
contempt and abhorrence. He did not state that the torture
could not, in any case, be inflicted in Old Spain; but applying
himself to the colonial law which he had studied, that he had
never found any trace of its existence in the West Indies.

My learned friend designated Mr. Vargas by the words
'this jurisconsult'; let us see what sort of *jurisconsult* has
appeared on the other side. You have had Mr. Gloster—to do
what? To disclaim any ability to throw light on the subject,
and to tell you that he cannot read even the title pages of the
books put in! When desired to translate a passage, which from
my acquaintance with the Latin and French languages, I
myself could have translated, he said he could not do so,
because of the law-phrases contained in it. And this man, who
cannot translate, without a dictionary, a single passage in

the Spanish books, who never looked into the Spanish law, who cannot explain the meaning of a petition, no longer than the oath which my lord's crier when he called you into the box administered to you, this man is the *jurisconsult*, whose testimony is to send Mr. Vargas out of court, and upon whose authority you are to assert the existence of a law, authorising the infliction of that torture which the unfortunate woman before me has suffered.

Let us see what Mr. Gloster's evidence is. Does it make these books receivable? I am bound to say it does, because they have been received; but his lordship will forgive me, when I say, without fear of contradiction, that they are barely within the pale of evidence; for they stand upon no better support than this,—that they were seen in an *escrivano*'s office in Trinidad, in 1803. This was at a time long subsequent to the cruelties of Governor Picton—at a time when he was beating up for any authorities in which such a law might be discovered, in consequence of his having been called upon to make retribution for his misconduct—and then, this gentleman comes forth, who has been acting under the mandamus as the counsel of General Picton, with what propriety and decorum I leave it to himself to determine, he being Attorney-General of Trinidad at the time, and says 'I saw these books lying in the *escrivano*'s office!' I beg his pardon, he goes further and says, 'I do think that once, at the council of which I have the honour to be a member, somebody did produce one of them, and quote something out of it, and treat it as an authority. Not being able to read Spanish, I am myself totally ignorant whether it is an authority or not, but I am ready to pour in upon you a wheelbarrowful of such authorities, in order to make out a justification of the infliction of torture.' Is this, gentlemen, the way in which a defendant is to be justified in an English court of justice?

I shall demand of you a general verdict of guilty, because I am sure I shall satisfy his lordship that (although he kindly anticipated the possibility of there being some written law which might make this a fit case for a special verdict), there is nothing left for you to determine but the plain naked question, guilty or not guilty, justified or criminal.

* * *

The Trial of Thomas Picton

The defendant should have recollected how the law is administered in England; which, if it has any particular excellence more remarkable than another, is distinguished for its extreme tenderness towards persons under accusation. What is the practice every day of the judges in our courts of law? If any syllable of confession is attempted to be produced against the accused, the judge immediately interposes in favour of the prisoner, and asks the witness, 'Did you say anything to induce him to confess? Did you use any threat? Did you give him the least reason to suppose that he would be favoured if he confessed?' And if anything was said to induce him to believe that his condition would be better or worse, the judge, even in crimes hazarding His Majesty's sacred life, would say that the confession could not be heard. Gentlemen, a learned friend reminds me of something, to which I believe I have already drawn your attention. The last answer of Mr. Farfan upon his cross-examination. You will remember that Mr. Farfan was a witness produced by General Picton, and examined by Mr. Gloster, the advocate of the General through the whole of his defence, and by whom Farfan was led during the whole of his examination-in-chief in a manner that would not be permitted here. Farfan's evidence concludes with these words, 'I have seen several transported during the Spanish time. I saw no other torture but imprisonment, in order to discover the truth from criminals.' You will say whether you are of opinion that there was any such law; whether you believe that General Picton has any justification, or even supposed that he was acting according to law. If such is your opinion, you will say so. But if you believe that there was no such law, and that it is a mere pretence raked up now that the day of retribution has arrived, you will find a general verdict of guilty. You will do so reluctantly, but you will do so because you are Britons, and feel the satisfaction that you can protect those, who by the prowess of the British arms have become your fellow-subjects; and you will show that the poorest individual in the territories of England has the opportunity of bringing his oppressor, however high his rank, to answer for his misconduct before a court of justice.

The Trial of Thomas Picton

SUMMING-UP

Lord Ellenborough. Gentlemen of the jury, it is my duty to advise you by all means to divest yourselves of everything which can possibly inflame your minds, with reference either to the defendant, or to the particular species of punishment which is so justly odious to Britons and which is the foundation of the present charge, in order that you may calmly consider a plain question of fact. *i.e.* At the cession of Trinidad to Sir Ralph Abercromby, what was the law of that island as confirmed by the English authorities? It is for you to determine whether the law by which the island was then governed did or did not invest the Governor, or chief magistrate, with the power of applying personal torture upon any occasion. In considering this subject, your attention should, in the first instance, be directed to the fifth and seventh articles of His Majesty's instructions to the defendant, which have been given in evidence.

* * *

The same judicial powers, therefore, which, previously to the cession of Trinidad to Great Britain, had been exercised by the Spanish Governor, were thenceforth to be exercised in the same manner by the defendant. A nice question of fact now presents itself for consideration. Viz. Did the criminal law, while Trinidad continued a colony of Spain, authorise the infliction of torture upon witnesses? It should be remarked that this island formed no part of Old Spain, but was at some period, subsequent certainly to the discoveries of Columbus, connected with that Kingdom as a dependency. Of the terms upon which this connection was formed, we have received no positive evidence. In the absence of any evidence applicable to this single island separately, the *Royal Schedula* has been produced, although it has not been read at length. It relates to the commerce and population of the West India colonies, but it does not appear that this *Schedula*, which was a communication of the royal pleasure, contained any regulations upon this subject. There is also a book called the *Recopilacion*, which relates to the islands generally. It does not appear that that contains anything relative to criminal punishments, or at least anything relative to torture. And therefore the right of a magistrate to apply torture to a person who appears in the character of a witness must, if it exist at all, depend only upon the authorities to be derived from the several law books that have been read. Being ignorant of the terms upon which this island, two or three centuries ago, was associated with Spain, we do not know whether the whole of the laws of Spain were introduced; but this is in some degree ascertained by several witnesses, whose memories reach a considerable distance of time back. One of them, M. Gourville, knew the island in 1774, now thirty-two years ago. Another witness has been examined who was born there, and who appears to have been an *alcalde* down to the period of his examination; and neither M. Gourville, nor M. de Vargas, nor Mr. Nugent, who speaks of knowing the island from 1781 to the present time, which comprehends a period of twenty years, nor any other person who has been examined in this cause, speaks to a single instance in which torture has been applied in the island of Trinidad. Not one witness from Trinidad who has been examined here, speaks to that fact; and in the absence of all positive proof (I mean from living witnesses) upon the subject, the question is, whether, without knowing the particular terms upon which this island became connected with Spain, you can say that the law of Spain was so fully and entirely, and in all its parts, introduced into the island of Trinidad, and domiciled there, as that torture formed a part of the law of the island? That is the question. I will state the evidence respecting that law, as it has been given by the several books recognised and stated to be law in that island; it has certainly been proved that these books are referred to and treated as authorities; but their existence in the island and the reference to them as authorities there, as far as Mr. Gloster's evidence goes, cannot extend beyond the period of his knowledge of the island, which commenced in January 1803, his appointment to the office of Attorney-General bearing date October 1802. But they have certainly been adverted to as having existence, and having been referred to in the island in 1801, when the punishment was inflicted; because prior to 1799 the instrument of torture was in the barrack yard. Mr. Begorrat knows no instance of its having been inflicted, and he is another to be added to the number of those who did not know it in the time of Governor Chacon. He adverts to what he conceived to be the law applicable to that island in 1801. And therefore the law in the books is to be weighed against the disuse of such a practice.

* * *

Taking all these facts into consideration, it is for you to say whether, although it is in evidence that such was the law of Old Spain at the time, you can from that circumstance necessarily infer that it was also the law of Trinidad: whether in the absence of all usage for thirty-two years, you are enabled to say that it was the existing law at the time of the capitulation. If you should be of opinion that it was the existing law at the time of the capitulation, that fact will be inserted in the special verdict. If you are of opinion that, as far as we have any knowledge of the subject, the practice of torture was not in use, and that no such law did exist, I shall have further observations to communicate to you.

At present you will consider whether torture could be applied at the discretion of the judge, and, if so, whether the application of torture to witnesses formed a part of the law of Trinidad at the time of the cession of that island.

Foreman of the Jury. We are of opinion that there was no such law as this existing at the time of the cession.

Lord Ellenborough. Then Governor Picton cannot derive any protection from that law. If no law obtained in that island at the time which authorised the severities that were practised upon this young woman, your verdict must be that the defendant is guilty.

A verdict of guilty was then pronounced by the jury, and recorded.

Mr. Dallas. Upon the other points I shall trouble your lordship hereafter upon a motion for a new trial.

Lord Ellenborough. The other points you know will be open to you upon that motion.

Notes

Introduction

1 Henry Boguet, *An Examen of Witches*, trans. E. Allen Ashwin, ed. Rev. Montague Summers, 1929, p. xxxv.
2 20 *State Trials*, pp. 1–82.

One   A Trial of Witches: Salem and Bury St Edmunds

1 William Goffe was one of those who signed the death warrant of Charles I.
2 The Westminster assembly of Puritan divines met in 1643 and continued its work for over five years. In 1646 it laid a confession of faith before Parliament, and though this acquired no legal status it was generally accepted by Presbyterians. John Cotton's *Milk for Babes, Drawn out of the Breasts of both Testaments* was published in 1646. John Cotton was Cotton Mather's maternal grandfather.
3 From Richard Baxter's preface to the 1691 edition of Cotton Mather's *Memorable Providences*.
4 Joseph Glanvill, *Saducismus Triumphatus*, 1681; William Perkins, *Discourse of the Damned Art of Witchcraft*, 1608. Glanvill, who upheld the traditional view of witchcraft, was to provide the Scholar Gypsy of Matthew Arnold's poem.
5 Richard Hathaway was convicted as a cheat and impostor in 1703, after pretending to be bewitched. *Cf.* 14 *State Trials*, pp. 639–90.
6 Matthew Hopkins (d. 1647) was a lawyer who began 'witch finding' in 1644. Edmund Calamy (1600–66) was one of the Commissioners of Oyer and Terminer for the Chelmsford witch trial of 1645.
7 William Douglass, *A Summary Historical and Political of the first planting, progressive improvements and present state of the British Settlements in North America*, 1747–50, vol. 1, p. 448n.
8 The new charter for the Province of Massachusetts Bay, following the Glorious Revolution of 1689.
9 Perkins, see note 4, above; Richard Bernard, *Guide to Jurymen in Cases of Witchcraft*, 1627.
10 1 James I cap. 12.
11 Robert Calef, *More Wonders of the Invisible World*, 1700.

12 Priestess of Apollo at Delphi.
13 A true bill, i.e., a case to be answered.
14 Here Hutchinson's account ends and is followed by an extract from Sir John Lauder, Lord Fountainhall, *Decisions of the Lords of Council and Session*, 1759–61.
15 Camerarius Philippus, *Meditationes Historicae Centuria Prima*, 1602.
16 Martin Delrio, *Disquisitiones Magicae*, 1720.
17 Gabriel Naudé, *Apologie pour tous les Grands Personnages qui ont esté faussement soupçonnez de Magie*, 1625.
18 The trial was published in 1682 by William Shrewsbury at the Bible in Duck Lane.

Two John Huggins

1 *A True State of the Proceedings of the Prisoners in the Fleet Prison*, 1729, p. 5.
2 *State of the Gaols in London, Westminster and the Borough of Southwark*, 1776, p. 10.
3 *The State of the Prisons in England and Wales*, 1777, p. 25.
4 *Ibid.*, pp. 158–9.
5 Star Chamber was abolished in 1641 by 16 Charles I cap. 10.
6 An Act for the Relief and Release of Poor Distressed Prisoners for Debt 22 & 23 Charles II cap. 20 (1670–1671).
7 A dealer in secondhand clothes or small articles of furniture.
8 Twenty-shilling pieces, used as an alternative after the introduction of the guinea in 1663.
9 Sir John Cheshire (1662–1738).
10 Proceedings in a suit between preliminary and final process.
11 Charles, Baron Talbot (1685–1737). Solicitor-General, 1726; Lord Chancellor, 1733.
12 A form presumably derived from the medieval practice whereby a 'languishing' tenant might depute another man to serve the King on his behalf.
13 Chief Clerks in the Courts of King's Bench, Chancery, and Common Pleas.
14 The first clause of the Insolvent Debtors Act of 1725 required gaolers to make out 'a true, exact and perfect list' of their prisoners.
15 One of the Companies of the City of London.
16 A member of a vestry representing the ratepayers of a parish.

Three Thomas Picton

1 H. B. Robinson, *Memoirs of Lieutenant-General Sir Thomas Picton*, 1836, vol. 1, p. 207.
2 *The New Newgate Calendar*, ed. Norman Birkett, 1960, p. 20.
3 William Blackstone, *Commentaries on the Laws of England*, 1769, vol. 4, p. 320.
4 Cesare Beccaria, *Dei delitti e delle pene*, 1764.

Notes to pp. 199–226

5 First published in 1786–8.
6 During the course of Picton's trial, a number of commentaries on Spanish law were referred to. They included Antonio Gomes, *Commentarium Variarumque Resolutionum Juris Civilis, Communis, et Regii*; Gerónimo Castillo de Bobadilla, *Politica para Corregidores y Señores de Vassallos, en tiempo de paz y de guerra*, as well as Elizondo, *Practica Universal* and the Commentaries of Juan Colom. The *Curia Philippica* was a compendium of such authorities. Among other sources of Spanish law mentioned in Picton's case, *Las Sieta Partidas* was a Castilian-Spanish compilation of 1255–65, modelled on Justinian. The *Recopilacion des Leyes des Indes* of 1681 dealt specifically with colonial law. According to the *New Newgate Calendar* (pp. 20–1), Picton had never seen this last book, since the only known copy in England had been in the Marquis of Lansdowne's library. At the sale of the library, the book was bought by the British Institution, but this was not until after Picton had been indicted.

The quotations from Spanish legal works in this trial are, of course, from translations made by the interpreter.

7 A special verdict might find that Picton had committed the acts alleged but that there was no criminality on his part.
8 The court of appeal for the Province of Caraccas.
9 For the Act of Process, see p. 163.